Strength in Numbers

Strength in Numbers

THE POLITICAL POWER OF

WEAK INTERESTS

Gunnar Trumbull

Harvard University Press

Cambridge, Massachusetts · London, England

2012

Library of Congress Cataloging-in-Publication Data

Trumbull, Gunnar.
Strength in numbers : the political power of weak interests / Gunnar Trumbull.
p.   cm.
Includes bibliographical references and index.
ISBN 978-0-674-06641-0 (hbk. : alk. paper)
1. Consumer protection. 2. Trade regulation. 3. Consumption (Economics)—
Political aspects. 4. Consumers—Political activity. I. Title.
HC79.C63T78 2012
381.3′4—dc23
2012009690

For Seema

Contents

CHAPTER 1

The Political Power of Weak Interests

CONVENTIONAL WISDOM and a deep tradition of academic research hold that concentrated interests dominate public policy. Through a combination of industry lobbying, campaign finance, direct interaction with compliant government agencies, and informal ties to elected officials, industry is said to dictate the outcome of national regulatory policy. Diffuse interests, by contrast, go underrepresented. The problem they face is one of coordination. Whereas a small number of companies may easily coordinate their lobbying efforts through industry associations, vast numbers of consumers face significant barriers to organizing to defend themselves. On this account, any new regulation that imposes concentrated costs and diffuse benefits should face strong, consistent opposition. Yet diffuse interests have historically nearly always found representation in public policy. Across the advanced democracies, diffuse groups like retirees, patients, and consumers enjoy strong protections— protections that were opposed by industry. In cases in which diffuse interests have failed to find representation, this was frequently because they lost to *other diffuse interests*. Even the most convincing cases of industry influence—in sectors such as pharmaceuticals and agriculture— reveal clear limitations on industry's ability to influence public policy. Given the organizational challenges facing diffuse interests, and the easy coordination enjoyed by concentrated interests, the question arises as to why companies have not been more successful in achieving their desired legislative and regulatory outcomes. How have diffuse interests come to be so consistently and strongly represented in policy?

The idea that industry gets the public policy it wants represents a fundamental misreading both of the historical record of group mobilization, and of the core logic of interest representation. Historically, even the most challengingly diffuse interests have managed to mobilize to pursue their common interests. And the most concentrated business interests have failed to forestall restrictive regulations. The emphasis that researchers have placed on coordination is heavily overstated. The problem is that the challenge in influencing public policy is not primarily one of coordination. Despite clear challenges, groups with shared interests do manage to organize; when they do not, other actors step in to advocate on their behalf.

The core challenge in shaping new regulatory policy is the need to make that policy appear *legitimate*. In certain cases, the requirement of legitimacy inverts the logic of collective action embraced by advocates of coordination models of public policy influence. On the one hand, diffuse interests may actually benefit from the organizational challenges they face. Given the real difficulties of organizing, groups that do manage to mobilize an activist membership enjoy a heightened (but not unlimited) degree of policy legitimacy. Successful mobilization serves as a signal that the policies being advocated represent real underlying interests that are deeply held. On the other hand, concentrated interests with easy access to policymakers are viewed with suspicion, and the policies they advocate necessarily attract critical scrutiny. To achieve their policy goals, concentrated interests must either attempt to obscure their influence, or, more commonly, present their preferences as representing broader societal interests. This need to link their narrow interest to a related diffuse interest provides more than just a fig leaf for raw economic interest: it places significant constraints on the discretion that even powerful economic actors enjoy in influencing public policy.

In the United States, where the coordination theory of regulation first took hold, views about the influence of concentrated interests on public policy have left their imprint on the regulatory culture. For the political

Left, the threat of business influence has been used to justify keeping industry as far as possible from regulators. For the political Right, the idea that policy was subject to industry capture was used to justify a broadly deregulatory view of government. Even in areas in which regulation might otherwise be warranted—areas like competition policy and product safety—the reality of business influence served as a warning that even legitimate interventions would inevitably be hijacked to fulfill narrow interests. The result was a regulatory culture that oscillated between deregulatory intuitions punctuated by periods of recrimination against industry for the consequences resulting from failures of regulation.

Collective Action and Policy Influence

Mancur Olson's 1965 *The Logic of Collective Action* launched a generation of research into the challenges of economic organization. His critique of earlier scholars of interest group pluralism was not new. Two years earlier, historian Gabriel Kolko had published an account of Progressive-Era reforms—rail, food, and banking regulation—that reinterpreted these reforms as the product of "business control over politics."[1] But Olson's bold theoretical framing became the rallying point for a generation of new theories of regulation.[2] From Mancur Olson and George Stigler to James Q. Wilson, our most noted—and most heavily cited—theorists of organization and regulation have argued that diffuse interests are therefore weak interests. The logic of their case was based on the problem of free riders. When the benefits of organization cannot be excluded from the general public, individuals will have insufficient incentives to support a collective lobbying effort. The larger the number of individuals in a group, the harder the group will be to organize, and the more potential supporters will have an interest free riding. This coordination problem makes organizing diffuse interests a harder job than organizing concentrated interests. Olson and the many regulation theorists who followed him saw in this coordination problem an explanation for the neo-Marxist insight that the concentrated interests of a few could outweigh the diffuse interests of the many.

Olson's emphasis on coordination was not the only explanation for industry dominance of public policy. In *Politics and Markets*, Charles

Lindblom attributed industry influence to the economic weight of industry. Because government relied on business for tax revenue, business always exerted an implicit holdup threat.[3] James Q. Wilson emphasized the size of the relative costs and benefits in motivating political influence. For him, what mattered about large constituencies was that the costs or benefits of regulation were spread thin.[4] But it was the coordination theory presented by Olson that would eventually dominate interest group theory in economics, political science, and sociology. Economist George Stigler took the argument to its logical conclusion, writing in his 1971 article "The Theory of Economic Regulation": "As a rule, regulation is acquired by industry and is designed and operated primarily for its benefit."[5] Stigler's idea of concentrated interest influence would be formalized in the work of Sam Peltzman, another Chicago-trained economist who was later appointed director of the Stigler Center at the University of Chicago.[6]

In political science, Russell Hardin's *Collective Action* elaborated Olson's insights in game-theoretic terms.[7] For Hardin, the challenge of coordination presented a prisoner's dilemma for individual actors, in which only irrational actors would contribute to providing collective goods. This coordination-based approach to the study of regulation is often described as the Chicago School of regulation, although it found its strongest exponents in the field of public choice centered in the so-called Virginia School, including members of the economics departments at George Mason University and the Universities of Maryland and Virginia.[8]

Almost immediately after they emerged, these theories began to face empirical and theoretical challenges. Empirically, there was increasingly strong evidence even in the United States that diffuse interests in fact *did* often manage to find representation in public policy. Consumers were benefiting from progressive trade liberalization and regulatory protections.[9] Competition policy was breaking apart concentrated producers with monopoly pricing power. Modern retailing was giving rural consumers access to an extraordinary variety of products at low prices. Small shareholders were enjoying legal protections against manipulation by powerful blockholders.[10] In fact, while Mancur Olson was writing his influential *The Logic of Collective Action*, three other authors were publishing books that would ignite the very sorts of collective movements about which Olson was so pessimistic: Ralph Nader's *Unsafe at Any Speed* (1965), Betty Friedan's *The Feminine Mystique* (1963), and Rachel Carson's *Silent Spring* (1962). The new social movements of the 1960s and 1970s for which these books became touchstones brought together a variety of diffuse groups that shared common social and progressive causes.

Advocates for the coordination model of interest representation responded by attributing noneconomic reasoning to the advocates of successful diffuse interests. Russell Hardin, who made an extensive study of the Sierra Club, attributed its success to "extra-rational motivations" of club members. Similarly, Terry Moe found that individuals who participated in representative associations understood poorly the costs and benefits of membership.[11] James Q. Wilson offered a similar analysis that focused on the motivations of regulators who advocated for diffuse interests. He focused on the role of policy entrepreneurship, a mode of policy-making in which "economic interests . . . are either not apparent or . . . are not of decisive importance."[12] On his account, policy entrepreneurs relied on cultural or educational backgrounds, rather than strictly economic criteria, for setting regulation. Wilson's idea of policy entrepreneurs would by the 1980s come to be widely embraced as a way to make the efflorescence of public interest legislation compatible with the Olsonian idea of interest coordination.[13]

Elsewhere in political science, various studies were finding that coordination might be far easier than Olson had supposed. Robert Axelrod found signs of decentralized coordination in iterated formal games.[14] Joseph Grieco and Kenneth Oye theorized that strategic trading would generate trade liberalization in the absence of formal transnational agreements.[15] Eleanor Ostrom discovered informal strategies of public goods provision in the absences of centralized solutions.[16] Each of these authors suggested that coordination was possible even in the absence of formal legal and political institutions. This finding posed a problem for the Olson thesis. If coordination was possible in the absence of formal political institutions, should it not also be possible in the densely institutionalized setting of advanced capitalist democracies? Research into neocorporatist institutions in Europe seemed to confirm this idea.[17]

What mattered in interest representation was not the diffuseness of the interest, but the institutions through which those interests were translated into public policy.

In retrospect, the evidence for systematic regulatory capture by concentrated interests was remarkably uneven. The issue is not only that diffuse interests have managed to organize effectively, but also that concentrated interests have not been able to dominate the policy process in the way that Olson and Stigler foresaw. To be sure, concentrated interests did lobby and achieve victories in public policy. The surprise is how relatively rarely that led to outcomes that directly undercut more diffuse economic interests.[18] Particularly challenging for the Olson view of policymaking was the move to industry deregulation that began in the United States in the late 1970s. If concentrated industry set regulatory policy, then regulation should be designed to increase the rents to incumbents in regulated sectors. But if that was true, then the small number of incumbent firms should have tried and succeeded in blocking deregulation.[19] This posed a dilemma for Olson and Stigler: either regulated firms did not get regulation that they wanted, and hence were not hurt by deregulation, or they benefited from regulation and should have fought to retain it. Researchers whose analysis was more closely engaged with managerial practice recognized that industry did not see the state as an amenable ally. David Vogel, for example, found that the American managerial class perceived that public policy was out of its control.[20] Research into lobbying and campaign contributions reinforced this view. Studies of lobbying by U.S. companies found that they invested a surprisingly small amount of funds to influence public policy given the potentially large benefits of regulatory manipulation.[21] One reason was that concentrated interests that exercised excessive influence against the broader public interest could quickly become the target of media contagion that would engender a broad public outcry.[22] Faced with the risk of public and policy retribution, narrow industry interests understood that they must ration their efforts to manipulate public policy.

If the influence of concentrated interests has been weak, the influence of diffuse interests has been one of the unheralded political trends of the postwar period. These interests—including environmentalists, women's groups, consumer groups, retired people, patient groups, gun owners, and any number of other diffuse groups—have defied the organizational obstacles theorized by Olson. Despite their large and diffuse constituencies, these groups mobilized around shared pragmatic interests and succeeded in having those interests transcribed into public policy. Since Olson's 1965 *Logic of Collective Action*, the voices of diffuse interests have driven the creation of countless new areas of policy and vast new government bureaucracies to administer those policies.

Diffuse Pragmatic Interests

For any issue of public policy affecting a large, diffuse group of shared interests, activation on that issue depends on a combination of individuals' perceptions about the potential benefits of acting, assessed both collectively and individually. The process involves a two-stage calculation. First, it must be determined whether a particular outcome, given the costs and benefits of achieving that outcome, is in the group's interest. This first stage is a pre-strategic assessment. Individuals are asked to assume for a moment that everyone could be compelled to pursue a project collectively, with no free riders. With perfect coordination, would the benefits of the project outweigh the costs? If so, the second stage is an evaluation of the project in terms of strategic interaction at the individual level. Here the expectation is that no individual would accept to undertake a project in which each individual also had an interest to free ride on the public benefit supported by others. In such instances, the project is unlikely to be achieved in the absence of coordination. The exception, adumbrated by hegemonic stability theory, includes cases in which the advantages to the individual are so great that free riders are grudgingly accepted. Thus individual actors may have two reasons to shy away from providing public goods. They may impose a higher cost *collectively* than the collective benefits they provide, meaning that they are, in a narrow economic sense, not really public goods. Or they are subject to free-rider problems, meaning that no individual has an interest in pursuing a collective outcome that would nonetheless improve the situation of all. For Chicago School regulation theorists, the failure of diffuse interests rested on the second, strategic assessment.

This emphasis is wrong on both empirically and theoretical grounds. Diffuse interests have typically failed to find representation in public policy not due to a failure of coordination, but because of a lack of perceived common interest. This has been especially true of idealistic movements that did not address pragmatic group concerns. Once pragmatic group concerns became recognized, diffuse actors could and did mobilize to represent their interests. Empirically, mobilization happened with relatively little delay following the recognition of a new public good. Nor did diffuse interests prove to be systematically weaker than concentrated interests. In many cases in which diffuse interests failed to find representation in the policy process, they succumbed not to concentrated interests but instead to other diffuse collective interests that were able to capture the mantle of legitimacy by defining and addressing alternative collective goals.

Interests held by groups may be concentrated or diffuse, and they may be pragmatic or idealistic (see Figure 1.1). Political science research on mobilization has tended to collapse these two dimensions. Diffuse groups were assumed to be idealistic, meaning they pursue policies that bring a social benefit at a cost to the material interests of the individual; concentrated groups were assumed to be pragmatic, meaning they pursue policies that meet the material interests of the individual, but at a social cost. This approach to mobilization research had its roots in the new social movements (NSMs) literature of the 1970s and 1980s.[23] These studies gave particular attention to lifestyle and environmental movements that confronted and questioned basic economic and social priorities. The most ambitious NSM researchers thought they were observing a new stage of social organization in which postmaterial values would transform the existing economic and social order.[24] Perhaps inevitability, such optimism was followed by disillusion. A generation later, Europe's 1968 movements were perceived by a new wave of social theorists to have abandoned their idealism for the healthy pensions they assumed as a social entitlement. But in the tumultuous rise and fall of NSM research, something important was also missed. By linking social organization mainly to idealistic social goals, the NSM literature tended to overlook the real, if diffuse, material interests that *did* find their voice in formal politics during this time. These were the interests that, while

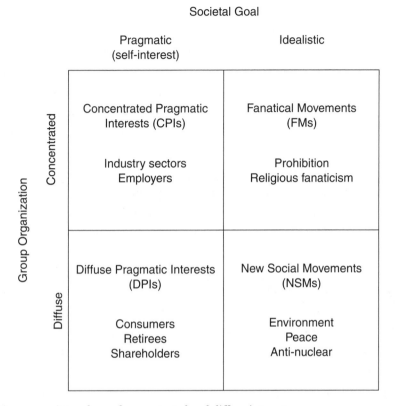

Figure 1.1. A typology of concentrated and diffuse interests.

the peace and student movements were rallying in the streets, were more quietly pushing their way into every aspect of economic and social policymaking. The success of these diffuse pragmatic interests may be the most enduring legacy of late twentieth-century interest organization.

By linking mass mobilization specifically to idealistic movements, and concentrated interests to pragmatic economic concerns, political scientists have tended to overlook important mixed forms of interest representation. On the one hand, concentrated interest groups might pursue their own idealistic goals through policies that affect society as a whole. Such efforts are different from social movements that pursue idealistic goals in that they make no effort to secure broader public support for their specific ideological agenda. They are also distinct from concentrated interest groups that pursue pragmatic goals that affect society as a whole. Indeed, their goal is pursued even though it is (1) understood that it is not in their own material (but instead idealistic) interest, and (2) that it may directly contradict the broader societal interest and/or ideology. Such movements of concentrated idealists might be defined as fanatical.[25] By this account, the class of fanatics includes not just religious fanatics, but also social campaigners who attempt to restrict self-interested (and therefore economically optimal) behavior without an accompanying effort to mobilize the broader public around the underlying social or personal ideal. Although fanaticism does not require violence, its goal of imposing a narrow set of idealistic goals not shared by most of society frequently places the fanatic in a position requiring compulsion.

The second category of interest group activity that traditional accounts of mobilization fail to capture is that set of diffuse interest groups that pursue policy outcomes grounded in their collective material interests. These groups have diffuse pragmatic interests (DPIs), and they are the focus of this book. Such groups are diffuse not only because they represent a large pool of unaffiliated individuals, but also because members of the group have multiple and cross-cutting identities and interests that make group identification on a particular dimension difficult. The individuals in these diffuse groups understand what they want, even if they don't conceive of their specific interest as being shared by a coherent if diffuse class of people. Because their interests are often multidimensional, diffuse pragmatic interests may end up being defined in different ways depending upon how the diffuse interest is first identified and "activated." Still, once a particular DPI *has* been identified, it is relatively easy to track the success of its implementation in national policy and practice.

Diffuse pragmatic interests, those interests that fall into the lower-left quadrant of Figure 1.1, have been the unspoken success stories of postwar mass mobilization. Diffuse but pragmatic consumer interests have systematically dominated national policy processes in trade policy, competition policy, retail liberalization, and labor policy for the past forty years. The same has been true for other diffuse groups, including women, welfare recipients, and the large and growing population of retirees. A testimony to their success is the difficulty in finding a diffuse interest group with shared pragmatic concerns that has *not* succeeded in organizing to have their shared interests represented. Failures of DPI representation do exist—in the cases of agricultural protections, drug pricing policies, and minority shareholder rights, for example. But these instances of failure seem to be exceptions rather than the rule. In a world of successful diffuse interest representation, such failures of representation deserve special attention.

The Surprise of Coordination

Empirical studies have consistently shown a capacity to coordinate when the collective interest is both material and evident. One of the early studies to assess the impact of group size on coordination to achieve pragmatic goals was conducted by sociologists Gerald Marwell and Ruth Ames.[26] In their 1979 study, groups of high school students were given funds to invest. Participants could opt to invest individually, at a relatively low rate of return, or to add some or all of their funds to a group pool, which would give a higher return. Regardless of how individuals invested, the returns to the group pool were then divided among all members of the group. Given the theorized impact of group size on cooperation, the authors expected larger groups to have fewer students contributing their funds to the group investing pool. Instead, they found no significant difference across group sizes.[27] Coordination was by no means complete. But a surprisingly high percentage of students, 87 percent on average, contributed at least some of their funds to the collective pool. Of those, 22 percent contributed only to the common pool. Just 13 percent invested only privately. "There can be little doubt," concluded Marwell and Ames, "that subjects in our experiment do not fit Olson's description of rational free riders in this isolated, abstract, but financially real situation."[28] Their criticism is perhaps too sharp. After all, coordination was not complete among these groups, and potential financial gains were lost due to a lack of sufficient coordination. The point is not that coordination is easy, or automatic. But when the group interest is material and evident, a fairly high level of coordination can nonetheless be achieved.

A real-world, and widely studied, example of this phenomenon is listener-supported public radio.[29] It is costly for public radio stations to coordinate their viewers so that they all contribute at a sufficient level, and stations put considerable effort into raising funds. With a reasonably affordable amount of effort, however, and with matching funds from non-profit organizations and the government, they are able to prod the listening public into contributing sufficient funds to sustain the public good.

A fascinating set of cases that clearly reflects the properties of diffuse pragmatic interest representation involves specific disease populations. Individuals that either are suffering from an uncured disease, or are in a particularly susceptible population, have material and evident interest in finding a cure. They also clearly face strategic reasons for letting someone else take on the task. What is important about these medical examples is that the collective interest is unambiguous. We know without question that AIDS patients have an interest in finding a cure for the disease, even if they choose not to participate in AIDS patient groups or contribute to funding AIDS research. Yet the U.S. mobilization around AIDS was highly successful. Nor is this a recent phenomenon. A classic disease-centered coordination success story was the effort of the nonprofit March of Dimes in the 1920s to raise funding for polio research. The organization's strategies to induce contributions relied heavily on social pressure. Popular culture icons such as Humphrey Bogart and Mickey Mouse appeared in March of Dimes advertisements. Although criticized as manipulative or exploitative, March of Dimes posters featuring cute children that were also clearly afflicted with polio (the original poster children) were effective. A strategy of "porch light" fund-raising campaigns applied powerful social pressure to encourage contributions. At exactly 7 P.M. on a specific night, households wishing to contribute to the March of Dimes were asked to put on their porch lights so that volunteers would know whom to visit—and also so that neighbors could see who was giving and who was not. The lesson of the March of Dimes success story is not that defending diffuse pragmatic interests is necessarily easy, but that it *is* possible. And when collective interests are both material and evident, they tend to evoke a rapid and effective collective response.

One of the most striking apparent counterexamples is in the area of environmental protection, and in particular climate change. Responses to climate change pit energy providers and manufacturers—for whom the costs of adjustment are likely to be high—against the general public interest in restraining temperature increases. In this contest, the concentrated interests appear to win. But a survey of responses across countries show that these responses mirror popular sentiment about climate change. For countries whose populations had come to see global warming as a pragmatic collective threat, efforts to promote the reduction of CO_2 emissions followed quickly. If we compare levels of reported concern about climate change in different countries with national commitments to reduce CO_2 output under the Kyoto Protocol, the correlation is evident (see Figure 1.2). In general, countries whose population perceived climate change as an important environmental issue also committed to significant CO_2 emissions reductions.

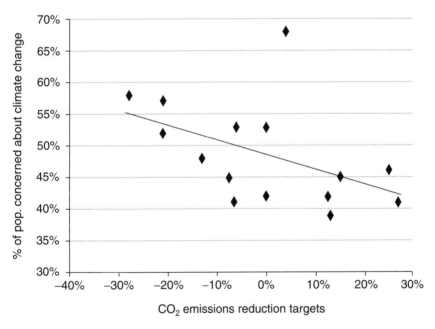

Figure 1.2. EU member-state views of climate change and national Kyoto targets for CO_2 emissions (2012 targets relative to 1990 emissions levels). The survey reports the percentage of respondents who identified climate change among the top five environmental problems their countries face. This survey question provides a useful means of identifying not just the fact of concern, but also the level of concern. Respondents who feel global warming is not among the top five environmental problems faced in their country would probably also prefer that political leaders focus their attention on other, more pressing environmental issues. The prominent outlier on this chart is Sweden. *Sources: Eurobarometer 217* (2005); European Council, Council Decision 2002/358/EC, 25 April 2002.

Of course, one might object that none of these countries committed to reducing CO_2 emissions sufficient to stem global warming. That is, in part, because global warming poses a coordination problem not only at the national level but also at the global level, and at the global level coordination remains a problem. We are only just beginning to develop the kinds of institutions that might promote the representation of global diffuse interests.

What we do not detect, however, is any sign of a coordination problem within national policymaking. Narrow industry interests have generally not thwarted diffuse public interests in reducing emissions. Rather, it is differences in the broad public perception of need that explain most of the variance in emissions reduction we observe across countries.

The point of these examples is not that diffuse interests will always find an adequate policy response, nor that coordination is at all easy. The fact of frequent, effective diffuse interest representation suggests that we must look more closely at the incentives and tools by which advocates overcome the very real obstacles to a coordinated response. We should also focus more critical attention on those cases in which diffuse pragmatic interests go *un*represented in public policy. For too long we have accepted an easy account of these failures based on the diffuseness of the underlying interest. The relative ease with which diffuse interests appear to find representation in public policy suggests that the reasons behind these exceptions may be more complicated and more interesting than we had previously assumed.

The Limits of Industry Capture

Not only do concentrated interests organize surprisingly effectively to address collective material concerns, it is also surprisingly common for concentrated interests to fail to achieve their goals, even when they commit significant effort and funds to the fight. Indeed, some of the most striking counterevidence to the Stigler/Olson theory comes from a historical moment when the implications of their theories should have been most evident, namely, during the two-term (2001–2009) administration of U.S. President George W. Bush. At first glance, the experience of industry under this explicitly pro-business presidency seems to confirm the idea that industry enjoyed broad influence across a range of policy areas.

This was a period when the stars should have been aligned to promote industry influence over policy. For the first time since 1954, pro-business Republicans controlled both houses of Congress and the presidency. They held this dominant position for six years, from 2000 to 2006—a sufficiently long period to design, negotiate, and pass even complex regulatory reform legislation. (The next previous Republican president to benefit from similar same-party congressional support was Dwight Eisenhower, who was elected in 1952 and enjoyed only two years of a Republican-led Congress before both houses were lost to the Democrats.) Furthermore, the leadership of both houses of Congress during President Bush's administration was ideologically aligned with the president. That ideology was grounded in a deep commitment to liberalizing the regulatory environment for business. The president himself held an MBA, had made his career mainly in business, and had made clear that he supported the business community. Political confrontation over congressional access to the list of attendees at the vice president's 2001 Energy Task Force meetings highlighted the degree to which industry enjoyed close ties with government policymakers. Finally, the attacks on the World Trade Center and Pentagon in 2001 placed the country on a war footing. Governments in time of war typically enjoy greater policy discretion than their peacetime counterparts. Wartime leaders also enjoy greater latitude to shift legislative priorities, especially if those are seen to be linked to security.[30]

Headline regulatory reform priorities for the incoming administration included pro-business changes to personal bankruptcy, environmental protection, and consumer protection regulations. Each reform had strong industry advocates, and those advocates were active in pushing for the reform. Given the propitious environment, what is perhaps most striking about this period are the cases of regulatory capture that did *not* occur. Automakers did *not* roll back fleet emissions standards, although they did lobby successfully to block California from proceeding with its own higher state-level standards. Superfund legislation for environmental cleanup was *not* repealed, although many sites were indeed removed from the list. The inheritance tax was *not* eliminated, despite sustained efforts to achieve this. Government lands were *not* widely privatized. And, in the highly publicized campaign to permit oil exploration in Alaska's Arctic National Wildlife Reserve (ANWAR), drilling was *not* allowed. This sort of counterfactual policy history is of course difficult to assess. But it evokes the feature of the 2000–2006 period that was perhaps most unexpected: the limited degree to which narrow interests managed to capture the regulatory process for their own benefit at public expense.

To be certain, meaningful pro-business regulation was enacted during this time. The Class Action Fairness Act (CAFA), signed into law in 2005, gave U.S. federal courts jurisdiction over class action suits in which the plaintiffs and defendants were in different states. Advocates argued the legislation would stop forum shopping, by which plaintiffs were able to select especially favorable states and districts in which to file their cases. In the same year, Congress passed the Bankruptcy Abuse Prevention and Consumer Protection Act that placed means-based limits on consumer access to automatic discharge via Chapter 7 bankruptcy procedure. The legislation was supported most strongly by the lobbying group of U.S. credit card companies, which had fought for eleven years to achieve bankruptcy reform. Yet, while acknowledging industry success in these cases, the gains seem relatively modest given what industry interests could have hoped for. Why didn't concentrated interests get more?

The case of the 2003 Clear Skies Act suggests some of the challenges that concentrated interests faced. This legislative initiative proposed to exempt power plants from certain emissions controls under the 1990 Clean Air Act, while loosening standards for reducing sulfur dioxide, nitrogen oxide, and mercury emissions. The reduced standards were to be tied to an emissions trading scheme modeled explicitly on the successful sulfur dioxide legislation of the 1990s. The primary advocate of the Clear Skies approach was the main association for the electric power utilities, the Edison Electric Institute. With close ties between the Bush administration and the energy sector, passage should have been easy. Yet the road was surprisingly rocky. When the bill came before Congress, in 2003, it did not find enough support to pass. In 2005, the key provisions of the bill were implemented through EPA regulation.[31]

The part of the legislation that was most important to coal power plants—the restrictions on mercury emissions—quickly ran into trouble. The 1990 amendments to the Clean Air Act called for power plants to apply the most effective technologies available to limit mercury emissions—so-called "maximum achievable control technologies." The EPA's March 2005 Clean Air Mercury Rule changed this approach. Rather than imposing technology requirements on a plant-by-plant basis, it moved to an interstate cap-and-trade standard. Under the new provisions, producers exceeding their allotted emissions budget would have to purchase additional emissions permits on the open market. These could come from other plants, even in other states, that had found ways to reduce their own mercury emissions below their allotted budget. This provision was particularly relevant to coal-powered plants, which produced an estimated 40 percent of U.S. mercury emissions.

Even as the new rule was being drafted, however, questions emerged. The EPA's own inspector general publicly criticized the agency for not comparing the cap-and-trade approach to other possible regulatory solutions, as required by law.[32] The *Washington Post* revealed on its front page that results of a Harvard School of Public Health study on the economic cost of mercury emissions were expurgated from the EPA's final environment assessment report.[33] The Union of Concerned Scientists warned that emissions trading was not suited to mercury emissions because mercury tended to accumulate in the area where it was emitted.[34] This created the risk of mercury hot spots around plants that opted to purchase emissions credits rather than reduce emissions. Even the *Wall Street Journal* chastised the EPA for ignoring its own internal impact findings. In June 2005, four national associations of public health and health providers sued the EPA for failing to protect children and fetuses.[35] In June 2006, sixteen states joined by dozens of environmental and public health groups filed suit in federal court against the EPA for not acting more decisively to limit mercury emissions.[36] What is striking about this case is the way in which even a relatively modest case of regulatory capture by the electricity-generating industry[37] set off a chain of public recriminations and legal claims that would eventually force the EPA to change its approach to mercury emissions.

As the mercury emissions example suggests, influencing regulatory agencies is not as easy as the Olson/Stigler model supposes. First, narrow interest representation is politically unpopular. Although it is difficult to separate the impact of other drivers of public opinion, public opinion of the leadership of the Republican Party fell to extraordinarily low levels of support during this period. Equally telling were the names given to pro-business legislative projects: the Clear Skies Act was lenient on power plant emissions; the Healthy Forests Act gave lumber companies new access to national forests; the Bankruptcy Reform Act had the phrase "and Consumer Protection" tacked onto its title. This Orwellian turn in legislative labeling is hard to interpret as a sign of overweening industry power. It has instead the feel of elected officials seeking shelter from the electoral ramifications of unpopular legislation.

A particular challenge for concentrated groups in achieving their narrow interests (those that impose a public cost) is that the small number of members they represent makes them easy to identify in the media. In general, the smaller the coterie, the easier they become to target and, often, to vilify. At least since Upton Sinclair's hugely successful 1906 account of conditions in the Chicago meatpacking industry, *The Jungle*, stories of narrow corporate malfeasance have been a boon to publishing. Whatever the potential benefits of lobbying for legislative "relief," the potential cost of being targeted for subverting the general interest is often higher. Even narrow economic interests that are not strictly susceptible to public disapprobation can face high indirect costs from unfavorable media attention. Electricity producers are a good example. Consumers have to buy electricity, and in general they have little choice among providers. But if providers become the focus of a media campaign assailing the regulatory benefits they achieved through effective lobbying, those benefits may quickly be reversed.

This experience is consistent with empirical studies of industry lobbying and campaign contributions that have shown that companies underinvest in favorable regulation. Noting the potentially large return on policy "investments," Gordon Tullock first asked why companies did not allocate more funds to shaping a favorable regulatory regime.[38] Stephen Ansolabehere, John de Figueiredo, and James Snyder confirm that companies contribute far less than might be expected given the potential returns in terms of favorable policy outcomes from campaign contributions: "Given the value of policy at stake, firms and other interest groups should give more."[39] The reason they do not, they find, is that donations have very little impact on specific legislator decisions, as revealed in the record of congressional roll call votes. But would higher levels of contribution have a greater impact? If the case of mercury emissions is typical, probably not. As the perception of illegitimate industry influence grows, the likelihood of media scrutiny also grows. And the perception of injustice seems to motivate environmental, professional, and consumer groups to target cases of undue influence. This is especially true when already unpopular sectors are perceived to be doing harm to the general public interest. This makes investment in lobbying a careful calculation. Firms and sectors need to exert enough influence to help shape policies, but not so much as to draw undue public scrutiny. We are far from the world of policy capture that Olson and Stigler envisaged.

Defending Diffuse Interests

Three different sets of actors have been the focus of efforts to explain successful diffuse interest representation. The most closely studied have been grassroots constituencies mobilized by social activists. Mancur Olson was skeptical of the potential for diffuse interest groups to mobilize quickly, but he did feel that they could organize given enough time. The tool he emphasized for overcoming the coordination challenges of mobilization was the selective benefit for membership. Although the benefits of public goods could not be excluded from nonmembers, advocacy organizations could provide other kinds of benefits that were exclusive. Olson was right to focus on selective benefits, which interest groups commonly provide, but he was perhaps wrong about their function. In principle, selective benefits should never be able to provide sufficient material benefits to encourage membership from individuals who would not otherwise be inclined to join a group. Assuming membership in an advocacy organization has a cost, in terms of time or membership fees, it is difficult to see how that group can provide selective benefits that will cover the cost of the benefits and also leave excess "profit" to dedicate to the group mission. The problem is that a selective incentive that is of sufficient value to induce group membership might be provided at a lower cost by a competing provider that was not also attempting to provide a public good. By contrast, if the selective incentive is not sufficient in benefit to cover the cost of the selective benefit *and* the cost of providing the public good, then it does not overcome the collective action problem. This implies that the organizers of social movements that rely on selective incentives must not themselves be acting in a self-interested way.[40]

Those who are induced to join a group by the provision of selective benefits were therefore likely to have already been inclined to undertake an activity that would impose an extra cost on themselves. Selective benefits may only work for potential activists who *already* have non-self-interested reasons for joining a movement. What seems to matter is that the selective benefits be related to the collective good that the group is also trying to secure. Trade unions secure credit access for their members in case of strike actions. Consumer groups provide comparative product evaluations and distribute warnings and recall notices. Environmental groups offer tools and strategies for limiting individual environmental impact. This link between selective benefits and a group's collective interest suggests that their primary purpose is affiliational. Because the selective goods embody the principles of the organization, they help to identify, attract, and retain potential members that are likely already to have noneconomic reasons for joining a group.[41] And because the motivations of individual members may have more to do with frustration and anger than with economic optimizing, specific outrageous events are important drivers of new membership.[42] Opposition from policymakers or producers can strengthen that sense of outrage and make an advocacy organization stronger. Motivations based in individual or social justice, when properly directed, have been especially powerful in creating movements to defend diffuse interests. Roy Kiesling, a U.S. activist who helped to mobilize consumers in the 1960s, explained: "The motivating spring of the consumer movement was anger . . . a peculiar, enervating form of anger that flourishes like some mold of fungus under conditions of frustration and impotence."[43]

A second approach to diffuse interest representation has relied on the economic interests of other actors, especially producers, to support and extend protections to unaffiliated sets of diffuse interests with which they share strategic objectives. In these cases concentrated economic actors—mainly those with interests related to production—adopt the goals of diffuse interests as their own. These concentrated economic interests may wish to extend or restrict markets, shape demand, or rally allies in conflicts between labor and capital. If diffuse interests can be enlisted to legitimize these efforts, the potential benefits may persist over time. In some cases, firms have embraced broader consumer goals as a means to enlarge or stabilize existing markets. U.S. advocacy groups in the 1970s pushed for commercial banks to extend retail credit to women and urban blacks. After initial resistance, banks quickly learned that these new customers were potentially highly profitable, and banks became strong advocates of credit access policies.[44] In France, early mass retailers like the Leclerc chain collaborated with consumer associations to lobby for permits to open new large-format retail sites that tended to offer goods at lower prices.[45] More recently, renewable energy generators in Germany have collaborated with environmental advocacy groups to promote government regulation supporting the adoption of new wind and solar generation technologies.[46] In such cases, industry-consumer coalitions help to open and shape markets in ways that benefit coalitions of narrow and diffuse interests.

Other instances of industry adoption have worked not to extend markets, but to protect them. Incumbents concerned about new entrants may push for policies intended to protect broad consumer interests in order to limit competition purely based on price.[47] One of the first to notice the role of producers in securing policies that also fulfilled public goals was David Vogel.[48] In *Trading Up*, he argued that producers might work with consumer and environmental advocates and regulators to support higher standards in order to raise barriers to foreign producers.[49] Although they would face new costs of compliance, those costs would be lower than for rivals, and could serve as a barrier to entry. In response, foreigners could be expected to import these higher standards in order to be able to create a competitive export sector. Over time, this logic might drive a competitive upgrading of regulations favoring diffuse interests. In Canada, for example, the logging sector has embraced lumber certification schemes to promote sustainable forest management.[50] This sort of industry support for regulatory upgrading, what Vogel dubbed the California effect, has also been deployed as a means to manage domestic competition. Higher standards can raise barriers to new domestic competitors by shaping the institutions of domestic competition.

A third approach to defending diffuse interests has relied on the logic of electoral politics exploited by policymakers within government. Early theorists of democratic competition were skeptical that politicians would act in the general interest. Both Anthony Downs' median voter theory and William Riker's theory of minimum winning coalitions suggested that politicians should ignore highly diffuse interests in order to target narrow constituency interests.[51] Yet recent research suggests that policymakers *do* work to defend diffuse interests—not because those interests will deliver decisive votes, but in order to preempt these issues from being adopted by potential opponents.[52] Other theories emphasize the role of policy entrepreneurs in identifying and defending new interests. Concerned about their own legitimacy, and imbued with a bureaucratic ethos to support the spirit of the laws from which they draw their authority, policy entrepreneurs have the ability to deploy existing regulatory authority in the broad public interest.[53]

Legitimacy Coalitions

These three kinds of actors—activists, firms, and policymakers—all have strong incentives to organize or to advocate for diffuse interests. However motivated they may be, each must overcome the challenge of presenting its own narrow interest as publicly legitimate. Concentrated industry actors face the clearest obstacle to legitimacy. Any perception of quid pro quo behavior, in which they support politicians in exchange for regulatory rewards, damages the legitimacy of the policy they are advocating. Although not as obvious as for concentrated industry interest, both policymakers and social activists also face challenges to the perceived legitimacy of the interests they advocate. Even legislators acting in the interest of the general public may face skepticism that they are pandering to narrow constituencies. At the agency level, concerns about capture—either by industry or by the "clientele" they are meant to be protecting—raise concerns about the legitimacy of regulatory responses.[54] Finally, social activists and their grassroots membership face questions of legitimacy. These are allayed in part by the very difficulty of mobilizing a diffuse group. But because successful mobilization frequently requires exaggeration, the general public may regard mobilizations with some skepticism.[55] To succeed, even successful social activists need to seek external sources of legitimacy.

One of the most important strategies for each of these groups has been to forge coalitions with each other. By working together, sets of interested actors can engender legitimacy around a new area of diffuse interest representation that would be difficult for any individual actor working independently to create. Most commonly, this occurs when two of the three potential main protagonists in securing diffuse interests—policymakers, social activists, and producers—collaborate to achieve common regulatory goals. In the case of consumer protection regulations, we observe each of the three possible coalitions emerging in different national settings. Figure 1.3 depicts the three major policy actors and the three kinds of legitimacy coalitions that they can form.

The first scenario is one in which government regulators interact with newly mobilized nongovernmental groups to promote a new set of diffuse interests. In this interaction, the government grants the groups either funds or formal status; the groups in turn help to define the scope of legitimate regulatory intervention by the state. The process is not typically directly collaborative, but interactive, with the pairs of actors playing one off of another. This sort of interaction may be supportive, as with the provision of funding or legal support for diffuse interests. It may also be adversarial, as when diffuse groups forge their own legitimacy through opposition to unfriendly regulatory stances. In cases in which advocacy groups do not already exist, the government may step in to provide resources that assist in their formation. Over time, this interaction between advocacy groups and regulators generates a bottom-up construction of a

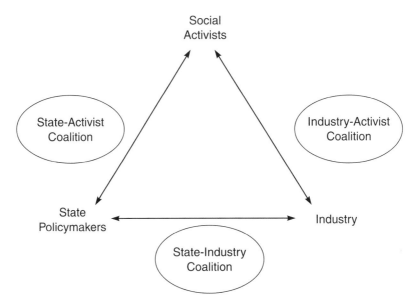

Figure 1.3. Policy actors and legitimacy coalitions. *Note:* Ovals describe coalitions of two actors.

new field of regulatory legitimacy where none existed before. The back-and-forth creates a sort of bootstrapping, in which new issues that had not previously been the focus of government attention become legitimate targets of public policy. When state-activist coalitions come to dominate, the concentrated interests of producers tend to be either ignored or intentionally excluded from the policy process.

In the second type of coalition, social activists and producers work together largely outside the regulatory purview of the state. They may choose to exclude state regulators out of an interest in maintaining organizational discretion, or out of a reticence to cede policy control. Alternatively, states may promote these sorts of independent negotiated responses in order to avoid being drawn into entirely new areas of policy or enforcement. For this sort of negotiated response to succeed, both producers and activists must be sufficiently organized so that decisions negotiated by top representatives will be accepted by the broad class of actors they represent and effectively implemented by targeted classes of producers. This may be accomplished through a balance of organizational power, or through a formal legal arrangement granting representative bodies authority to negotiate on behalf of their constituencies. This set of negotiated responses to diffuse interests I call industry-activist coalitions.

Industry-activist coalitions have typically emerged between diffuse interest groups and company management, but they may also be based on ties with workers. This sort of collaboration occurs only when it provides benefits to both groups. For diffuse interest groups, organized labor has a lot to contribute. It typically has mastered the technology of mobilization, and maintains mailing lists of potential grassroots constituencies that may be mined for related issues. These labor groups may in turn have reasons for supporting other diffuse interest groups. Two types of cases are possible. On the one hand, organized labor undertaking wage negotiations may use other diffuse issue areas as leverage against employers. This occurred periodically in France, where union-affiliated consumer groups often coordinated their consumer boycotts with protests over wages or working conditions. But the collaboration with diffuse interests need not be a tool for confronting employers. In high-skill employment settings, organized labor may choose to support certain kinds of regulatory responses that favor high-skill, high-wage production. Unions in high-skills environments, for example, have commonly perceived an educated and informed customer base as a bulwark against low-quality, and therefore low-wage, manufacturing.

A third type of policy coalition does not rely on diffuse interest mobilization. Rather, in this approach, governments work directly and interactively with industry. Typically, regulation or the threat of regulation by the state stimulates industry self-regulation, reinforced and delimited by background regulations and legal principles that grant legitimacy to the self-regulatory strategy. Although these types of industry-state regulatory strategies are commonly perceived to be the result of regulatory capture, they do not typically have their roots in industry lobbying. More commonly, new government regulatory efforts intended to defend diffuse groups receive support from industry over time. As industry groups come to recognize their interest in the regulation—as a means to extend markets or to raise regulatory barriers to new entrants—they then promote further efforts at protection. In Germany, industry faced pressure from the economics ministry to design voluntary product safety standards within the country's main standards-setting body, Deutsches Institut für Normung (DIN). As it became clear that these new standards tended to favor Germany's large and most technically capable firms, industry pushed for them to be made mandatory in the 1980 Equipment Safety Act.[56] Similarly, U.S. pharmaceutical firms in the 1990s actively resisted proposals by Newt Gingrich's Republican Revolution to liberalize Food and Drug Administration (FDA) efficacy standards—of which the pharmaceutical industry was initially highly critical—out of concern that the liberalized standards would open up the industry to new competitors. Industry-state coalitions can be an attractive regulatory approach for governments that are apprehensive about entering new and highly technical areas of regulation. The dangers of regulatory capture are in turn limited by the institutions that promote diffuse interest representation: effective democratic elections, a free press, watchdog groups that monitor the effectiveness of self-regulation schemes, and regulators that stand ready to intervene if the self-regulatory solutions are perceived to have abandoned the broad public interest.

The Role of Narratives

Diffuse groups that organize do so around legitimating narratives that define the shared interests of their broad class. These legitimating narratives, in turn, set the framing of current and subsequent policy discourse. They determine, into the future, what interests might legitimately be supported in the group's interest and which may not. Legitimating narratives play a pragmatic as well as a normative role in policy formation. Pragmatically, they help to coordinate highly dispersed actors around a unified set of policy initiatives. The role of policy narratives in helping to coordinate around a specific set of issues has been noted in other areas of policy.[57] In this pragmatic role, they are a critical tool for diffuse interest representation, in two respects. First, advocates of diffuse group interests, whether inside or outside the political process, need a narrative that allows them to show constituencies that they do indeed share a set of concerns that deserve public redress. This makes legitimating narratives especially important in cases of highly diffuse interests. The larger the group that shares a common set of interests, the more these common interests are likely to be tied to other and conflicting interests. The second pragmatic role of legitimating narratives is the way in which they define and structure policy responses.[58] Most diffuse interests are sufficiently complex that they require a plurality of policy responses. These may include new substantive rights, new rights to organize and access the courts, or new kinds of market regulation that structure economic competition. Legitimating narratives help to organize a consistent set of policies from among this diverse, and technically complex, set of individual policy responses. In this pragmatic mode, legitimating narratives coordinate both interests and responses.

Legitimating narratives also play a normative role. From a range of potential policy goals, they define both what is in the broad public interest, and in which areas a public policy response is demanded. By defining parameters of the public good, these narratives provide a basis for policy legitimacy that is tied neither to formal aggregative procedures (so-called input legitimacy) nor to explicit outcomes that generate improved efficiencies (so-called output legitimacy).[59] Rather, legitimating narratives define the boundaries of public and private interest within which even unsuccessful policies may derive legitimacy based on their intended goals. And, as distinct from the purely coordinating function of legitimating narratives, the normative role places limits on the narratives that may be defined as legitimate. Not every potential coordinating narrative can be considered legitimate. Rather, it must meet a broad test of public good that constrains the potential discursive space.

For diffuse interests, two classes of narratives provide the dominant discourses of legitimate policy response: narratives of access, and narratives of protection. Narratives of access define policy benefits as an expansion both of the number of individuals gaining access to goods and services, and of the quantity or price of goods to which they are gaining access. Access to credit, access to inexpensive consumer products and food, access to drugs—in each of these markets, regulatory policies have been fought for and justified on the basis of availability and/or affordability. The rhetoric of access is not aligned solely with economic or policy liberalism. Indeed, early legitimacy of Europe's agricultural policy was premised on access to products in the context of a significant balance-of-payment problem. Similarly, U.S. mass retailers like Walmart have defended themselves against charges leveled by traditional retailers and labor unions by vaunting the unprecedented access they offer to low-priced products. By contrast, narratives of protection define risks against which diffuse interests must be defended. They typically invoke government regulation or industry self-regulation to restrict access to a sector in the interest of safer or more orderly competition. The rhetoric of protection can be a tool for aligning consumer interests with protectionist goals of producers. It most commonly takes the form of restricting competition in the interest of maintaining quality.

As these cases suggest, the narratives of access and protection are initially highly malleable. Who is being protected, and from what? Who is gaining access, and to what? As new diffuse interests emerge and are defined, a decisive struggle takes place over definition of legitimate common interests. Such struggles pit alternative visions of the common interest against one another. In credit markets, for example, the poor may be seen as needing greater access to credit, or as needing to be protected from exploitation in the form of high interest rates. Once established, however, narratives of access or protection come to define both how diffuse interests are perceived in public policy and how individual members of a diffuse interest group perceive that group's common interests. Because they serve a role in coordinating the expectations of policymakers and the public, such narratives tend to exhibit historical persistence.

At this point, one might object that the strategies I describe as generating legitimacy for new policies—coalitions forged through legitimating narratives—are merely a fig leaf covering the raw influence of concentrated interests in society. There are two reasons to think this is not the case. First, the priorities expressed by consumer groups were not merely veiled industry aspirations. In many countries, industry worked closely with consumer groups to negotiate a mutually acceptable response, but they did so in the shadow of a greater threat from direct state intervention. In countries in which consumer groups worked with state regulators to bootstrap new policies, regulators also gave material and other kinds of support to help the consumer groups. In general, the experience of the consumer protection movement across the advanced industrial societies offers evidence that the diffuse interests being defended were real. Industry in every country initially preferred the status quo—a regulatory regime in which they retained autonomy in production and sales decisions. The outcomes that emerged, and the legitimating strategies they relied upon, were in every case something different from the original preferences of concentrated industry groups.

Second, even in cases in which concentrated interests clearly participated in the design of a policy, the need to justify their preferred policy in terms of a narrative that linked their specific preferences to the interests of a diffuse group placed limits on their policy discretion. The point is not that concentrated interests are powerless, but that their investments in policy influence have long time-horizons and may embody genuine trade-offs. In European agricultural policy, for example, we observe a powerful political interest that is bound by its historical legitimating narrative. The success of European agriculture in the early postwar period was in linking the idea of farmer supports to the broad public goal of food abundance. The target audience was the general public, and the narrative emphasized the logic of access. By the 1990s, however, European agricultural officials were trying to change the narrative of agricultural support. The new narrative would emphasize agricultural supports as a means to achieve rural land conservation. However, in attempting to shift from a narrative of access to a narrative of protection, the agricultural authorities seemed to be undermining the basis for their own internal support. The challenge was not with the general public but with their constituency, as farmers across Europe balked at the new approach.

The Role of Institutions

This book explores five sets of comparative studies that focus on the ways in which concentrated and diffuse interests interact in the context of new government regulation. The cases are diverse in their emphasis, and range from instances in which diffuse interests have been successful—especially in general consumer protection legislation passed during the 1960s and 1970s—to other cases in which concentrated interests have been most influential. The latter cases, focused on pharmaceutical and agricultural regulation, provide the strongest evidence for an Olsonian approach to collective action. Yet, as I show below, they also reveal important limits on producer influence in public policy. Two final cases, focused on the regulation of retailing and consumer credit, point to further weaknesses of size-based organizational theory in explaining cross-country differences in regulatory outcomes. Taken together, these cases identify key deficiencies in the Olsonian interest-group approach to public policy analysis. They also suggest the possibility of a more productive approach to interest group politics that emphasizes the role of coalitions in determining which interests come to be reflected in public policy. Based on these case studies, I propose an alternative approach to interest group influence that emphasizes the role of coalitions built around legitimating narratives.

One virtue of this alternative approach is the emphasis is places on the institutional context in which legitimacy coalitions are forged. Two kinds of institutional variation in particular appear to matter. First, core national institutions of capitalism—including labor market and capital market institutions—can influence relative support for competing diffuse interests.[60] For countries that rely more heavily on nonmarket allocation of human and productive capital, so-called coordinated market economies (CMEs), product market competition tends to emphasize competition on the intensive margin. Their firms, operating with highly structured labor training systems and close ties between capital and management, tend to compete more effectively on dimensions of quality and engineering. By contrast, countries that rely more heavily on market mechanisms to coordinate human and productive capital accumulation, so-called liberal market economies (LMEs), tend to favor product market competition that emphasizes competition on the extensive margin. Firms in this liberal setting compete by expanding markets, both into radically new kinds of product markets, and by aggressively extending their customer base. Other things being equal, the extensive competition in LMEs should favor more highly diffuse interests. Conversely, the intensive competition in CMEs should favor the merely somewhat diffuse interests.

Second, electoral systems may influence politicians' incentives to favor different kinds of diffuse interests. Ronald Rogowski and Mark Kayser have found empirical evidence for this tendency based on comparative price level data.[61] They argue that the low proportionality of majoritarian, two-party electoral systems pushes politicians to favor consumer votes over producer campaign contributions. My own research suggests that the important factor is the possibility for cross-class alliance formation in proportional electoral regimes. Majoritarian electoral regimes, because they generate a struggle among two dominant parties to capture the political center, tend to favor highly diffuse interests over merely somewhat diffuse "sectoral" interests. By contrast, proportional systems with multiple political parties tend to enable the defense of sectoral over highly diffuse interests. In practice, national economic and electoral systems tend to be highly coordinated.[62]

Taken together, the institutional setting in which politicians and producers operate may tend to favor one set of diffuse interests over another. In countries like the United States, with winner-take-all elections and a liberal market economy, "universal" diffuse interests associated with consumption and citizenship have tended to win out over sectoral interests of workers or declining economic sectors. In continental European countries like Germany, proportional representation and coordinated institutions of market competition have tended to favor sectoral diffuse interests over universal diffuse interests. This is the case in part because sectoral interests are institutionalized through intermediate associations; they tend to prevail over the highly diffuse interests of groups like consumers and women. As usual, France enjoys an unstable status on both of these institutional dimensions.

The point of this framework is not to link structures to outcomes in a deterministic way. On the contrary, choices about narratives and coalitions offer broad opportunities for creative agency.[63] Social activists, industry, and policymakers all enjoy significant discretion in defining the narrative that legitimates a particular policy. In the United States, seemingly narrow interests can be redefined in terms of universal public interests in order to succeed. Gun rights, for example, are defined in terms of general public safety rather than in terms of the narrow interest in gun owners to be able to continue to shoot recreationally. By contrast, in countries like Germany, with proportional elections and a coordinated market economy, universal diffuse interests can be framed in narrower sectoral terms. Early defenders of longer store hours in Germany, for example, emphasized the benefits that longer store hours would give for women workers. The focus was not on a broad narrative of market access, but instead on the narrow social issue of female workers who had a hard time fitting in shopping at the end of their day. Although national institutional setting places constraints on the narrative logic by which both narrow and diffuse interests come to be defined, it leaves ample room for creativity in constructing narratives to legitimate alternative policy outcomes.

The import of the legitimacy coalition framework is twofold. First, it defines the major axes of contention. In any regulatory fight, opposing sides may confront each other across each of these dimensions. By isolating critical decision points, the focus on legitimacy coalitions defines the "elements of the drama" that allow us to make meaningful analytical comparisons across different countries and cases.[64] Second, this common framework allows us to generate testable causal claims that can be applied across a range of comparative cases. If narratives matter for the legitimacy of a particular policy, then they should show persistence even when firms or policymakers attempt to make changes. If the selection of a coalition partner matters, then we should observe competing interests defining their arguments in those terms. The cases presented in this volume provide preliminary evidence for both of these claims.

CHAPTER 2

Three Worlds of Consumer Protection

Aᴄᴄᴏʀᴅɪɴɢ ᴛᴏ ᴛʜᴇ ʟᴏɢɪᴄ of organizational theory, consumers are the quintessential weak interest group. They are large in number, which should itself make them difficult to organize. Mancur Olson himself cited consumers as the broad but unrepresented interest group *par excellence*.[1] They confront regulatory issues that are overwhelmingly technical and complicated in nature, which should further reduce their ability to engage the broad class of consumers in policy activism.[2] Consumers share their identity as consumers with their other identities—as workers, small business owners, welfare recipients—that intersect and potentially conflict with their perceived consumer interests.[3] Finally, the space of potential consumer interests is multidimensional. It includes diverse concerns, including access, price, quality, safety, social status, and environmental impact. The diversity of potential consumer interests makes it difficult to agree on a unified agenda.[4] Taken together, these barriers to effective interest representation make consumers a powerful test case for theories that posit a failure of collective action. If anywhere, the collective action problem should manifest itself in the case of consumers.

Beginning in the mid-1960s, the advanced industrialized countries experienced an efflorescence of mobilization, policy activism, and industry accommodation focused on the defense of consumers. Nearly every advanced economy in the 1970s and 1980s moved to provide legal, legislative, and administrative protections for the consumer. What is striking about these cases is both how systematic consumer defense was, even across distinctive national regulatory and institutional contexts, and how the timing of the defense was tied to economic context rather than the organizational capabilities of consumers. Once it became clear that the new age of affluent consumption entailed its own grievances and injustices, legislatures, activists, and judges moved quickly to respond to these concerns.[5]

What follows is a comparative historical account of the rise of consumer protection policies in eight countries: Sweden, Norway, Denmark, Germany, Japan, Austria, Britain, and the United States. These case studies record the historical fact of broad success in consumer interest representation. Consumer interest representation was not an exceptional phenomenon, limited to the efforts of Ralph Nader in the United States. It occurred *everywhere.* Each of these countries, despite diverse historical and political contexts, found strategies for representing the highly diffuse consumer interest in public policy. Further, the move to advance the consumer agenda happened quickly—in most instances over the course of a single decade. Once consumer grievances became apparent, very little time elapsed before new regulations and institutions were erected to promote the newly perceived interests. Because these changes involved complex areas of policy that impinged heavily on concentrated industry interests, this rapid response was especially surprising.

By studying more closely how the consumer interest was translated into public policy across many countries, this chapter raises questions about possibilities for collective action in industrialized democracies. It suggests that collective action even among broad and highly diffuse interests may be more common and more effective than social scientists have conventionally expected. The experience of the parallel consumer movements shows that, when material self-interest was at stake, even weak interests shared among an extremely large and diverse part of the population appear to have been quick to achieve a regulatory response. If diffuse material interests were truly difficult to mobilize, as Chicago School regulation theories suggest, we should not observe such systematic policy response.

Yet the story of consumer policy in the advanced economies is a story of variation as well as of uniformity. A comparative look at the origins of consumer protection measures in the advanced economies reveals that these policies, though widespread, emerged at the instigation of different agents in different cases. To be sure, each of the three policy actors discussed in this chapter—consumer activists, industry representatives, and government officials—played a part in furthering the consumer agenda in all cases. But each national context featured a coalition of two policy actors primarily responsible for the direction of consumer policy. One reason for the success of consumer protections across such diverse national settings may be the variety of regulatory coalitions that emerged to advocate for them. If consumer groups failed to negotiate solutions directly with business, then regulators could step in. If businesses failed to engage with regulators, then activist consumer groups would become a more critical policy partner. This variety in possible regulatory coalitions meant that national regulatory approaches embodied a strong experimental element. If one set of approaches seemed not to be achieving the desired consumer protection goals, another set of approaches would be attempted. Nor was the emergence of one coalition or another a purely arbitrary process. The nature of a country's institutions and traditions—its economy, electoral system, and political culture—proves to be closely tied to the question of which two groups emerge as policy prime movers, which in turn has implications for the types of consumer protections and advocacy measures that are ultimately implemented.

The Scandinavian countries, with their tradition of openness, egalitarianism, and the negotiation of conflicts, are notable for a strategy of industry-activist coalition (see Table 2.1). In this approach—which we observe in different variations in Sweden, Norway, and Denmark—industry associations and individual companies negotiated directly with consumer associations to set important areas of consumer policy, including contract terms, advertising norms, labeling standards, and mechanisms for addressing consumer complaints. Although the state is far from absent in this process, its role is primarily to facilitate negotiation and arbitration rather than to set norms and enforce them. For example, rather than focusing their energies on establishing standards or prosecuting offending companies, the Scandinavian countries tended to create

Table 2.1. Legitimacy coalitions for consumer protection

Industry-activist coalition	Industry-state coalition	State-activist coalition
Sweden	Japan	United States
Norway	Germany	United Kingdom
Denmark	Austria	France

councils and other deliberative bodies in which industry representatives and consumer activists could negotiate. These were backstopped by special tribunals and administrative ombudsmen in cases in which negotiation failed to result in agreement.

Countries with more liberal economies and majoritarian electoral systems—including the United States, the United Kingdom, and France (discussed in detail in Chapter 4)—relied on state-activist coalition, in which organized activists and accommodating government regulators interacted over time to create and legitimate a new area of regulatory activism in favor of the consumer. Compared to the Scandinavian countries, with their emphasis on negotiation, these countries adopted strong legal and regulatory protections for injured consumers and an energetic approach to setting and enforcing standards. New statutory protections for consumers were designed through an interaction between consumer activists and state regulators, with little input from industry. This approach to consumer protection led to regulations that placed the overwhelming burden of consumer safety on producers.

We also observe a third mode of regulatory policymaking that emerged in cases in which industry worked closely with the regulatory state. In Japan, Germany, and Austria, consumer policy was the product of a close industry-state interaction. This mode based on an industry-state coalition is closest to the Stigler model of regulatory capture. Even in these cases, though, business faced considerable constraints. First, industry was uniformly opposed to any consumer protection policy. The very fact of regulatory intervention by the state was initially perceived by industry as blocking their interests. Only later did they come to see consumer protections as creating benefits for incumbent firms, primarily by creating barriers to entry for potential competitors. Second, in no case was business able to enforce its agenda unilaterally. As one would predict for these relatively coordinated market economies with their systems of proportional representation, what looks like industry capture was in fact a coalition between industry and regulators in which the latter frequently held the upper hand. In Germany, for example, the government used the threat of negotiations with consumer groups to compel real reforms from industry. Compared to either the Scandinavian countries or the French and Anglo-American cases, the three countries that embodied industry-state coalitions— Japan, Austria, and Germany— tended to emphasize product labeling and consumer education, coupled with relatively weak legal protections. The remainder of this chapter focuses on these three alternative coalitional mechanisms of diffuse interest representation.[6]

Industry-Activist Coalitions: The Scandinavian Experience

The Scandinavian countries developed a distinctive approach to regulating consumer markets in which strong and centralized consumer movements negotiated directly with industry representatives to set the terms on which consumers would interact with industry. National governments saw their role primarily as supporting this sort of negotiation, and they intervened to varying degrees to support negotiated outcomes. Sweden was the early innovator in the creation of industry-activist coalitions, but the other Scandinavian countries quickly followed. Four kinds of outcomes were distinctive to this Scandinavian approach: a focus on providing consumers with accurate product information, an emphasis on prenegotiation of contracts and advertising standards, informal dispute resolution managed by joint consumer-industry entities, and an office of the consumer ombudsman that could provide independent consumer representation in public policy matters and in negotiations with producers.

Sweden

In Sweden, industry-activist coalitions took time to emerge. In fact, credit for the earliest successes of Swedish consumer advocacy, mainly in product labeling and consumer information, goes to a coalition of producers and the state. Immediately following World War II, Swedish producers and government officials began discussions to create a system of informative product labels that would help consumers to discern useful product qualities. In 1951, with financial support from the state and from industry, a new private labeling office was created, the Institute for Informative Labeling (VDN). Within the VDN, a fourteen-member board composed of consumers, producers, and distributors worked to design informative product labels tailored to narrow classes of products. Although they set no minimum standards on overall quality, these labels indicated where each product fell on specific measurable dimensions as compared with the full range of comparable products.[7] Products adopting the labels were checked each year for accuracy. The impact of this labeling scheme appears to have been quite significant. By 1963, French observers concluded that, as a result of the labeling scheme, "the Swedish consumer is among the most demanding in terms of product quality and is particularly attracted to innovations."[8] The Swedish labeling model was also internationally influential—by the 1970s, nearly all of the advanced industrial countries were designing informative labeling schemes broadly modeled on those originated by the VDN.

Under pressure from consumers, the Swedish state began to take a larger role in the work of informing consumers. In 1957, the state household information agency Aktiv Hushållning (founded in 1940) and the private home economics research institute Hemmenes Forskningsinstitut (founded in 1944) were merged into the new Institute for Consumer Issues. This new institute was melded in 1973 with the formerly private labeling institute, VDN, to become the new National Board for Consumer Policy (Konsumentverket). Iselin Theien describes the process as part of a "clear development towards centralization [of consumer policy] under state leadership."[9] The 1970s also saw the rise of local consumer advice centers to disseminate prepurchase information to assist with product selection, as well as advice on legal rights and means of redress. In 1975, there were consumer advice centers in one-third of Sweden's municipalities (95 out of a total of 278). By 1984, 80 percent of all municipalities had them (230 of 284).

It was in the late 1960s and 1970s that Sweden shifted its strategy from a more top-down system of labeling and consumer education to one that sought to facilitate direct negotiations between purchasers and producers. The rise of inflation in the late 1960s began to reveal the limitations of the purely informational approach to consumer protection. If better information worked to the advantage of everyone, inflation disproportionately hurt consumers and workers. In 1966, Swedish trade unions and the ruling Social Democratic Party collaborated to form a joint committee on consumer politics. Out of these discussions emerged a proposal for the creation of a set of negotiated agreements between consumers and producers. In a 1972 report on Sweden's consumer policy, the author summarizes the new approach: "In applying consumer policy, bringing influence to bear on producers is . . . often a more efficient means than providing information for consumers in securing improvements of various conditions. In the first instance, an attempt should be made to cooperate with producers on a voluntary and informal basis. Only when this fails to protect essential consumer interests, should other methods be considered."[10]

Accordingly, the government's next move was to create mediated forums for negotiations between consumers and industry. On the consumer side, a new Consumer Ombudsman, created in 1971, would represent the consumer interests with producers. In cases of disagreement a new Market Court would settle disputes. In 1976 these new institutions were integrated into the Konsumentverket. Like the VDN, the Consumer Ombudsman would become an influential model for other countries trying to construct their own institutions of consumer policy. Operating under provisions of the 1970 Marketing Practices Act, the 1971 Unfair Contract Terms, and the 1974 Consumer Sales Act, the ombudsman was empowered to negotiate "voluntary" guidelines (*riktlinjer*) with sectoral industry associations. Guidelines covered standard consumer contracts, the content of warning labels, toy safety standards, pricing information, the content of direct mailings, as well as narrow issues like the safety and packaging of hobby glues. Although such guidelines were not legally binding, they could be enforced by the Market Court through fines. In practice, producer compliance was extremely high. The ombudsman also undertook to settle disputes against producers based either on grievances reported by individual consumers or on concerns raised by the ombudsman's own staff. In its second year in operation, 1972, the ombudsman took on 4,500 such cases, and one-quarter of these were initiated from within the office of the ombudsman. Although most cases were settled through direct discussion with producers, those that were not went to the Market Court for settlement. In particularly grave cases, the Market Court could issue an injunction or, from 1976, force a product recall.

The success of the Consumer Ombudsman and the Market Court in promoting close cooperation between the state, producers, and workers led legislators to shun more aggressive approaches to managing potentially risky products. As in other countries, the 1970s were a period of active consumer legislation in Sweden, which saw new regulations on door-to-door sales (1971), food safety (1972), general product safety (1973), small claims (1974), and consumer credit (1978). This regulatory activity was mirrored by growing budget allocations for consumer protection over the course of the 1970s. Yet Sweden's consumer protection legislation continued to stress cooperation rather than the punitive enforcement mechanisms of France or the United States. For example, the 1973 Products Control Board, created to enforce the Act on Products Hazardous to Health and the Environment, was a tripartite organization with producer and employee representation alongside consumer and government interests.[11] Sweden also resisted imposing a strict standard of liability on manufacturers of products that caused injury. When, in 1973, a committee convened to consider product liability reform recommended that Sweden adopt a strict standard of producer liability, industry instead created a no-fault insurance solution for specific sectors of the economy.

Norway

The Swedish approach would be seen as a model for the other Scandinavian countries, with important differences. The Norwegian approach, for example, involved earlier and more significant state intervention in consumer policy setting, though the creation of institutions for consumer-producer negotiations also played a prominent role.

Norwegian consumers enjoyed representation at the ministerial level already in 1956, with the creation of the Ministry of Family and Consumer Affairs. Although the consumer portfolio was moved a number of times—eventually ending up in the Consumer Affairs Department within the State Pollution Control Agency (SPCA) under the Ministry of Environment—its main functions remained the same. Divisions included the Consumer Council, a formerly private consumer institute with broad responsibilities pertaining to consultation, advocacy, and product testing; the Committee for Informative Labeling (discussed later); a State Institute for Consumer Research; and, beginning in 1973, a Consumer Ombudsman modeled on the Swedish office. Like its Swedish counterpart, the ombudsman worked with industry sectors to negotiate standards for advertising, labeling, and consumer contracts. It also took on consumer complaints, which could be brought before a dispute settlement body called the Market Council. In 1972, a National Consumer Congress was formed that, through yearly meetings, helped to set the trajectory of national consumer policy. Its fifty-seven delegates represented a combination of consumer, government, labor, and producer interests.

The early 1970s saw a surge in domestic consumer protection legislation in Norway that mirrored their Swedish counterparts. These included legislation related to compulsory price labeling (1968) and door-to-door sales (1972), and the Sale of Goods Act (1974). The 1977 Product Control Act imposed a general requirement on producers to exercise care in product design and manufacturing. In the same year, a report to the Parliament on consumer policy in Norway laid out for the first time the essential principles of consumer protection. This regulatory activism was mirrored by a boom in government funding for consumer protection that peaked in 1979.

Even more than in Sweden, information became a key element in Norway's consumer protection strategy. The goal was pursued through three main pillars. The first was comparative product testing. Whereas Swedish policymakers were somewhat skeptical because of the cost and perceived inefficacy of such tests, in Norway they became a central element in consumer policy. In 1953, the Consumer Council began publishing the results of comparative product tests in *Consumer Reports* (*Forbruker-Rapporten*). In 1972, the publication enjoyed a circulation of 230,000. Circulation peaked in 1979 at 255,000 then fell off (in part due to an increase in subscription fees) to 210,000 by 1982. Labeling and consumer advice centers were also avidly pursued. In 1972, a new Committee for Informative Labeling (CIL) was created, on the model of Sweden's VDN, to elaborate quality labels for products. These would be of two kinds. One, "Type A," would set no minimum standard and would apply initially to certain dairy products and canned vegetables. The second, "Type B," would set a minimum cutoff threshold for specific product qualities and would initially be applied to a wide range of products—stainless cutlery, dishwashers, macaroni, frozen vegetables, and so on. Such labels were to be negotiated between consumer and producer interests. Formats for the first batch of labels were issued in 1974. In 1983 the CIL was absorbed into the Consumer Council.

Norway's Consumer Council also maintained a set of county offices around Norway that proved popular. Between its main office in Oslo and these county offices, the council offered information and legal advice to a large number of consumers. By 1975, the council offered purchasing guidance to 8,400 consumers and handled 36,000 consumer complaints. In 1983, 26,000 visitors came for purchasing advice, and 80,000 consumers lodged complaints. In the late 1980s, the offices were receiving a combined total of over 150,000 inquiries. In 1980, Norway also introduced an ambitious consumer curriculum in its schools. These efforts to provide accurate information made the Norwegian approach something of a hybrid between the Swedish system and the German model described later in the chapter.

Though Norway possessed fewer institutions designed to facilitate negotiation between producers and consumers than did Sweden, even consumer activists perceived a willingness on the part of business to work with organized consumer groups as central to the nation's consumer protection system. As a former head of the Norwegian Consumer Council explained, "In Norway after World War II, the cooperative feeling was immensely strong. Business has been receptive to working with the Ombudsman to negotiate solutions. Today, those who want to do business in the country have to work with [consumer groups]."[12]

Denmark

The Swedish model, with its characteristic emphasis on negotiation, was also influential in Denmark. But unlike in Sweden and Norway, where the state was instrumental in creating and maintaining forums for consumer-producer encounters and dispute resolutions, Denmark's broad-based grassroots consumer groups took the initiative in liaising with industry.

The earliest Danish efforts at consumer protection were almost entirely private, carried out by a combination of women's groups, consumer groups, and, increasingly, trade unions. These groups were gathered under the umbrella of the Consumer Council (Forbrugerrådet), created in 1947 by Danish housewives' associations and enlarged in the 1960s to include unions, cooperative societies, civil servants, and individual consumer members. The Consumer Council became one of Denmark's two most influential independent consumer associations and was instrumental in creating coalitions with industry. By the early 1980s, half of Denmark's twenty-eight voluntary consumer groups (representing 75 percent of the Danish population!) belonged to the Consumer Council. The council's functions were multiple. It negotiated with industry and trade groups to develop codes of practice, contract terms, invoice formats, and fee structures. It undertook price surveys, advocated for the consumer interest with the government, ran twelve consumer information sites around the country, and provided assistance with consumer complaints.[13] In 1964, the council began publishing the results of comparative product tests in its magazine *Taenk*. It also began working with schools to develop a consumer curriculum. The Consumer Council was not an entirely private endeavor, however: by 1972, the Danish state provided half of the funding for its activities.[14]

Consumer labeling in Denmark also began as a voluntary consumer-producer initiative, only later taken up by the state. The effort was launched by the country's second important private consumer group, the Danish Institute of Informative Labeling (Dansk Varefakta Naevn, DVN), which promoted voluntary quality labeling schemes for consumer products that mirrored Sweden's VDN labels. DVN was founded in 1957 in a collaborative project by the Consumer Council and Home Economics Council and a broad contingent of economic actors: the Federation of Danish Industries, the Council of Danish Handicraft, the Economic Board of the Danish labor movement, the Joint Representation of the Danish Traders' Association, the Danish Standards Association, the Joint Council of Danish Retailers, the Royal Danish Testing Institute, and the Danish Cooperative Wholesale Societies. Labels issued by DVN included descriptive scales for qualities relevant to each class of product, with minimum thresholds set for some of these values.

As described by the Danish representative to the Organisation for Economic Co-operation and Development (OECD) in 1967: "The DVN mark itself is not a guarantee of quality, but DVN demands that the goods must be 'fit' for use to be labeled, and therefore there is a lower limit to the quality. Consequently a number of minimum-quality standards have to be incorporated in the specifications stipulating what information is to be given on the label."[15] Despite high hopes for its implementation, the DVN system was not widely used. The number of DVN labels grew from 15 in 1968 to 109 in 1978, covering only 3,400 individual products produced by 238 firms.

In the early 1970s, the Danish government launched a program of direct administrative involvement in consumer policy. In doing so, however, it built on the practice of consumer-producer negotiation begun by the independent groups. In 1972, the government issued its "First Danish Report on Consumer Policy."[16] Active government intervention in consumer protection began in 1974–1975 with the passing of the Marketing Practices Act. That law placed most responsibility for consumer policy under the Ministry of Industry. Three separate bodies would manage consumer issues: the Consumer Complaints Board, the Consumer Ombudsman, and the Home Economics Council. The first two were created by the Marketing Practices Act, and they worked to frame the context in which consumers purchased goods. As in Sweden, the ombudsman headed negotiations between industry and organized consumer groups to cover consumer contract terms, codes of conduct, and fair advertising. Further, the Marketing Practices Act specifies that the ombudsman "shall, on his own initiative or in consequence of complaints or applications made by others, use his best endeavors by negotiation to induce trade or business to comply with the provisions of this Act. In urgent cases the consumer Ombudsman may issue an interlocutory injunction."[17]

Consumer grievances filed with the ombudsman were passed to the Consumer Complaints Board (Forbrugerklagenaevnet). This board was a tripartite group with equal consumer, retail, and producer representation. It provided arbitration on consumer cases, and worked with producers to develop private, sector-specific arbitration boards.[18] By 1981, eleven such boards had been created, and all relevant cases were being handled by them.[19] Cases not settled in arbitration went on to be tried in regular courts. In practice this two-tiered arbitration system proved highly successful at settling consumer cases against producers and service providers. In 1975, Danish consumers were granted group status for legal suits, as they were in a number of other countries around that time, but the sectoral arbitration system worked to limit the number of cases that made it to court. In 1977, two years after starting, the office of the ombudsman received 2,112 cases—half filed by private individuals, half by public authorities—and settled all but thirty.[20] By the early 1980s, the ombudsman was receiving upward of 15,000 cases per year, with the vast majority being settled in arbitration.[21]

The third consumer function within the Ministry of Industry was the Danish Government Home Economics Council (HEK). Created in 1935 with a goal to improve nutritional, hygienic, economic and technical aspects of household management, the HEK was reorganized in 1960 to address new consumer challenges. It began conducting consumer product tests, and published test results in the magazine *Rad og Resultater* (*Advice and Results*), a direct competitor to *Taenk*. It also tracked technical consumer issues and published these in *Tekniske Meddelelser* (*Technical News*).[22] In 1988, these three bodies were consolidated in the National Consumer Agency (NCA) and, in 2004, the NCA was moved to a newly created Ministry of Family and Consumer Affairs.

Food safety and labeling was managed by the Ministry for the Environment. The 1973 Food Act gave the ministry broad powers to regulate food content, to restrict or block sales, to limit pesticide use, and to regulate food labeling. Policies within the ministry were set in consultation with a newly created Council on Food. Like other government functions concerning the consumer, the council was tripartite, with an equal share of representatives from consumer groups, trade groups, and the government ministries. The placement of food safety within the Ministry for the Environment forged a link between consumer and environmental policy that persisted in the Danish politics of consumer protection.[23]

The Scandinavian approach to consumer protection based on direct consumer-producer interaction offered a seductive vision for responding to the regulatory challenges facing increasingly complex consumer product markets. Not long after they were being introduced as models for consumer protection in the Scandinavian countries, industry-activist coalitions were being copied by most of the other advanced industrialized countries. France's efforts to promote consumer-producer negotiations were inspired by the Swedish experience. Germany closely studied the Scandinavian experience to assess if it could be deployed there, as did the United Kingdom. Many countries borrowed parts of the model. Consumer ombudsman offices sprang up all over Europe. Sweden's private informative labeling system, the VDN, was copied—rarely with much success—in nearly every advanced industrialized country.

Yet it is striking how few of the historical efforts to emulate the Scandinavian model succeeded. Two key features appear to have made consumer-producer negotiation successful in Sweden, Norway, and Denmark. First, the model rested on willingness by business to work together with organized consumer groups. All three countries were small, relatively homogenous nations with strong traditions of nonadversarial conflict resolution. Producers accepted that the outcomes of negotiations with consumers were a legitimate expression of public interest, and generally abided by them. Second, the government provided legal backing to enforce the negotiated outcomes. Although most consumer complaints were settled in dispute settlement bodies staffed jointly by consumers and producers, cases that failed to be settled eventually found their way into the national court systems. Similarly, producers that failed to negotiate with the consumer ombudsman on issues related to product safety, contract terms, or truth in advertising quickly found themselves before their national market courts. Industry-activist coalitions did not emerge in the absence of a state response; rather, the state was instrumental in bringing both parties to the negotiating table and encouraging settlements.

Industry-State Coalitions: Japan, Germany, Austria

Certain advanced industrialized countries have seemed to cede the initiative in setting consumer protection policies to industry. These producer-oriented consumer policies most closely correspond to the vision of Chicago School regulation theories that posit the power of concentrated industry interests. Yet, even in these cases of strong industry influence—including Japan, Germany, and Austria—the role of independent state initiatives has been important. In Germany and Japan, electoral pressures for more adversarial consumer policies were largely absent. In Japan, this was due to a lack of real competition under the effective one-party rule of the Liberal Democratic Party. In Germany, a cross-class alliance of workers and producers favored policies that would reinforce Germany's quality-focused production strategy. Strategies of consumer groups also mattered. In Austria, organized labor and the country's chambers of commerce essentially co-opted the consumer movement. In all three countries, consumer groups that did organize adopted organizational strategies that accommodated rather than opposed industry interests. Thus, for a combination of reasons, all three of these countries embraced consumer policies that reinforced rather than challenged the product strategies of industry.

Japan

In Japan, consumer interests came to be represented through a combination of business self-regulation and regulatory treatment by the state. Labor unions, which were in any case closely tied to the interests of producers, did not take significant interest in the consumer plight. Governmental regulatory solutions drew only in narrow instances on the grassroots capabilities of the local and regional consumer groups. Without outside allies, the consumer movement remained relatively weak. This left national policy to be dictated largely by the interests of industry, which interpreted consumer protection primarily as requiring a more highly educated consumer base. This resulted in consumer protection policies that emphasized consumer advisory services, consumer education, and elaborate product labeling and certification schemes.

Japan's consumer movement mobilized relatively early, partly in response to an early consumer product crisis. The watershed case concerned the Morinaga milk company, which in 1955 distributed dried milk laced with arsenic that ended up killing 130 children and leaving a further 12,131 mentally damaged.[24] The early consumer groups that formed in response to this crisis had their roots in existing women's and family groups. Local dedicated consumer groups formed a national umbrella group (Shodanren) in 1956. The national association of women's groups (Shufuren), which had formed in 1948, also became active in consumer issues. But these representative associations never coalesced into powerful players at the national level, and their efforts were primarily oriented toward educating consumers and promoting "rational, sound consumption," rather than influencing producers or policy.[25] The Japanese government, which saw consumer activism as potentially harming industry, did little to encourage a grassroots movement around consumer citizenship.[26] A noteworthy exception was the Consumers Union of Japan (Nisshoren), founded in 1969. Nisshoren brought suits against producers, lobbied the government for regulatory reforms, filed a class action lawsuit against the oil industry cartel, and even invited Ralph Nader to speak in Japan. Still, with only 10,000 readers of its publication, Nisshoren was a small island of radical activism amid a broader consumer movement intent on educating consumers rather than suing producers.

Administrative bodies focused on the consumer did arise, but these often treated consumer protection as a means of promoting other economic goals. The first of these, formed in 1958 within the Japan Productivity Center in the Ministry of International Trade and Industry (MITI), was called the Consumer Education Committee, and it incorporated individual consumer representatives. In 1962, the Ministry of Agriculture created its own consumer division. In 1965, the Economic Planning Agency (EPA) created a Citizens' Lifestyle Bureau that helped to coordinate consumer policy across the government. In 1968, the first comprehensive consumer legislation, the Basic Law for Consumer Protection, created a Conference on Consumer Protection that was chaired by the prime minister and had representatives from all seventeen government ministries. Operationally this new group fell under the EPA, which undertook research on consumer issues at the behest of any of the ministries.[27] In 1970, two new offices were created with the dual goals of assisting consumers and supporting producers. MITI created a Consumer Products Guidance Office—later the Japan Consumers Association (JCA)—that launched a training and qualification system for consumer advisers. In the same year, the EPA formed the Japan Consumer Information Center (JCIC) to educate consumer leaders, provide consumer advice, and mediate disputes. By the mid-1970s, the two groups were conducting comparative product tests (both with government support) and publishing the results to a wide consumer audience. MITI's Better Living Information Center (BLIC) published its test results in *Tashikana Me* (*Critical Eyes*), and the JCA published its own test results in *Gekkan Shohisha* (*Monthly Consumer*). Each of these administrative bodies sought to protect consumers, but in ways that assisted the overall economic development trajectory of the country.

The 1960s and especially the 1970s saw an outpouring of consumer legislation in Japan: on advertising and rebates (1962),[28] a basic statement of consumer policy called the Consumer Protection Basic Law (1968), followed by new legislation governing consumer credit (1972), automobile safety (1973), product liability (1973), unit pricing (1975), and door-to-door sales. These new laws were backed by rapid growth in government funding for consumer protection policies during the 1970s. Most of the laws, however, reflected the interests of producers over those of consumers. Product liability retained a negligence standard that continued to favor producers. Product safety standards were defined by industry itself. The weakness of consumer representation led to a perception of the Japanese consumer movement as passive and co-opted by government and industry. Political scientist Patricia L. Maclachlan argues that it was in part the "wide range of administrative access points" that complicated the process of consolidating consumer interests at the national level.[29]

The most active consumer protection programs in Japan emerged at the local and prefecture levels. In 1961, Tokyo set up the first Consumer Lifestyle Policy Advisory Council, with consumer representatives, to make recommendations to the governor.[30] The following year the council convened a group of one thousand consumers called the Consumer Lifestyles Monitor to track new consumer concerns. Two years later the council formed a consumer consultation center. In 1965, Hyogo Prefecture created the Citizens' Lifestyle Science Center, which undertook consumer education programs. Such centers quickly spread across Japan, with their numbers growing from 94 in 1972, to 217 in 1980, to 266 in 1984.[31] Half of these information centers had their roots in the "lifestyle school" movement; the other half were formed beginning in 1970 under the MITI-sponsored Better Living Information Centers

(BLIC) program. In 1982, the centers collectively provided 182,000 consumer consultations.[32]

The emphasis on consumer information was mirrored by a strong focus on product standards and quality labeling. By the 1970s, these had become core strategies of consumer protection in Japan. Since the 1950s, product standards had been an important element of Japan's postwar industrial resurgence. The Japanese Standards Association, established in 1945 under MITI, helped manufacturers to coordinate design features in ways that ensured technical compatibility, helped to disseminate new technology, and created informal barriers to trade.[33] Quality labeling was also launched in Japan as an element of its industrial policy. In 1957, a Good Design Award (G-mark) was created by MITI for products judged to have "an excellent design . . . easy to use, safe, durable, unique and attractive." These were given in thirteen product categories, with an emphasis on supporting medium and small enterprise products. By the mid-1970s, 65 percent of Japanese people were aware of the "G-mark" and what it meant.[34]

Beginning in the 1970s, quality labels proliferated as a form of consumer policy. Under the Industrial Standards Act, certain consumer products that were potentially dangerous were required to comply with standards set by Japanese Industrial Standards (JIS). Other JIS standards that were voluntary allowed participating producers to indicate their compliance by displaying a "JIS-mark." In 1973, a similar system was created for agricultural and forestry products. The Japanese Agricultural Standards (JAS) Council, formed under the Ministry of Agriculture, promulgated both a compulsory quality label, for particularly dangerous types of food, and a voluntary set of standards indicated by a "JAS-mark." Whereas the JIS-mark was set primarily by leading producers, consumers participated actively alongside industry, distributors, and academic researchers in designing the JAS-mark agricultural standards. Similar to the JAS, the Excellent Housing Parts Certification System created Better Living standards (signified with a "BL-mark") for prefabricated housing; this system addressed a range of issues, including the prevention of disasters and crimes, and thirty interior decorations for reinforced concrete apartment houses and condominiums.

The popularity of labeling, and its broad acceptance by industry, made it an attractive way to deal with potentially risky products. With rising concerns about manufacturer liability in the 1970s, Japan launched a product certification scheme that linked compliance with technical standards to a new no-fault product liability regime paid out of sector-organized providential funds. Created in 1976 by the Consumer Product Safety Law, the new "SG-mark [safe goods]" was to be administered by a new Consumer Product Safety Association.[35] By the end of 1984, sixty-four product types carried the SG-mark. By 1991, an estimated 55 percent of all consumer products were covered by an SG-mark.[36] More than half of these were electronics, insured by the Electrical Appliances Compensation Insurance fund. Although successful, the scope of the SG-mark remained limited, and new pressures for product liability reform were growing.

Sectoral safety labeling schemes also proliferated, often with input from consumer groups. The Toy Safety Measures Commission, for example, brought together consumers with producers to develop a system of safety labels for toys (the "ST-mark"). Similar groups emerged for labeling textiles (the Textile Products Safety Measures Conference), sporting goods (the Sporting Goods Measures Committee), and ceramics (the Ceramics Safety Maintenance Control Committee). Finally, the Consumer Product Safety Law created a general "S-mark" (for "specified product") that would apply to classes of products that were especially dangerous but not covered by an insurance scheme.[37]

If government efforts placed a strong emphasis on labeling to achieve consumer safety, access to legal recourse in case of injury proved more difficult. Efforts to reform Japan's product liability system began in the early 1970s, but reform did not occur until the Product Liability Law of 1995.[38] Prior to the reform, Japan embraced a negligence standard for producer liability that placed a high burden of proof on the consumer. In fact, only 150 product liability cases were filed in Japanese courts from the turn of the century up until passage of the 1995 legislation. Instead, consumers seeking redress typically dealt directly with companies through their consumer grievance procedures (*aitai kosho*). In the automobile sector, a strict auto inspection standard made liability claims less important.[39] And, for products covered by the SG label, consumers sought direct compensation without demonstrating producer negligence.[40] The Japanese pharmaceutical sector also developed, in 1979, the Relief Fund for Sufferers from Damages Due to Adverse Drug Reactions. Although such schemes were typically effective at compensating injured consumers, they did little to punish the companies that produced dangerous products.

Germany

In Germany, like Japan, a coalition of industry and the state took the lead in formulating consumer policy. As with other countries where business was influential, Germany's approach to redressing consumer grievance rested heavily on consumer information. In Germany, however, the success of business in influencing the direction of consumer policy to accommodate its product strategies rested on a narrative that portrayed the consumer as a partner to industry: the choices of the educated, discerning customer had the power to protect consumers, strengthen business, and improve the nation as a whole. Both governmental and nongovernmental groups subscribed to this notion of "consumer sovereignty": educated and informed consumers could help themselves, and increase the competitiveness of German producers, by making informed product choices when they shopped. Efforts to provide useful consumer information combined the work of nongovernmental consumer associations with formal legal provisions of the government. In general, consumer protection measures in Germany were depoliticized. Consumer groups advocated product boycotts in a narrow set of cases, but they shunned political activism or even direct policy influence. Most groups were semiprofessionalized and discouraged grassroots membership. The result was a consumer movement that viewed itself as a partner to industry rather than an opposing force.

Germany's consumer groups coalesced from women's groups early in the postwar period. Organized into state-level associations in the 1950s, they became increasingly active in providing consumers with useful product information. Beginning in the 1960s, the state associations began to create local consumer information centers that would offer free technical advice on specific product types and attributes. The activities of the centers were funded through a combination of state and federal money. One of the important sources of information for the advice centers was Germany's influential comparative product test organization, Stiftung Warentest. Formed by government statute and with public financial support in 1964, Warentest proved extremely popular. Circulation of its magazine, *Test,* grew from roughly 100,000 in 1970 to 500,000 in 1980, and reached 1 million for the first time in 1995. Unlike U.S. and British comparative product testing organizations, which retained scrupulous separation from industry, Warentest was designed specifically to work with manufacturers at every stage of product test design and evaluation. In return, consumer product manufacturers overwhelmingly employed Warentest testing criteria in designing and testing their own new products.

Accuracy of product information became a dominant theme in German consumer protection policy. Regulations governing truth in product advertising and consumer contracts were unusually strict in both the level of transparency and the accuracy they were required to provide. Consumer groups became active partners in policing these standards, although they were not given central roles in influencing the content of the regulations. Consumer representatives were incorporated into Germany's standard-setting body, DIN, in 1974, initially over the objections of industry. They sat both on the general advisory board and on each of the technical standard-setting committees for product standards relevant to end consumers. Consumer representatives also participated in Germany's quality labeling scheme, called RAL-Testate. The experience of quality labels also revealed the limits of consumer group influence. In 1974, RAL-Testate began to set minimum standards for granting quality labels. These standards were generated through equal negotiations between industry and consumer group representatives. Industry members of DIN saw this approach as a threat to the autonomy of DIN, and quickly prevailed on the economics ministry to withdraw its financial support from the RAL-Testate program.

If product information was a centerpiece of German consumer protection, legal protections against product-related damage tended to be pursued less aggressively. Product safety standards were established not by an independent government office but by industry itself in the context of technical standard setting. National legislation passed in 1978 mandated that consumer product standards set by DIN be enforced as national safety standards. Legal responsibility for product-related damages was also not aggressively pursued. In a watershed 1968 bird flu case, a German court found that producers, not consumers, faced the burden of proof to show that they had not acted negligently in case of product failure. This procedural shift made it possible for consumers to sue producers, but left open a range of exculpatory options for producers. Moreover, German consumers were not granted status as a legal class for such liability cases, making it extremely difficult to organize groups of plaintiffs in cases of product-related damage. For the most part, Germany's independent consumer groups did not pursue such legal cases for concern of the consequences of crossing industry. In one of the few cases in which consumer groups did protest government policy, in the interest of reduced agricultural prices under the Common Agricultural Policy, Germany's powerful farm association pushed to slash federal funding for consumer advocacy groups.

Austria

Austria, too, was home to a consumer policy shaped in large part by business interests, but several key features made Austria's consumer policies more than a simple case of regulatory capture. Though Austrian business did manage to forge a consumer policy friendly to their product management strategies, they did not achieve this on their own. Rather, an alliance between producers and trade unions set the main direction of policy. Athough Austria's consumer protection regime was hardly as extensive as that of the Scandinavian or the Anglo-American models, the Austrian experience shows consumers achieving favorable outcomes. Even in the absence of a major grassroots movement, an interest group as diffuse as consumers did achieve representation in public policy.

From its outset, Austria's consumer movement was deeply embedded in the country's syndicalist structure, with significant input from all of the major social interests. The primary consumer association, the Association for Consumer Information (Verein für Konsumenteninformation,

VKI), was founded in 1961 by the Chamber of Labor (Österreichischer Arbeiterkammertag, ÖAKT) and the Austrian Trade Union Federation (Österreichischer Gewerkschaftsbund). Each of these groups had previously sponsored its own independent consumer information activities, but these were merged to avoid competition.[41] In 1964, the Federal Economic Chamber (Wirtschaftskammer Österreich) and the Austrian Agricultural Chamber (Landwirtschaftskammer Österreich) joined as supporting members of the VKI. Initially, the four groups contributed 80 percent of the VKI's operating funds, though over time the government share grew to nearly half. Other groups representing the environment, youth, and family also eventually became members of VKI. Notably lacking were any independent consumer groups. And, as with the German consumer group AgV (Arbeitgemeinschaft der Verbraucherverbände), the VKI permitted no individual members. This situation led Hans Peter Lehofer to observe that "a 'consumer voice' in the form of an independent consumer organization was significantly absent."[42]

As its name suggests, the VKI focused on providing consumers with useful product information. From its founding it was active in product testing. Results were published in the magazine *Konsument,* whose circulation grew from 25,000 in 1969, to 70,000 in 1980, to roughly 100,000 in 2000.[43] Hans and Sarah Thorelli, in their authoritative survey of national comparative product testing magazines, called *Konsument* "by any standards one of the world's outstanding consumer information and education journals."[44] Like other testing organizations, *Konsument* was frequently sued by unhappy producers, but the courts consistently found in its favor based on the professional manner in which it was operated. The VKI also provided individual advice through four public information centers, located in Vienna, Innsbruck, Lanz, and Eisenstadt. At its main Munchnerhof center in Vienna, the VKI displayed products and hosted special exhibitions. In 1976 it received some 300,000 visitors. By 1982, the VKI was seeing an average of 1,500 consumer visits and 300 phone enquiries each day.[45] It also began publishing an influential consumer handbook in 1972, called the Consumer Manual. This publication, which included a range of advice for consumers, was widely distributed, periodically updated, and translated into several languages, including

Serbo-Croatian. In 1977, the VKI launched the monthly TV magazine *Argumente* dealing with consumer complaints. Finally, during periods of high inflation, the VKI was active in undertaking price surveys. In 1976, for example, the group surveyed 200,000 consumer product prices throughout Austria.

The information emphasis of the VKI served to structure the broader response to consumer grievance in Austria. Apart from its participation in the VKI, the Chamber of Labor also became active in providing consumer advice through its own offices, located in each of Austria's nine federal states. In 1975, the Labor Chamber of the state of Lower Austria transformed a bus into a mobile information facility that visited 300 villages and 130 factories. The mobile advice bureau proved popular, and by 1980 it could be found parked near street markets and shopping areas throughout Austria.[46] Individual state governments also maintained consumer protection units, and these undertook important safety and information functions. In 1978, for example, the Consumer Protection Unit of the Vienna Land held its first Consumer Film Days, at which it screened consumer-related films from Switzerland, Germany, and the United Kingdom.[47]

Formal legislative initiatives to protect consumers were enacted only in the wake of VKI initiatives, and they tended to replicate the information model that was at the core of the VKI approach. They also embraced the VKI as a partner in implementing and enforcing the new legislation. One example was the regulation of consumer contracts. Beginning in 1979, a Consumer Policy Council composed in equal parts of VKI and industry representatives began negotiating standard contract terms that could be adopted on a voluntary basis by businesses selling to end consumers. The standard contracts were widely used. For companies not using these standard contract terms, the Consumer Protection Act of 1979 provided a "black list," modeled on earlier German legislation, of terms that could not legally be included in any standard consumer contracts. The VKI was empowered to enforce this law, and did so with some success.[48] In 1981, the Trade Licensing Act required that companies employing standard consumer contracts give a copy of the form to the VKI for review. In cases of producer wrongdoing, the four main members of the VKI were empowered to bring legal suits before the Austrian courts on behalf of consumers.[49]

In an effort to extend the Austrian syndicalist tradition to the realm of consumption, the VKI was invited to participate actively in a variety of other regulatory functions. It joined the Working Party on Labeling created to draw up templates for a voluntary labeling system called Product Description (PD). In this product labeling scheme, the content of labels was set through consultations between the VKI and representatives of different product sectors. The first and most important sectors to receive such labels were electronics: televisions, radios, tape recorders, and dishwashers.[50] The VKI was also invited to participate in a variety of sector-specific arbitration boards that gave consumers a forum in which to have product disputes mediated.

While such semiprivate strategies of consumer information provision dominated the 1970s, by the 1980s, Austria had begun to place more emphasis on direct regulatory control. Administratively, consumer policy was upgraded in 1979 from the minor Special Section on Consumer Policy within the Ministry of Trade and Industry to a full Secretariat of State, headed by Anneliese Albrecht. In 1983 it was further upgraded, to the newly created Ministry of Family, Youth, and Consumer Protection headed by Elfriede Karl.[51] A new Product Safety Advisory Board was constituted under the new ministry, with working groups on specific consumer issues. Still, the new administrative services remained highly consultative, and the VKI nearly always had a place at the policy table. The Austrian government also created an independent Advisory Council on Consumer Policy (Konsumentenpolitischer Beirat). The council convened specialized working parties on current issues, including such topics as misleading advertisement, textile quality and labeling, and competition policy. These working parties met roughly twice monthly. The council also organized a twice-yearly Consumers' Forum. These forums, in which consumer activists were invited to participate, served both as a means of informing consumers of the activities of the council, and as a tool for identifying and launching new council initiatives.[52]

As with nearly all other countries, product safety was a central concern of legislative action in Austria beginning in the 1970s. A 1975 Food Law ensured food safety and labeling. It led to the opening of the Vienna

Food Institute, which yearly checked five thousand different food speci-
mens for their fitness for consumption.[53] The 1979 Consumer Protection
Act created a Product Safety Council to consider new product safety challenges. Its members were nominated by representatives of labor, employers, and farmers. Finally, the 1983 Federal Products Safety Law imposed a
general standard of product safety on all consumer products. This emphasis also extended to the legal sphere. In 1987, Austria became one of the
four signatories to the Strasbourg Convention on Product Liability (with
France, Belgium, and Luxembourg) that endorsed an unusually strict
standard of producer liability. This approach was not pursued, however,
and 1988 legislation adopting the European Union product liability directive embraced a less stringent standard of producer liability.

In Japan, Germany, and Austria, producers were able to fend off significant regulatory intrusion into important aspects of product design
and safety. This was due in part to the strength of business in these
countries, but also to particular features of the consumer movement itself. In each case the consumer movement shunned a more radicalized
approach to mobilization that might have allowed them to impose stricter
standards on producers. Similarly, the governments in each of these
countries opted not to antagonize business with overly aggressive legislative solutions. These cases represent the strongest evidence for the
policy influence of concentrated economic interest, but they also show
that this power was limited more to agenda-setting power than to outright policy control.

Two features of these industry-state coalitions are worth emphasizing.
First, these cases are significantly different from a simple explanation
based purely on industry capture. In both Japan and Germany, industry
did not initially support *any* of the consumer protection policies that
were imposed on them by the state. Only over time, as it became evident
that policies that reinforced consumer information about product quality could create barriers to new competition, did industry groups come
to support the new consumer protection policies. As we will see in the
following chapters, instances of regulation that have been interpreted
as the consequence of industry capture commonly have their roots in
very different constellations of economic and political interests. Second,
even in these cases of industry-state coalition, in which industry and regu-

latory agencies worked together to define the consumer interest, consumers nonetheless showed signs of organizing. In Germany and Austria, organized consumer groups were largely co-opted by industry and labor interests, respectively. In Japan, an activist consumer movement was kept out of politics by government policies that discouraged their engagement in national policies. This suggests that certain strategies of mobilization, especially those that shun grassroots activism, may be particularly susceptible to being subsumed into a regulatory response that emphasizes interactions between industry and regulators.

State-Activist Coalitions: Britain and the United States

So far we have seen strategies that involved high levels of industry engagement in consumer protection policy, either through direct negotiations with organized consumers, or through intensive interactions with regulatory policymakers. We now turn to two countries in which business was largely inactive in the policy process, leaving organized consumer groups and consumer-friendly legislators to work together to create a strong and legitimate policy response to consumer grievances. The result in each case was a move to create strong administrative standards of consumer protection, legitimated through close interaction between regulators and nongovernmental consumer groups.

Britain

Consumer protection emerged in the immediate post-World War II era in Britain as a set of non-governmental initiatives that, like the early Swedish model, emphasized the provision of accurate product information as a strategy of consumer protection. In 1950, the National Council for Women (NCW) approached the British Standards Institute (BSI), a non-governmental body composed mainly of representatives from industry that created standards for engineering and other products, to propose consumer representation in standard setting for consumer products. The resulting Consumer Advisory Council (CAC) was the first instance among all of the advanced industrialized countries in which consumers participated formally in standard setting. Out of this initiative emerged a particular view of the role of the consumer in society. As described by

Matthew Hilton: "[It] was predicated on the belief that the consumer was an individual and that ultimately individual choice was the most fundamental and basic consumer protection that existed."[54] Yet the NCW was an entirely voluntary organization, and its impact on specific technical decisions relating to standards was viewed with some disappointment. The most enduring product of this collaboration was the BSI Kitemark indicating that a consumer product met relevant BSI standards.[55]

The first professional consumer group in Britain, Consumer Association (CA), was launched six years later. Modeled explicitly on the U.S. Consumers' Union, CA focused its early efforts on publishing comparative product test results in its magazine *Which?* From the publication of its first issue in 1957, *Which?* circulation grew rapidly: from 50,000 in its first year to 250 million by 1961, 500 million by 1968, and 1 million in 1987. Like its U.S. counterpart *Consumer Reports, Which?* maintained strict separation from business.[56] Results from comparative product tests were also disseminated, beginning in 1969, through CA-sponsored consumer advice centers. Inspired by the Austrian VKI, these centers provided consumers with useful product information and were located in popular shopping areas.[57] The advice centers were funded primarily by local governments. By 1975, Britain had seventy-four consumer advice centers, including several mobile rural units. In 1976, the number had nearly doubled to 120, with a combined budget approaching £4 million. All of the centers were shut under Prime Minister Margaret Thatcher's reform initiative in 1980.[58]

Shortly after its founding, the CA also began to sponsor affiliated local consumer groups. The first of these, established in Oxford in 1961, held meetings and published a local journal, the *Oxford Consumer.* As more of these local groups formed, the CA proposed a new National Federation of Consumer Groups to act as an umbrella organization. Fifty local consumer groups had formed by 1963, with a total of five thousand members. The number of these groups doubled over the next four years, and total membership increased to eighteen thousand.[59] Yet the 1970s saw a gradual disbanding of these groups. Hilton attributes their decline partly to the "individualist" consumer agenda they espoused, and partly to their own reluctance to participate in radical forms of organizing.[60] Their organizational strength was also undercut by an ethic of volun-

tarism that placed consumers in a weak position with respect to producers. At a time when other national consumer groups were professional-
izing, the British consumer movement strongly resisted this trend. By
the early 1980s, only thirty or so local consumer groups remained. By
then, the government had fully taken the initiative in furthering the consumer agenda.

Britain's early official forays into consumer protection were tentative.
The government's first act in this sphere was the convening of the trade-
and industry-dominated 1959 Molony Commission on Consumer Protection, whose findings, unsurprisingly, emphasized the value of education and information as a tool of consumer protection.[61] Its main impact
was the founding of the state-financed Consumer Council, established
in 1963, to conduct research into the consumer interest and to represent
that interest to the government. The council was restricted in important
ways. Its statute blocked it both from conducting comparative product
tests and from giving direct advice to consumers. It considered undertaking comparative price surveys, but balked at the expense and the potential political controversy such surveys might generate. The council
did launch, in 1965, the "Teltag" system of quality labels for consumer
goods. This strategy was modeled directly on the successful Swedish
VKN labels. British producers never accepted the idea, however, and
Teltag use was eventually limited to the tufted carpets market.[62] With
growing uncertainty about its benefits, the Consumer Council was closed
in 1970.

In the wake of these policy failures, the 1970s marked a consumer
protection renaissance in Britain, and a shift to a more aggressive regulatory response. New legislative projects included the Trade Descriptions
Act covering misleading advertising (1968), the Unsolicited Sales Act
(1971), a small claims procedure (1972), the Supply of Goods Act imposing an implied warrantee on producers (1973), the Counter Inflation Act
restricting price increases (1973), a Consumer Credit Act (1974), a Unit
Pricing Act (1975), the Resale Prices Act banning retail price maintenance (1976), and an Unfair Contract Terms Act (1977). New government
bodies were also created. In 1972, a Minister of Consumption was
appointed to the Board of Trade. In 1973, a new Office of Fair Trading
(OFT) was created to oversee competitive conditions. The OFT became

a strong advocate for voluntary codes of business conduct. Most of these reforms embodied what Roberta Sassatelli has called a fair trading agenda of consumer protection.[63] The Labour Party's return to power in 1975 led to a brief experimentation with a still more activist vision of consumer protection. A new National Consumer's Council (NCC) was established in 1975. The head of the NCC, Michael Young, represented the consumer interest on the National Economic Development Council, an economic planning forum composed of representatives from industry, organized labor, and government. The NCC also launched a yearly Consumers Congress that grew to include about two hundred consumer-related groups. Young even proposed, as had been suggested in Germany, that consumers be represented on companies' boards of directors.

It is a striking testimony to the strength of consumer advocacy in Britain that the successes of the postwar period, achieved in turns by consumer activists and government officials, survived the changing political fortunes of the Labour Party. Though the activist consumer vision largely disappeared from government policy when Margaret Thatcher took over in 1980, the deregulatory efforts of the Thatcher government did not dismantle a single regulatory protection for consumers. If anything, the Thatcher revolution emphasized the benefits to consumers of policy reforms that would introduce competition into a variety of formerly regulated sectors.

United States

Consumer protection policies in the United States emerged from a creative interplay between regulatory and independent activist initiatives. Politically, the consumer protection movement in the United States began with President John F. Kennedy's "Consumer Bill of Rights" speech of 1962. Although nearly every president since has announced important consumer protection programs, the Kennedy administration, and its Democratic Party, retain the legacy and credentials of consumer protection. Outside of the government, Ralph Nader published his landmark book *Unsafe at Any Speed* in 1965. His subsequent fame was based on the movement that emerged out of the public response to that early work. Indeed, Nader became the leader of a sort of global consumer movement, and he was invited to speak in nearly every country that came to struggle with consumer protection policy during the 1970s.

The case of U.S. consumer policy is challenging to capture in such a brief format. Many actors were involved; important policy innovations occurred at both the national and state levels; and a variety of activists, politicians, and regulatory agencies were central to its evolution. Furthermore, excellent accounts have already been written.[64] The United States is also distinctive in that it led other countries in many of the watershed regulatory reforms, including consumer class action suits, product liability reform, the regulation of consumer contracts, and the innovation of comparative product testing for the public benefit. Yet, even a cursory look at consumer protection in the United States helps to illustrate three dynamics of diffuse interest representation: the back-and-forth dynamic of the state-activist coalition, the role of early activists in defining the relevant consumer interests and defending the consumer interest, and the surprising speed with which the newly identified consumer interest came to be represented.

Beginning in the early 1960s, politicians and nongovernmental activists worked interactively to elaborate an extensive set of regulatory protections for consumers. Although repeated proposals in the 1950s and 1960s for a dedicated "Consumer Department" were defeated out of concern that the consumer interest was simply too broad to be represented by a single body, a total of thirty-five separate federal agencies had by the mid-1960s been tasked with representing consumers in specific policy areas.[65] The emphasis of the consumer advocates that emerged to work with these agencies was less on grassroots mobilization and more on research and the publicizing of specific crises. Consumers Union, which published *Consumer Reports,* periodically conducted exposés that launched new product safety issues into the public debate. The independent Public Interest Research Groups (PIRGs) sponsored by Ralph Nader undertook more detailed policy studies and engaged in aggressive public lobbying. Many independent consumer groups funded themselves not through membership dues, but from the fees on class action lawsuits filed on behalf of consumers. As one observer described the U.S. consumer movement: "[Their] strength . . . came not from the direct mobilization of a large number of people or groups, but from the capacity to provoke and channel indignation, for example, about unsafe cars or of accidents resulting from children wearing flammable pajamas, and translating these in legislation that congress could not easily ignore."[66] Legislators, for their part, responded positively to these external pressures, passing 120 legislative projects focused on consumer protection between 1969 and 1976.[67]

It is also striking in the U.S. case how quickly representation of consumer interests seems to have followed perception of their collective need. In the area of consumer protection—arguably the most diffuse of material interests—mobilization was rapid. Historian Lizabeth Cohen dates the first public awareness of consumer protection as a regulatory issue to Vance Packard's 1957 book *Hidden Persuaders,* a fictitious account of research on the impact of subliminal advertising.[68] Senator Estes Kefauver began assailing the pharmaceutical industry for price collusion in 1959. Revelations about the damage done by the drug thalidomide that started to become public in 1960 would launch a series of legislative hearings into drug safety. John F. Kennedy also raised consumer protection as a part of his campaign platform in 1960. Yet these early signs of concern about consumer issues as a diffuse material interest are probably clearly identifiable only in hindsight. To make a more neutral assessment of public attention to consumer protection over time, Figure 2.1 plots the number of *New York Times* and *Wall Street Journal* articles in which consumer protection was discussed in each year from 1950 to 1990. This tabulation of news reporting provides an indirect indicator of public interest in consumer protection.[69]

The graph in Figure 2.1 suggests that consumer protection as a public concern did not emerge until the early 1960s. Most of the important consumer protection legislation was then passed within ten years. These projects included the Child Protection and Safety Act (1969), the Fair Credit Reporting Act (1970), the Consumer Product Safety Act (1972), the Consumer Product Warrantees Act (1974), and many others. Consumer legislation tends to be complex, is often arcane, and yet has a direct and occasionally dramatic impact on producers and distributors. These traits should have made it a difficult area for quick legislative victories against the concentrated interests of industry. Nonetheless, within a decade of the publishing of *Unsafe at Any Speed*, the legal and regula-

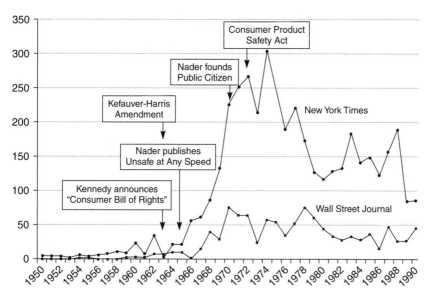

Figure 2.1. Number of newspaper articles about consumer protection by year, 1950–1990.

tory environment for consumers had been radically transformed. It is this sort of rapid policy response to diffuse material interest that requires explanation.

The record of newspaper articles in the United States also emphasizes the political logic of consumer protection policies. Reporting on consumer protection during the 1960s exhibits a strong cyclicality. The two-year cycles, with peaks on even years, match high levels of activity with congressional election years. A review of the content of these articles shows that the bulk of reporting did indeed relate to new legislative proposals. This suggests that there was an electoral logic to supporting consumer protection policies. Moreover, that electoral logic emerged rapidly, at least four years before the Kennedy "Consumer Bill of Rights" speech. Nor does this cyclicality seem to reflect partisan bias. The election-year bias persisted into the Nixon administration. And it is reflected in the publishing record of both the *New York Times* and the (less voluble and more conservative) *Wall Street Journal*. Interestingly, the pattern breaks down by the 1980s. If anything, election years in this later period receive lower consumer protection coverage.

Strikingly absent from the postwar U.S. consumer protection debates was a good-faith effort by industry to reach out directly to consumer advocates in order to make a separate peace that would allow regulators to take a step back. One reason for this failing may have been the legacy of an earlier effort by U.S. industry to co-opt the fledgling consumer movement. Beginning in the late-1930s, U.S. business associations began forming affiliated consumer groups, including the Consumer-Retailer Relations Council and the retailer-financed Consumers' Foundation. Most observers agree that these groups were intended more to muddy the waters than to forge genuine negotiation.[70] At the same time, industry was working to portray consumer groups as fronts for organized labor and even communism—a 1939 investigation of the House Committee on Un-American Activities investigated the fledgling consumer movement. A 1954 survey of business leaders found that 10 percent still saw consumer associations as "communist fronts."[71] Historian Lawrence Glickman notes that the very term *consumerism* was coined in 1966 by a business lobbyist eager to draw the link with communism.[72] These early red-baiting campaigns may have made it especially difficult for industry to come back to the negotiating table in the postwar period when consumer protections became a reality. The consequence of this failure was not a defeat for consumer protection, but resulted in a strategy of consumer protection that would bring policymakers and consumer activists together in opposition to industry.

Three Worlds of Diffuse Interest Representation

According to the austere model of interest group representation advocated by Mancur Olson, larger groups should be harder to organize, and their interests therefore less well represented in public policy, than the concentrated interests of industry. This argument has been influential, in part because of the organizational logic that motivates it. When large groups of individuals share an interest in a common policy outcome, no single member of the group will be willing to provide the effort needed to secure the common benefit. More technically—and the technical has been a defining feature of the Chicago School public policy analysis—

when marginal costs to the individual exceed marginal benefits from acting together, shared interests go underprovided. As Olson argued, larger groups face ever greater organizational challenges to overcome this impediment to adequate representation. By these accounts, consumers should be a hard case for mobilization. Yet the striking feature of postwar consumer mobilization, representation, and protection was how pervasive and diverse the phenomenon turned out to be. Diffuse but practical consumer interests came to be represented not just in one way, but in many.

Three dominant logics appear to have acted and interacted to make this possible. First, consumers *did* mobilize, although not equally in all countries. The form of this mobilization varied widely. Some organized consumer groups were professionalized while others remained intentionally nonprofessional. Some groups engaged in grassroots mobilization and political protest, whereas others worked closely with government and business associations, often shunning grassroots memberships as radicalizing or at least distracting. Some consumer associations allied with trade unions, a move that could lead toward either radicalization or accommodation, depending on the nature of the national trade union movement.

A second logic of consumer mobilization was a strong political focus on consumer protection. Under pressure from political constituencies, governments executed elaborate legislative programs to defend consumers. Although in some cases these initiatives were strongly shaped by the preferences of industry, this was only sometimes the case. In Japan, for example, politicians faced little in the way of electoral pressures that would lead them to oppose industry interests. In other countries, like Germany, labor and industry reached across the political spectrum to block more activist consumer legislation. More important, even in cases in which industry was able to exert a strong influence on the form of emerging consumer policy, the move to regulate the consumer sphere was clearly not something that industry had advocated or desired. Only after industry had failed to block regulatory initiatives did they begin to work to shape the new regime in ways that would favor their own product market strategies. If there is a surprise in the consumer movement, it was how willing governments were, especially beginning in the early 1970s, to take on industry groups and enact legislation of which many if not most producers clearly did not approve.

The third logic of consumer mobilization came from a recognition and acceptance by business that if consumer markets *were* to be regulated, advantage might be gained by participating in the process. In some cases, business associations were able to work closely with organized consumer groups to shape negotiated outcomes that met a combination of producer and consumer needs without excessive administrative oversight. This was the Scandinavian model. In other cases, business interests were able to adapt the policy process to favor their dominant product market strategies. In Japan and Germany, an emphasis on labeling and consumer advice services was seen by companies as a response to consumer grievance that could also create a more knowledgeable consumer base. At a time of growing competition from newer, and sometimes lower quality, products, a more discerning group of customers was seen as a key to brand loyalty. Critically, however, the influence of business went only so far. And in countries in which business was unable to organize sufficiently to represent producers collectively, such negotiated solutions typically did not generate lasting solutions.

These cases of parallel policy emergence suggest an informal system of policy borrowing and collaborative-discursive policy elaboration that had emerged even before formal intergovernmental institutions—including the European Commission, the United Nations, and the OECD— embraced agendas for consumer protection. In this informal process, the forms and types of policy responses adopted in one country commonly found their inspiration in the experiences of others. Ideas and instruments for protection were studied in foreign settings, then adopted in modified form for domestic purposes. The result, however, was not a trend toward progressive policy convergence. Borrowing worked and failed in nearly equal measure. And similar policies were often adopted with very different functions. As foreign models and domestic experiments mixed to form national approaches to regulating consumer markets, distinctive national consumer and shopping cultures emerged and evolved.

Yet all of the country models shared two common features. First, each of the main policy actors—industry, activists, and the state—sought out coalitions to promote their narrow interests as publicly legitimate. Those coalitions differed depending on the institutional context, but resulting policies were the product of interaction between pairs of actors. Second, these coalitions were forged around a common narrative that described the social identity of the consumer and the nature of the problems from which consumers needed to be protected. By defining the status of the consumer, the coalitions also conferred legitimacy on a set of regulatory interventions that corresponded with that status. In fact, the goals of both consumer groups and producers were mediated by the need to form co-alitions with other actors that would allow them to present their interests as being the legitimate target for public intervention. How such legitimacy coalitions emerge, and the role that political and economic institutions play in constraining coalitional outcomes, is the focus of the following chapter.

CHAPTER 3

Consumer Mobilization in
Postwar France

T HIS CHAPTER CONSIDERS the successful mobilization of consumers in postwar France to explore how, contrary to the predictions of organizational theory, broad and diffuse interest groups may organize and translate their agendas into public policy. For political scientists, the fact of consumer interest mobilization in France is doubly unexpected. That is because France has traditionally been seen as skeptical of the political and economic influence of intermediate associations. This charge has been leveled by scholars from Alexis de Tocqueville, who thought overweening state authority had strangled associational capacities, to sociologist Michel Crozier, who rued the lack of alternatives to state decree as a means of transforming French society.[1] More recently, political scientist Peter Hall writes of French policymaking: "Aggregations of individuals and formal organizations outside the state cannot pretend to speak for the general interest. Their political status is suspect."[2] This aversion to independent societal groups, compounded by the inherent challenges in organizing consumers, would appear to make France a poor environment for dynamic consumer mobilization.

Yet beginning in the 1970s, France saw the rise of an active and popular consumer movement. As early as 1972, a survey conducted by the National Consumption Institute (INC) found that 20 percent of French people over age fifteen said they were "ready to belong" to a consumer organization.[3] By the late 1970s, French consumer groups had become numerous, dynamic, and increasingly well funded. Another survey in 1978 found that interest in joining a consumer group had increased to 27 percent, and that two million French citizens (4 percent of the population) had already become members.[4] Many of these were simply passive members, subscribing to consumer magazines or sending in yearly contributions. But a growing number were grassroots activists. By 1980, France had more than one thousand local consumer unions that undertook price surveys, organized product boycotts, and provided consumers with remediation services. By 1982, a survey conducted by the journal *Nouvel Observateur* found that 76 percent of the French trusted consumer groups, compared to only 32 percent who trusted labor unions.[5] How do we understand the associational dynamism of the French consumer movement, especially in a country characterized by formal relations linking citizens directly to the state?

Mancur Olson explained the successful representation of large latent groups as a by-product of the provision of selective benefits. Those benefits, available only to members, created a positive inducement to join the organization. Olson explains, "Large pressure group organizations must derive their strength as a by-product of some nonpolitical functions."[6] The case of consumer mobilization in France shows the limitations of this account. French consumer groups did provide benefits to their members. These primarily took the form of advice and product information published in monthly magazines distributed to group members. But these benefits were not central to the groups' organizational success. Rather, successful consumer groups interacted with the state and with industry in ways that emphasized their societal importance. Critically, the main benefits from these interactions—described in more detail later in this chapter—were not limited to members of the consumer groups. Nonmember consumers could address grievances to any consumer association. Consumer associations negotiated advertising and product standards with producers for which the benefits accrued to the entire consuming public. Moreover, these activities in the broad public interest seem to have attracted new membership by emphasizing the important societal function of the organization. Larger memberships, in turn, made consumer associations more credible and legitimate interlocutors for industry and the state.

Although the French state did eventually become heavily involved in furthering the consumer agenda, its approach to consumer policy was not initially statist. Inspired by the Swedish model, French leaders on both the right and the left worked to promote independent organization of consumer associations, and then to encourage efforts to represent the interests of consumers through agreements negotiated directly with producers and their trade associations. On issues ranging from product labeling and safety to features of product design, this associational approach brought together consumer associations with producers and their trade associations to agree to mutually acceptable solutions to various consumer concerns. Policies related to issues as diverse as truth in advertising, product labeling, consumer contracts, product design, and retailing all became the focus of consumer-producer negotiations. By cutting out the government, this strategy of negotiated responses to consumer grievance was intended to lower the cost of regulatory oversight, while empowering consumer groups to represent their own interests in society. The idea, based on the Scandinavian approach to consumer protection, was to grant consumers the same collective agreement provisions that workers already enjoyed. It would extend the principles of associational liberalism to consumers. Doing so, however, first required that consumers be adequately organized to represent their own interests. The French state therefore provided funding and legitimacy that it hoped would help to promote a vibrant and independent consumer movement.

Ultimately, the experiment with a Scandinavian model of consumer protection failed, but not because consumers were unable to organize. Contrary to size-based theories of interest organization, French consumers did organize. Through their interactions with industry and with the French state, they took on a social legitimacy that in turn helped them to attract new members. This is an important departure from the Olsonian approach to collective action. French consumer groups cultivated membership *not* by providing selective benefits, but by emphasizing their public purpose. Moreover, the regulatory outcome that emerged in France had more to do with the institutional context in which consumer groups operated—and in particular the organization of industry—than with their own organizational capacity. The relatively weak organization of industry in France led individual companies to flout consumer standards that were negotiated between consumers and producers. Researchers seeking to understand the success of diffuse interest representation would do well to place greater priority on such institutional factors than on the putative organizational challenges that face large groups of individuals.

Consumer Nongovernmental Organizations (NGOs) and the State

How were France's consumer associations able to overcome the collective action problems supposedly inherent in their large size? The French case suggests several conclusions. The first is that the organizational-theory approach considerably overstates the difficulties. The interests of broad groups enjoy the advantage of a natural and easily established legitimacy. Nor are they particularly demanding of their members: unlike most of the new social movements more often studied as archetypal diffuse interest groups, the consumer movement did not require its participants to stage Gandhi-style hunger strikes, for example, or risk arrest or personal violence sitting in at a Woolworth's lunch counter. The second conclusion concerns the importance of partnerships between consumer groups and the state, both for increasing the legitimacy of the consumer cause and for expanding its organizational potential.

Broadly, three organizational strategies can be identified in the French consumer movement, each involving different levels of government support. The first strategy used dedicated consumer advocacy groups: one exclusively private, the second formed and supported entirely by the French state. The former, the Union fédérale des consommateurs (UFC), was independent and adopted an often contentious stance with respect to industry and government regulation. The latter was the state-sponsored Institute national de la consommation (INC). INC was a government administrative body tasked to support consumer associations and inform consumers. These two institutions represent different sides of the story of consumer mobilization in France. Each confronted the challenge of supporting a dynamic and emerging independent consumer movement in the context of the regulatory state. Each interacted in complex ways with the state, sometimes embracing it and sometimes playing a more oppositional role. Taken together, the emergence and interaction of these two groups shaped the form and focus of the French consumer movement. A third breed of consumer organization consisted of groups formed up to a generation earlier around other interests that later took up the consumer agenda with state funding and encouragement. The French consumer movement drew much of its strength from the diversity of its organizational structures and their interactions with the state.

The Federal Consumers Union (UFC)

Many of the most dramatic achievements of the French consumer movement can be traced to one group: the Union fédérale des consommateurs (UFC). From the 1960s through the 1980s, the UFC prided itself on being a thorn in the side of French industry. It launched a comparative product testing magazine, *Que Choisir?*, in 1961. In the early 1970s the group began to sponsor affiliated local consumer unions. By 1980, *Que Choisir?* was distributing the results of comparative product tests to 400,000 subscribers, and the UFC boasted 170 local unions with 50,000 active local members. This nation-wide manpower gave the group a strong voice in regulatory policy. During the week beginning November 20, 1979, for example, members of 110 local UFC unions were able to survey 27,735 store windows and shelves in 160 cities in France for compliance with a new price labeling law. Mobilized under the slogan "not seen not bought" ("*pas vu pas pris*"), they found that 38 percent of the stores visited had not displayed prices on their products.[7] Given the diffuseness of the interests that the UFC was attempting to represent, how did this sort of mobilization and activism arise?

The secret was that the UFC—in this regard a useful microcosm of the French consumer movement as a whole—did not act alone. It emerged and grew through a protracted back-and-forth interaction with the French state. These interactions were sometimes amicable but also frequently antagonistic. Although it was France's most independent consumer group, throughout its lifetime the UFC relied heavily on the government, sometimes for financial support but often also as a foil. The state helped the UFC to grow; the UFC gave new legitimacy to regulatory actions of the state. Even during episodes of real antagonism, and there were many of these, the UFC assisted state policymakers by showing that consumer protections had a constituency in the general population, and that they corresponded to real, independent interests of consumers.

The UFC was, at its founding in 1951, closely tied to state policy. Its origins lay in state institutions created to administer European Recovery Plan (ERP) funds granted by the United States under the Marshall Plan, which formally went into operation in 1948. To assist in allocating ERP funds, the French government formed a National Productivity Committee (NPC) that included two separate subcommittees dealing with consumer issues: the Production, Distribution, Consumption Committee and the Trade, Consumption, Quality Committee.[8] The idea that consumption and productivity were closely tied was expressed explicitly in 1951 by an administrator of the NPC: "To the extent that the consumer is more or less informed, advised, active, and far sighted, the economy stagnates or progresses. . . . Growth in productivity, which leads to an increase in quality of life, depends less today on progress in production techniques than on determining the precise final service to render to consumers and on adapting the economy to this imperative."[9]

On the recommendation of the Trade, Consumption, Quality Committee, two new state-funded institutions were created that would provide better information about consumption both to consumers and to the state. One, called Crédoc and created in 1953, collected systematic data on household consumption. The second, the UFC, was intended to represent all of France's consumer groups.[10] Article 2 of the statute that created the UFC set out its goal: "to create a permanent link among the groups and individuals who, for whatever reason, are interested to help consumers and users to maintain their position in economic life." With this broad mandate, the UFC was envisioned as an umbrella organization for women's groups, consumer cooperatives, and labor unions interested in consumer policy. It was headed by André Romieu, a lawyer by training who had previously headed the Consumption Office of the economic ministry's Direction on Economic Planning.[11] This earlier group had

primarily collected data on consumption patterns and worked with
family, women, labor, and cooperative groups to conduct consumer surveys. By the time Romieu was appointed to head the UFC, he was already deeply knowledgeable about French consumption patterns and
challenges.

But the consolidated, state-run approach to consumer policy did not
last long. Soon after the UFC was formed, affiliated groups began breaking away. In 1954, the cooperatives left the UFC to create their own
product testing lab, Laboratoire cooperatif d'analyses et de recherches
(LaboCoop). In 1958, the trade unions pulled out of the UFC to create
their own independent consumer group, the Organisation générale de
consommation (ORGECO).[12] Following suit, the UFC itself broke ties
with the government in 1959, forming itself as the newly independent
Federal Consumers' Union. To support itself, it began publishing the
results of comparative product tests in its monthly magazine, *Que Choisir?* (*What to Choose?*). Comparative product testing would eventually
become a core activity of the UFC, and an important source of its internal finance.

Although the UFC vaunted its growing circulation as a sign of increasing membership, it was broadly understood that this sort of membership was not analogous to membership in other mobilization efforts.
Que Choisir? would eventually become a source of revenue for the organization, but before that happened, it served two other organizational
functions that proved essential to the UFC's remarkable success. First,
the UFC used circulation data from *Que Choisir?* to launch its first affiliated local consumer unions. Selecting communities with particularly
dense readership, it found it was able to increase its chances of success in
local mobilizing. In 1973, the UFC formed its first 10 local unions based
in areas of particularly high subscription rates. The following year, 18
local unions were added, raising total participation to 5,000 members.
These early groups proved highly successful, and more were added each
year, reaching 100 local unions by 1977 and 170 by 1980. Unlike the general *Que Choisir?* readership, members in these unions were active.
They assisted local consumers with advice and complaints, and joined
broader national consumer protection initiatives. By 1980, the local
unions had become a dynamic force both within the UFC, through their

representation in the General Assembly, and outside of the organization. Half of the local unions had between 50 and 200 members; 15 local unions had more than 500 active members. All together, 50,000 grassroots activists had joined the UFC's local unions across France. Most members were women, although increasingly men began to join as well. In 1980, these local unions handled 35,000 consumer complaints related to products ranging from cars, white goods, and furniture to lodging and insurance.[13] Their members sat on regional consumer councils, on municipal committees approving new store openings, and on departmental committees that implemented France's complex price-fixing scheme.[14]

The second organizational benefit of *Que Choisir?* was the platform it gave the UFC for establishing its independence, and hence its legitimacy as the voice of French consumers. The magazine's most common conflicts occurred when its product reviews criticized producers, often resulting in protracted court cases that the UFC sometimes won but also regularly lost. These cases—against aerosol can producers whose cans exploded at high temperatures, against the tire producer Kléber-Colombes for tires that exploded, against medical test labs for faulty test results, and against condom producers for micro-perforations—provided the UFC with a continuous stream of publicity. French courts were not particularly sympathetic with the UFC, and the organization often lost such cases. In the November 1978 edition, for example, *Que Choisir?* showed on its cover the picture of three medicines produced by the Laboratoire Beaufours, with the text: "We demand the recall of these three medicines." When Beaufours sued the UFC in a Paris court, the court found for the plaintiff and required the UFC to pay 50,000 francs and also publish the court's verdict in *Que Choisir?* and in five national newspapers selected by Beaufours. An appeals court upheld the decision, citing the need for testing organizations to act "without passion and with prudence." Yet each time such cases became publicized, both the magazine's circulation and its public esteem seemed to grow.

Nor did the UFC hesitate to criticize the French government. These conflicts often escalated into political battles that further raised the profile of the UFC as not just economically but also politically independent. In February 1970, for example, the UFC published in *Que Choisir?* results of a study conducted by a government lab (CERBOM) showing that French beaches were highly polluted. Speaking before the National Assembly, the mayor of the resort town Deauville accused UFC of having shown themselves "incompetent and irresponsible" in publishing the results of the study. When a new test was conducted in 1975, CERBOM refused to give the results to UFC. In 1976, the UFC used its own funds to conduct an environmental survey of thirty beaches in France, at a cost of 25,000 francs. They repeated these tests in 1977, and then in 1978 following the *Amoco Cadiz* oil spill off the coast of Brittany.[15] Based on the results of these tests, they also filed suit against Amoco for the resulting environmental damage. Through such cases, *Que Choisir?* gave the UFC a public voice. The impact of such dramatic critiques of industry was then amplified by the French courts—whether or not UFC actually won the case—and by the invective of political leaders.

Almost certainly, the research and warnings issued by *Que Choisir?* led to the dramatic growth in the UFC's grassroots membership. But this was not achieved by providing selective benefits, in the way that Olson has suggested that groups might mobilize. Rather, the UFC uncovered and publicized egregious behavior by firms as a means to promote outrage among its readers, and it was that outrage—not charts comparing the performance of household appliances—that seems to have led to greater membership. By focusing public attention on flagrant abuse or corporate misbehavior, *Que Choisir?* was able to identify and motivate activists who did not otherwise have meaningful economic incentives to mobilize.

The National Consumption Institute (INC)

State involvement in the French consumer movement did not end when the UFC, the cooperatives, and the trade unions broke away from the ministerial program. Not content to leave consumer policy in the hands of independent advocacy groups, the French government in 1966 launched a new National Consumption Institute (INC) with state funding and a mandate to conduct research, inform consumers, and support independent consumer groups. INC published the results of comparative product tests, distributed information about product and consumer regulation to independent consumer groups, and helped to train consumer activists. Funding for INC came directly from the government budget, with a growing share deriving from sales of the INC's own consumer magazine, *50 Millions de Consommateurs.* From its inception, the idea of state-supported consumer protection was contentious. Observers worried how objective a government-sponsored institute could be. Industry worried that the new institution might work to the detriment of French producers. In an effort to provide balance, the advisory council of the INC was constituted half of industry representatives and half of consumer representatives.

Even before its founding, the apparently anodyne informational goals of the new institute were viewed with suspicion by other consumer groups. The labor group ORGECO objected to the participation of producers on the advisory council; the employers in turn arranged to have all union-related consumer groups banned from the INC. Women's groups questioned the value of a government office focused on advising mainly women consumers and, more generally, viewed the measures as condescending. In National Assembly debates on the new institute in 1966, Jeannette Prin, a member of Parliament, explained the concern: "We are hostile to the creation of a new national consumption institute that will bring nothing to consumers. Raise our salaries; improve family services. Housewives and heads of family do not need advice; what they need is sufficient purchasing power."[16] In the subsequent Senate debate, Robert Boulin noted the lack of support among women: "It is curious; all of the women are against the consumption institute. There is some sort of hysteria[17] when we want to defend the household." His colleague Pierre de la Contrie replied (shouting): "That is because they are [already] competent!" Senator Irma Rapuzzi interjected: "It would be more helpful to lower the consumption tax!"[18] The commitment to provide consumers with better information was perceived both as patronizing to women, and, more important, as a distraction from meaningful improvements in household finances. Finally, the UFC also actively opposed the creation of the INC, although for more self-serving reasons. Concerned about competition from a rival product testing magazine, it argued that the INC "weakens the position of consumers by channeling their claims into an organization controlled by the government and by producers."[19] Accordingly, the UFC refused to sit on the INC's governing board, despite periodic entreaties by the government, and boycotted INC activities, including the once-yearly public convention called the Salon des Consommateurs.

Underlying these critiques was a genuine tension in the mission of the new institute. At the first meeting of the INC's advisory council, in January 1968, economics minister Michel Debré spoke of the institute's double responsibility: "A responsibility of mobilization, extending the actions of groups that represent you . . . but at the same time, you will have a program for information and education."[20] The conflict between these two goals became increasingly evident. The idea of protecting consumers by informing them, after all, implied a depoliticized and relatively passive consumer movement. This contradicted the idea of providing support for independent consumer groups that were becoming progressively more politically engaged. Especially as independent consumer groups began cultivating a grassroots following in the mid-1970s, this tension emerged as a profound organizational crisis.

The institute's first director, Henri Estingoy, was a strong consumer and consumer-group advocate. Indeed, Estingoy may have been the closest that France came to its own homegrown Ralph Nader. As a 12-year-old, he is said to have sold candy canes at school at half the price they were sold by the school's concierge. Formerly employed in the Paris police, he quickly came to see his position in the INC as defending the increasingly active but also vulnerable independent consumer groups. Although the INC was not nearly as aggressive as the UFC, Estingoy nonetheless showed that he was willing to side with consumer interests against those of producers. When he publicly criticized chocolate makers for packaging their products with too much air, he was banned from further appearances on the government-run television station on which his statement had aired.[21] He invited Ralph Nader—a radical activist by the standards of the French consumer movement at the time—to speak at the first annual Salon des Consommateurs held in Paris in 1972. He was a strong defender of product testing and aggressively defended INC's comparative product testing magazine *50 Millions de Consommateurs* against attacks. He opposed industry efforts to have greater influence on testing standards, and responded strongly to criticisms of *50 Millions* product reports. In one noteworthy case, INC sued the magazine *Hi-Fi*

Stereo for criticizing a comparative test that INC had conducted of thirty-five different stereo systems. (The cover of the *50 Millions de Consommateurs* in which the results were published proclaimed: "50 Million Dupes.") The court found in favor of INC and required *Hi-Fi Stereo* to pay INC 50,000 francs in compensation.[22]

Estingoy was also a vociferous supporter of the right of consumer associations to call for product boycotts, and such boycotts had become progressively more common. They ranged from a near halt of lamb purchases in 1978 out of concern over the use of artificial hormones, to a retaliatory consumer boycott against fruit and vegetable vendors who had stopped selling produce for nearly a week as part of a price negotiation with their own suppliers. Meanwhile, the legal status of calls to boycott was still being contested. In its July 1978 edition, *50 Millions de Consommateurs* published an editorial making clear its position: "The right to boycott has no exceptions. It is not a question of whether the call to boycott is well founded or not. In the same way that an employer cannot judge the timing of a strike, so a producer or distributor may not contest a consumer association's right to call a strike, that is to say, a boycott."[23] For the third government of Raymond Barre and his pro-business economics minister René Monory, this appeared to be a step too far. Estingoy was fired in 1978 and replaced with Pierre Fauchon, with instructions that "the institute (INC) does not and should not have the militant stance [of the consumer associations]."[24] To emphasize the point, Monory wrote to Fauchon asking him to "watch personally for any circumstance, in order to dissipate any event that could give the impression that the Institute is an organization of consumers or that it represents consumers."[25] On taking office, Fauchon announced that the INC would not take political positions against the government. "The role of the institute is not to represent consumers, as many wrongly imagine, but to protect them. This justifies certain types of actions, but rules out others." Of particular concern were consumer boycott actions. Fauchon warned: "The boycott . . . should only be understood as a tool to inform the public and to warn them in case of danger." In particular, he criticized a UFC boycott of Shell to protest high oil prices as illegitimate—claiming that it was intended merely as retaliation for the *Amoco Cadiz* oil spill. Christiane Scrivener, the former secretary of state for consumption who had backed Estingoy, warned that INC risked becoming "a technical center without a militant spirit."[26]

The new orientation imposed by Fauchon left the INC without a clear organizational direction and, with the election victory of François Mitterrand in 1981, the INC was again restructured. Under the new leadership of Laurent Denis, the INC's advisory board invited union-affiliated consumer groups to join, and business was, in 1983, kicked out.[27] But a series of crises ensued that left the INC on shaky ground. The general budget austerity of the Mitterrand fiscal U-turn also reduced funds for INC. A report leaked by France's regional development commission (DATAR) revealed that there had been pressure to move INC out of its Paris office to Lille.[28] And, in 1984, Laurent Denis threatened to fire the longtime editor of *50 Millions de Consommateurs* in response to rumors that the test magazine was contemplating breaking away from its parent group, INC.[29] INC writers went on strike in response. Business was pushing for, and eventually achieved, greater influence on the process of product selection and testing. And the UFC continued to criticize the INC as creating unfair competition to their privately funded comparative testing journal. Marie-José Nicoli, then head of the UFC, wrote in March 1988 to the secretary of state for consumption and competition, noting the "unfair competition from *50 Millions de Consommateurs*—a magazine created and financed by the state—for our independent magazine, *Que Choisir?*"[30] INC weathered these problems and emerged by the 1990s a strong and respected consumer information center. By this time, however, the core activities of consumer protection had shifted away from INC and comparative testing and toward new efforts to directly regulate issues of product quality and safety.

Other Organizations

Beyond the UFC and the INC, the French state-activist coalition manifested itself in the form of government support to nonconsumer groups that took up the consumer agenda. Some of the organizations that began to pursue consumer protection in the 1970s had their origins as family associations founded in the 1940s, with a focus on defending family life and values.[31] Traditionally these groups addressed subsets of family issues:

women's issues, rural family life, trade union families, and Catholic family issues. Others, including the Fédération nationale des cooperatives de consommateurs (FNCC) and its product testing lab, LaboCoop, had emerged at the turn of the century from France's consumer cooperative movement. Originally organized as distribution channels for cooperative producers, these groups began reorienting themselves in the 1970s toward the broad consuming public. A third source of consumer mobilization came from the labor union movement. The Organisation generale des consommateurs (ORGECO) was the first of these, created in 1959 to represent all consumers with union affiliation. By the mid-1970s, France's individual labor unions began breaking away from ORGECO to create their own consumer advocacy groups. In 1974 Force ouvrière (Workers' Force) broke from ORGECO to form the Association force ouvrière consommateur (AFOC). In 1979 the communist trade union Confédération générale de travail (CGT) followed suit, creating the affiliated consumer group INDECOSA-CGT. In 1981 the CFDT trade union created ASSECO-CFDT. Each of these groups used organizing skills developed in the context of labor mobilization to attract and motivate their own activist consumer memberships. By the early 1980s, each of these groups had expanded their scope of activity to include consumer information and advocacy efforts.

Why did these groups move into the realm of consumer protection? One reason was the direct government funding they began to receive during the 1970s and 1980s for undertaking consumer advocacy work. Combined government funding for consumer activities by family associations increased from 125,000 francs in 1974 to over 1.5 million francs by 1983 (in current francs).[32] Funding to consumer groups affiliated with labor unions increased from 35,000 francs in 1974 to over 1.6 million francs in 1983. Consumer groups that focused exclusively on consumers, including the UFC, Confédération syndicale du cadre de vie (CSCV), and Association des nouveaux consommateurs (ANC), also saw their government funding increase over the same period, from 80,000 francs to 1.3 million francs. Even taking away the effects of inflation, total government support to independent consumer associations increased by seven times between 1974 and 1983.[33] (See Figure 3.1.)

France's consumer groups were enticed in part by government financial support, but they were also given opportunities to engage directly

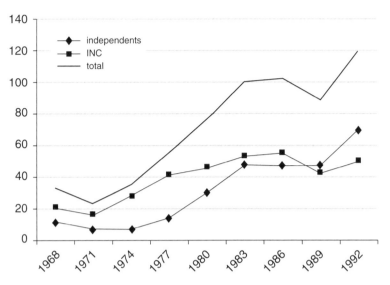

Figure 3.1. Government support to consumer groups (in millions of 1971 francs).

with consumers through new regulatory schemes that delegated quasi-government functions from the state to these associations. Groups that might potentially support consumer interests were initially invited to participate in the National Consumer Council, formed in 1960, to discuss ways in which the government should respond to consumer issues. By the 1970s, the government was giving them a more active role in direct relations with consumers. A government-sponsored *Opération vacances*, launched in the summer of 1976, brought consumer groups together to sponsor 2,500 consultation points in 248 locations in the south of France in order to assist tourists with consumer grievances.[34] A consumer complaint service launched in November 1977, called "Boîte postale (BP) 5000" for the address to which letters of complaint should be sent, relied in part on consumer associations to help resolve disputes. Although the program was popular with consumers who used it, it was not uniformly embraced by consumer groups. Six national consumer associations, including all of the major family-oriented associations (CSCV; CSF; Fédération des familles de France, or FFF; Fédération nationale des associations familiales rurales, or FNAFR), the labor union association ORGECO, and the dedicated consumer associations UFC and UFCS, boycotted the BP 5000 program by refusing to handle BP 5000 cases referred to them.[35] Their complaint was that the central distribution system treated consumers individually, and thus hurt their own efforts to promote consumer mobilization.

Apart from the government-sponsored services in which these groups participated, they were also drawn into undertaking their own activist agendas. The dozen or so national consumer organizations published their own weekly or monthly journals. In 1974, journals of consumer and family groups enjoyed a joint circulation of nearly 2 million, of which 1.5 million was accounted for by *Le Cooperateur de France* published by the FNCC, and 320,000 by *Que Choisir?*, the comparative testing magazine published by the UFC.[36] Most of these consumer groups also ran active public campaigns. Product labeling was a repeated theme for these groups. They frequently mobilized their participants to visit stores to evaluate the extent to which the regulations were being heeded. And they increasingly coordinated price surveys and product boycotts.

Those consumer groups that had their roots in the representation of families, women, and workers were not able to shed their founding interests entirely. Groups with roots in the trade union movement, for example, were typically hesitant to join in boycott actions that might result in worker layoffs. Groups rooted in the cooperative movement had similar concerns. When the cooperative publication *LaboCoop* began undertaking comparative product tests, the editors shied away from publishing the actual names of the products tested (referring to them anonymously as "product A" and "product B") for fear of hurting cooperative producers. Still, such consumer group activities were in general well received, and the groups themselves appeared to enjoy the trust of the French population. A survey conducted by Sofrès in 1976 found that 4 percent of respondents trusted manufacturers to assure consumer safety, 20 percent trusted themselves, 37 percent trusted the state, and 34 percent trusted consumer organizations.[37]

The experience of the family associations and other French groups involved in consumer activities echoes the experience of the UFC: the state-activist coalition in diffuse interest representation was both essential and surprisingly interactive. Sometimes the government spurred consumers to mobilize, as with the founding of the UFC and the funding of consumerist activities on the part of independent associations. But on other occasions it was the independent groups that pressured the government to further the consumer agenda. Either way, the opportunity structure of postwar France proved a conducive environment for the broad consumer interest, despite the nation's historic hostility to voluntary associations.

The Rise and Fall of an Industry-Activist Coalition

Less successful than the various manifestations of the government-activist coalition was the French government's attempts to resolve consumer grievances by facilitating direct encounters between consumers and business. Remarkably, both consumers and producers were initially interested in collaboratively negotiated standards. Through the mid-1970s, France's major consumer associations were pushing for a more active role in promoting product safety: a 1977 survey found that 81 percent of consumer groups wished for a consultative role with industry.[38] French businesses and industry associations, too, appeared increasingly willing to come to the bargaining table. Indeed, much of the initial contact between business and consumers took place at the initiative of companies themselves. Their efforts to reach out to consumer groups were motivated in large part by a concern to meet consumer demands. A survey conducted by the École supérieure de commerce of Lyons in 1976 found that one-quarter of the 550 French companies they contacted reported having engaged in dialogue with consumer associations, although half reportedly still viewed consumer groups with hostility.[39]

Consumer efforts to reach out to companies were frequently greeted with acceptance. One example was the case of Citroën. In 1978, two Citroën owners, a printer and a marketing specialist, joined forces to create the Comité de défense des citroënistes. They began by placing 10,000 notices posted on the windshields of Citroën model CX automobiles in the parking lot of a car show in 1978, asking for the car owners' feedback and experiences with the car. Two thousand Citroën owners responded. Drawing on this initial pool of consumers, the Comité de défense des citroënistes began compiling complaints and requests of users, which it then submitted to the company. By their own account, their goal was not to hurt the company, but rather to improve the quality of its products: "We will not accept for Citroën to produce below its reputation." Citroën took these requests seriously, and worked to solve the particular problems they had raised. "We accept this sort of confrontation," said Citroën, "it is part of our brand image."[40]

When France established its first ministerial position focused on consumers in 1976, its new secretary of state for consumption, Christiane Scrivener, emphasized the value of incorporating consumer interests within the firm itself. She urged France's large companies to introduce what she called "Monsieurs et Madames consommateurs." These would be company employees who, by representing the interests of product users, would play "a role of constructive criticism" within the firm. This seemingly unusual government initiative represented an early commitment by the state to step back from invasive regulation: "The problems of consumption cannot be solved by a systematic intervention by the state," said Scrivener.[41] It did not, however, prove particularly successful. Despite the pressures that were placed on firms to create such consumer advocacy departments, surveys showed that only seventeen companies had such departments in 1976; that number grew slowly, to twenty-five in 1978 and thirty in 1979.

At the same time that individual companies were increasingly interacting with groups of consumers, industry associations were also interested in making contact with France's officially registered consumer associations. One early experiment suggested that such negotiated approaches to consumer protection could work. Beginning in September 1970, France's largest employers' association, the Conseil national du patronat français (CNPF), collaborated with INC to create the Association française pour l'étiquetage d'information (AFEI), a nonprofit organization in the public interest that designed and distributed model product labels.[42] AFEI quickly became the standard-bearer for sectors interested to employ common labeling formats. In 1973, consumer associations also gained access to the board of directors of Association francaise de normalisation (AFNOR), France's product-standard-setting body, where they worked side by side with industry representatives to help design product specifications for products destined for end consumers. Some early regional agreements also showed promising signs of success. In the early 1970s in Alsace, for example, the consumer association ACOR (Associations des consommateurs organisés), with 130,000 families as members, signed agreements directly with retailers calling, among other things, for them not to charge more than 25 percent profit margins, and for them to open their accounts to a new Commission of Users. In exchange, ACOR provided them with its label to be included in their advertising, and publicized participating retailers in their own journal, *Le Consommateur*, which had a circulation of 80,000.[43]

These early success stories led France's central industry associations to open ongoing discussions with consumer associations. Initial efforts, though promising, were inconclusive. Over the period between 1971 and 1973, for example, the national association representing small proprietors, the Confédération générale du patronat des petites et moyennes entreprises (CGPME), met with INC, UFC, and ORGECO to discuss consumer issues, but without coming to any agreements.[44] In 1973, the Paris Chamber of Commerce and Industry (CCIP) proposed the creation of a new Centre de concertation industrie commerce comsommateur (CCICC) that would bring together consumers and producers within the context of the CCIP. One of its goals would be to show "that the protection of consumers is an essential goal of producers and distributors and that state intervention is not always indispensable for resolving problems of consumer information and defense."[45] This initiative was also never achieved.

Real progress was made in 1974, when, in the context of the first oil shock, CNPF president François Ceyrac announced that the CNPF wished to work together with consumers.[46] The following year the CNPF appointed Paul Simonet head of a new Commission on Industry, Commerce, and Consumption (CICC), with the goal of presenting a united front to consumer organizations. Simonet appears to have been open to constructive discussions with consumer groups. "Consumerism is a deep and durable movement that corresponds to the evolution of society," he announced, "and with which we must establish an open and constructive dialogue."[47] The CNPF was, in the words of Simonet, ". . . very open to all forms of negotiation, especially in the domain of information. . . ."[48] It was a view shared by many CNPF member companies. Jean-Georges Marais, for example, the director of customer relations at Air France, affirmed in 1977 that negotiation with consumer groups was "indispensable."[49]

Government Support for Consumer-Producer Negotiations

By the mid-1970s, the French government also began to take an interest in consumer-producer negotiations. In 1974, National Consumer Committee (CNC) president Francis Pécresse requested the creation of a special working group on "Commerce-Consommation" to consider approaches to consumer protection. That group proposed to put in place in Toulouse a trial forum for consumer-producer negotiations. The new organization, called CRICC (Comité de recours et d'information commerce consommation), was set up in 1975. Consumers were represented by two family-focused consumer groups, as many national consumer groups still refused to sit down at the negotiating table with business. On March 24, 1976, the first meeting took place, with Christiane Scrivener, the secretary of state for consumption, attending. It was the first truly equal meeting of consumers and producers in France, and resulted in agreements covering clothes laundering and furniture retailing.[50] In another signal of growing government interest in consumer-producer negotiations, the Commisariat du Plan created in 1975 a new Consumption Committee that would address consumer issues for the first time in the Seventh French Plan. Consisting of consumer and producer representatives, the committee concluded that France should support the development of a dialogue between consumers and producers—although business representatives to the committee also reported a "certain climate of hostility" among the consumer representatives to the Consumption Committee.[51]

The third Barre government, inaugurated in 1978, placed consumer groups firmly at the center of its consumer protection policy. Instead of relying on government administration to meet consumer demands, the new economics minister René Monory called instead for consumer associations to function as a counterforce to industry: "the consumer counterforce must be developed."[52] The innovation of the Monory program on these earlier efforts was to encourage collaboration on all aspects of the production process, something that the CNPF had long opposed. Although critical of the formerly militant stance of the INC, Monory nonetheless called on the group to support consumer associations by helping to "counterbalance the technical skill of producers and the effects of advertising."[53] Consumer associations in this new approach were to be full partners in the production process, not just in providing product information, but also in defining product quality and price.[54] To this end, Monory called for state funding to consumer associations to be quadrupled, from 1 million francs in 1978 to 4 million francs in 1979.[55] Monory, who commonly refered to himself as the "minister of consumption," gave actual authority over consumer issues to Danièle Achach, head of the newly created consumption mission within the economics ministry's competition and consumption agency.[56]

By 1979, the CNPF had announced that it was ready to discuss broad consumer protection issues with consumer groups. Under the new initiative, the CNPF's CCIC held regular meetings with consumer associations from November 1979 to March 1981. They discussed standards for advertising, auto sales, after-sale service, furniture, and many more topics.[57] Although decisions arrived at through these discussions were voluntary, companies that accepted negotiated standards could advertise their compliance as a selling point. Still concerned about the voluntary nature of these agreements, consumer groups were not content to limit their negotiations to the CNPF. They therefore also approached sectoral and regional industry associations to draw up separate negotiated agreements. By 1989, forty-nine voluntary accords had been signed between consumer associations and professional associations. Of these, 36 percent treated house construction, 20 percent used-car sales, 18 percent small retailing, 8 percent furniture, and 6 percent dry cleaning.[58]

One such sectoral agreement addressed standards of advertising. Between 1980 and 1983, the Conseil national de la publicité (CNP) negotiated with consumer associations to set standards for the advertising industry. The meetings brought together eleven consumer organizations and eleven representatives of the media, plus the INC and two prior authorities on advertising (Bureau de vérification de la publicité and Régie française de publicité). The professionals favored the discussions, saying that it helped them among other things to keep track of the interests of consumer groups on subjects that could change over time.[59] Another voluntary agreement was negotiated between consumer associations and the Union des artisans commerçants (UDAC), France's largest retail store association at the time. According to this agreement, retailers following a set of negotiated guidelines would be allowed to post in their storefront a sticker of a blue, white, and red fleur-de-lis that read: *"Engagement du commerce, j'adhère"* ("I participate in the retail agreement").[60] The negotiated guidelines included marking rebates as a percentage of the proper price, indicating prices *"tout compris"* (including services and other charges), posting information about service after sale, and a guarantee to replace goods that did not function properly or were damaged in delivery. Like many such accords, the program was well received but not very widely used. A survey conducted in April 1981 of 663 stores in Marseilles found that only twenty-seven stores (4 percent) had placed the *fleur tricolore* in their storefront windows.[61]

Industry was happy with these early experiments with negotiated consumer protection so long as they applied primarily to issues of consumer information. But Monory intended to extend their scope to aspects of product quality as well. One such effort focused on integrating consumer associations into the process of setting product quality standards. The law on consumer information of 10 January 1978 provided for so-called quality certificates (*certificats de qualification*), a set of standard product labels intended both to guarantee a reasonable minimum level of quality and to provide an objective measure of certain dimensions of quality.[62] Research centers that issued these certificates would be approved by the Ministry of Research and Industry, and were required to include all of the social partners (producers, labor, consumers) in the design process.[63] Consumer groups were invited to sit on the committees that decided on appropriate measures of quality and set minimum quality thresholds. The government's goal was to have all products labeled in this way by 1981. But the project became increasingly contentious, and studies revealed that hundreds of existing product brands were unlikely to meet even the minimum quality thresholds set by the design committees.[64] As it became clear that the labeling program might put businesses and their employees out of work, the program was quietly eliminated.

The Search for Binding Agreements

By the time François Mitterrand was elected president in 1981, tensions over voluntary consumer-producer negotiations had come to a head. Producers were concerned that consumer groups wanted increasingly to participate in negotiations bearing on product design decisions. Initiatives like the quality certificates, although formally a labeling program, increasingly impinged on product quality and features in a manner that industry felt was unduly intrusive. Consumers, for their part, were frustrated with businesses' unwillingness to adopt the voluntary standards negotiated by the industry associations to which they belonged. In January 1980, eleven national consumer associations wrote a public letter renouncing participation in collective agreements until a formal enforcement mechanism was established.[65] Their answer came with the victory of the Socialist Party, which in 1981 put a new emphasis on collective agreements as a means of consumer protection. Mitterrand signaled the importance of this initiative by creating a ministry of consumption, to which he appointed Catherine Lalumière as minister.[66] In September 1981, Lalumière affirmed her support for the negotiation approach to consumer protection: "I believe that we can do nothing with individual consumers in the state of nature, nor if all effort is concentrated at the state level."[67]

Her efforts focused on ways to make agreements negotiated between consumer and professional groups legally binding. One approach, advocated by many consumer groups, would treat the consumer-producer relationship as analogous to the worker-employer relationship, with the state enforcing binding collective agreements.[68] Lalumière therefore proposed to model consumer-producer negotiations on the 1936 labor law, which granted labor unions the right to negotiate contract terms at the sectoral level. Jacques Ghestin, a lawyer and spokesman for consumer groups, argued that the government should delegate authority over all aspects of consumer products, including product quality and the terms of consumer contracts, to negotiations among professional associations. "In reality," he argued, "I don't see why professional organizations that are able to speak legitimately for their members about work conditions could not do the same in relation to sales conditions."[69] Because a corporatist strategy of this kind would have ramifications for all areas of consumer regulation, even some that had already been regulated, Lalumière created a committee, headed by the lawyer and consumer advocate Jean Calais-Auloy, to rewrite the full body of consumer law in France. Tellingly, no industry representatives were included on the committee.[70]

While the initiative to make negotiated agreements at the associational level binding was being designed, the government was also pursuing a more direct means of making consumer-producer agreements binding. Rather than devolving state powers to sectoral actors, this second approach sought a legal contractual status for agreements negotiated between consumer groups and individual companies. In December 1982, Lalumière modified the quality certificates program created under the previous government to enable "contracts for the improvement of quality." Under this new legal provision, products or services conforming to the norms established in negotiations between management and officially recognized consumer groups would be indicated with the *Marque approuvé,* a symbol including a hexagon (for France) inscribed with the letter *A* (for *approuvé*).[71]

These agreements had a mixed reception among consumer groups. Those groups affiliated with the socialist and communist labor unions strongly favored quality agreements, and some companies even negotiated them through the consumer groups affiliated with the unions representing their own work force. Because these agreements took the form of contracts that were legally binding, consumers could resort to the court system to hold companies to their agreed standards. But not all consumer groups were satisfied. The UFC remained critical of the *approuvé* program because it felt that the program produced few results for consumers, and supplanted the more effective quality certificates initiative that had been attempted by the Ministry of Industry.[72] By contrast, the communist-affiliated consumer group INDECOSA-CGT complained that the government was not applying sufficient pressure on France's large nationalized companies to sign quality contracts with consumer associations.[73] Nor was the system as successful as its designers had hoped.[74] By 1985, only fifty-nine companies had signed quality contracts with consumer associations, most with a duration of only one to two years.[75] Of these,

thirty-three companies signed contracts to improve the quality of services; twenty-six companies signed contracts that applied to a total of
305 different manufactured products. A survey in 1986, four years after
the program was begun, showed that only 16 percent of the population
recognized the *approuvé* certification.[76] Although many judged the individual agreements to have succeeded, it became increasingly clear that
such company-level negotiations could not satisfy the broader need for
consumer protection.

Meanwhile, the effort to make negotiated agreements legally binding
was meeting strong opposition. Both the business community and the
Ministry of Justice found problems with the corporatist solution to enforcing consumer agreements. The business community argued that the
analogy with labor contracts was a false one. They argued, first, that
consumers were not dependent on producers in the way that employees
were on their employers because consumers could shop around.[77] Second, as delegates to the Paris Chamber of Commerce and Industry objected, the variety of interests in the professional community, which encompassed production, wholesale, retail, and services, could put industry
associations at a disadvantage when they sat down at the negotiating table with consumers.[78] Jean Levy, who succeeded Paul Simonet in 1982
as head of the CICC, felt that binding collective conventions could inad-
vertently hurt producers, and therefore also ultimately hurt consumers.
His concerns extended even to labeling. In response to a negotiated
proposal that retailers post the price-per-kilo and price-per-liter for foods,
for example, Levy argued that this could lower the quality of products in
the market by focusing consumer attention on price: "This would lead to
an invasion of products of mediocre or bad quality."[79]

France's ministry of justice supported industry in opposing a corporatist approach to consumer regulation. Although they felt that agreements between consumer groups and professional associations should
be encouraged, they emphasized that these must remain voluntary. Consumer groups, they argued, were not sufficiently similar to trade unions.
Whereas workers had a "unity of life, unity of training, class consciousness, and direct impact on their work environment," consumers remained
necessarily dispersed and disunited.[80] Perhaps more threatening, a corporatist devolution of control of the sort being designed by the Calais-

Auloy committee risked to undermine important administrative authorities. Bodies such as the recently created Commission on Abusive Clauses would find their authority displaced to consumer and producer groups negotiating beyond the scope of the state. In place of devolution, the ministry of justice advocated nonbinding approaches to enforcement, arguing that consumer-friendly brands such as the music cooperative FNAC and the Leclerc store chain had done very well in the marketplace by promoting a pro-consumer image. By 1982, the movement to promote corporatist solutions to economic regulation, formerly a key component of the Mitterrand initiative, was being scaled back.

But the failure of Scandinavian-style consumer-producer agreements in France did not mean the defeat of the French consumer movement. Quite the contrary: abandoning the negotiation model freed the government to implement its consumer policies more directly. As the first "contracts for the improvement of quality" were being signed, the Mitterrand government was already undertaking a consumer policy U-turn, abandoning the negotiation approach to consumer protection in favor of direct state intervention.[81] Growing consumer frustration with the limited impact of the negotiation initiatives on business practice finally led the French state to step in to fill the regulatory void. It dismissed the Calais-Auloy committee to rewrite the consumer law. In its place the government enacted strict regulations, enforced by new regulatory agencies, focused on consumer safety. The 1983 law for consumer protection created the Consumer Safety Commission (Comission pour la sécurité des consommateurs, or CSC), modeled on the U.S. Food and Drug Administration, to enforce a standard of product safety.[82] Under the law, government ministries were granted extraordinary rights to survey the consumer market and set product standards. A new General Direction of Competition, Consumption, and the Elimination of Fraud (Direction générale de la concurrence, de la consummation, et de la répression des fraudes, or DGCCRF), created in 1985, enjoyed extensive powers to visit and investigate companies, to seize documents, and to require that potentially dangerous products be recalled. Through these new agencies, and others that would follow, the French government quickly earned a reputation as one of the strongest voices for consumer protection in Europe.

The new statist regulatory approach to consumer protection brought benefits, but also posed challenges. The apparatus of the state did not always work rapidly or efficiently. The government's slow response to the risk of HIV infection through the distribution of untested blood to French hemophiliacs highlighted the risk of bureaucratic slowdown, and raised concerns that the consumer interest might be hijacked by national industrial goals. But it also emphasized the new responsibility held by the French state, as several officials and a minister lost their jobs when tainted blood entered the public supply. By the time the mad cow (bovine spongiform encephalopathy) scare emerged in the mid-1990s, French administrators were quick to take the risk seriously, and pushed for a prolonged ban on the import of British beef. Subsequently, on topics such as hormone-treated beef and genetically modified foods, France embraced the studiously cautious precautionary principle of consumer safety to justify blocking these products from the country's markets.

Theory-Building from a Least Likely Case

In methodological terms, the French experience with consumer mobilization represents a least likely case study of diffuse interest representation. Even in this least likely case, diffuse interests managed to mobilize effectively. As in other liberal market economies with majoritarian electoral systems, French consumer activists achieved policy representation primarily by means of collaboration with the state. State-activist coalitions manifested themselves via a number of organizational structures, ranging from independent groups to state agencies to state support for family associations and other nonconsumer groups that participated in activities that promoted the consumer interest. Though consumer activists also worked closely with business associations and individual businesses, the industry-activist alliances so successful in Scandinavia failed to produce useful negotiated solutions. Defending the highly diffuse consumer interest was clearly not easy or inevitable. But it nonetheless seems to have been sufficiently important to attract sustained effort from the state, from non-state associations, and—at times—even from industry. If this sort of response occurred in the least likely case, then we should not be surprised to find diffuse interests defended in more favorable institutional settings.

How did groups mobilize? At first glance, the circulation of the results of comparative product tests would seem to correspond exactly to the sorts of selective benefits that Olson identified as creating incentives to mobilize. On closer inspection, however, it appears that they played a very different role. On the one hand, results of comparative product tests helped the UFC to identify a population of consumers who were more likely to be already predisposed to engage in grassroots mobilization. On the other hand, the publication of test results gave the UFC a platform for identifying and publicizing specific cases of egregious producer malfeasance or product failure, and established the UFC as a legitimate independent voice of the French consumer. Specific cases of this kind, to the extent that they created outrage among consumers, seem to have helped to draw new members. Indeed, the UFC appears to have been most successful when it was being sued in the French courts, because even a loss in court served to signal that the group operated independently from the interests of industry and the government.

Influenced by the logic of organizational theory, researchers of public policy have often viewed national consumer protection policies as an instance of narrow producer interests that have captured the public debate. Blinded by the assumption that consumer interests are too diffuse to organize, they have typically understood consumer protection policies as industry protectionism. From this perspective, the high degree of state involvement in consumer protection in France—as in the strong restrictions on hormone-treated beef and genetically modified organisms—was viewed as a form of protection for domestic producers against foreign imports. But French consumer protection has a complex history, one involving interest-group mobilization, policy contestation, and experimentation. Industry influenced policy, but rarely from a position of strength. Rather, the considerable organizational capacity of French consumers lent the causes they pursued considerable legitimacy. Moreover, in a majoritarian electoral system such as France's, the consumer agenda was frequently attractive to policy entrepreneurs seeking political platforms likely to garner broad support. This history makes industry capture an unsatisfying explanation for the sustained success of consumer protection in France. As Thomas Bernauer and Ladina Caduff have shown in their study of hormone-treated beef, France's opposition to the practice had its roots not in producer protectionism, but in a sustained consumer boycott orchestrated in 1979 by French consumer associations against *French* producers.[83] By assuming industry capture of the regulatory process, we miss the deep legitimacy that such legislation draws from the contested political process out of which it emerged.

CHAPTER 4

Interest Group Coalitions and
Institutional Structures

O NE OF THE ATTRACTIONS of organizational theory is the simple
elegance of its formulations. Mancur Olson expresses the logic of
collective action as a streamlined equation of group size and individual
material interest: the larger the interest group and the more nonexclusive
the benefits it seeks, the less any individual will be motivated to expend
time and energy securing those public goods. Conversely, small groups
will enjoy influence out of proportion to their size because their members
are individually more motivated, and their organization correspondingly
superior. It is an argument that takes little if any heed of context: the key
variable is the size of the groups involved, and even there it does not ac-
knowledge that a given dispute might concern not two but three or more
interest groups of various sizes. Thus, organizational theory does not
encompass the possibility that similar situations might produce different
results in different contexts.

How, then, can we explain the widely varying success of traditional
retailing in France and Germany against the advent of hypermarkets and
other large-scale distributors? Traditional small retailers in each of these
countries were demographically similar: numerous, geographically dispersed, and disorganized. Although most were politically conservative,
small retailers were typically not perceived as a core constituency of any

of the mainstream political parties. By contrast, the new modern mass retailers, including Carrefour and Leclerc in France and Metro and Kaufhof in Germany, constituted a numerically small and highly concentrated interest. In the Olsonian logic, their small numbers should have made them politically influential. Moreover, they entered both countries at similar times and enjoyed similar early successes. Yet, by the end of the century, the French and German retail landscape had diverged dramatically. In 2000, French hypermarket sales were more than double those in Germany—1,300 euros per capita compared to just over 600 euros per capita.[1] Combined food sales through hypermarkets and supermarkets accounted for 75 percent of total food sales in France in 1998, compared to 32 percent of total food sales in Germany that year.[2] And, in a useful indicator of suburban retail development, regional shopping centers in France had 4,000 square meters of shopping space per 100,000 people in 1998, compared to only 1,300 square meters per 100,000 in Germany.[3] Whereas French small retailers faced serious and debilitating assault from large-format sellers, their German counterparts retained a healthy portion of the retail market.

Organizational theory fails to explain these outcomes in at least two respects. First, the success of small retailers—more numerous and less organized than the hypermarket interests—in Germany does not follow the logic of collective action. How did German shopkeepers keep the hypermarkets at bay? Second, an excessive focus on group size as the key variable does not account for the success of small retailers in one country but not in the other. The numbers of small shopkeepers in France and Germany were comparable both in their totals and in their relative size within the population at large. Yet in this regard Germany represents a case of diffuse interest success. Traditional small German retailers were highly effective at representing their diffuse interests against new concentrated retailers. In 2010, western Germany still had only approximately two thousand large-surface-area retail sites in the entire country, and that number was not expected to increase in the coming decades. France represents a case of diffuse interest failure. Despite major political mobilization and resulting legislative protections put in place to protect traditional retailing, shopkeepers ultimately failed to insulate themselves

from the growth of mass distribution. The explanation appears not to
reside with the mobilization skills of small retailers. In fact, French traditional retailers were far better organized than their German counterparts. Given this difference in militancy, how do we explain their relative weakness relative to the new large-scale retailers?

I argue that the story of postwar retailing in France and Germany was
a story of legitimacy narratives, coalitions, and institutional contexts as
much as—if not more than—a story of individual material interests and
organizational capacity. The importance of policy narratives is particularly apparent in the shopkeepers' efforts to reframe the general interest
in ways that highlighted their specific contributions to society. German
shopkeepers successfully cast themselves as the champions of family life
and leisure time against the uncaring hypermarkets that forced their
employees to work long and uncongenial hours, and as the saviors of the
vibrant old city centers against the suburban shopping centers. Alliances were a key determinant of outcomes in Germany. Small retailers
were able to forge alliances with labor and the Catholic right that allowed them to emphasize their own diffuse interests over those of the
more general consuming public. Regulations restricting retail opening
hours and store surface area effectively curbed the growth of Germany's
large-format retail sector.

Coalitions were another key factor in determining outcomes in French
and German retailing. Where the new mass retailers prevailed, as in
France, it was because they embraced and advocated for the interests of
an even more diffuse interest group than traditional retailers: consumers. With few exceptions, the retail innovators of the 1950s and 1960s
fashioned themselves as populist outsiders rather than power-wielding
political insiders. They touted the convenience of one-stop shopping, the
benefits of lower prices at a time when bouts of inflation were eating away
family purchasing power, longer opening hours than family-run stores
could manage, and the greater product selection they could provide.
Consumer groups often agreed, and advocated for policies that favored
the large distributors. France's mass retailers won not because they were
concentrated, but because their purpose addressed an extremely general
but unmet set of practical needs.

One of the important drivers of national difference was the institutional context in which the traditional retailers organized. Two dimensions in particular seemed to matter. First, the particular configuration of the German multiparty system favored cross-class political coalitions that supported traditional retailers. The Catholic right and Social Democratic left agreed on shorter shop hours that hurt large-format distributors—the former to limit the impact of shopping on family life, the latter to limit evening and nighttime working hours. Further, the right and the environmental movement came to an accommodation on highly restrictive land use policies that would both preserve urban community and spare outlying rural areas from the impact of urban sprawl. In France, presidential elections were majoritarian. This created a context in which pursuing broad consumer interests was a rational calculation on the part of politicians.

A second critical institutional dimension involved the strategic priorities of production. For Germany, smaller-scale quality production strategies led producers to favor smaller retailers that emphasized product quality. In France, with its administrative emphasis on Fordist manufacturing, mass distribution was seen to be the critical counterpart to mass production. This led government regulators to embrace pricing and zoning policies that would promote modern mass retailing. In each case, institutional priorities pushed policies toward defending different kinds of diffuse interests.

The Transformation of Postwar Retailing

Whereas manufacturing has retained the same basic principles—standardization, workflow management, division of labor, and outsourcing—throughout the postwar period, distribution has undergone dramatic changes. The retail environment has liberalized; retailers have consolidated both selling and purchasing; small shopkeepers have either been displaced or moved into new niche markets; over-the-counter sales have been displaced by self-service buying. These changes in industry structure have taken place against a backdrop of related transformations in urban geography, power relations between producers and retailers, and, most important for the present argument, a significant decline in the number of stores.

Two major developments mark the emergence of modern retailing. The first was the rise of the self-service retail format. Rather than having to ask shopkeepers for goods that were typically stored in the back or behind a counter, customers were free to browse and select for themselves among goods that were laid out on shelves. The second was the creation of the so-called hypermarket, a store combining the functions of a food store and large department store in a large physical facility that dwarfed the small storefronts of traditional retailers. France's Carrefour created the first hypermarket in 1963 in the suburbs of Paris, with a size of 2,500 square meters. In Germany, the retailer Globus opened the first hypermarket in 1966. The new format offered significant advantages to consumers in terms of both price and selection. Self-service stores allowed retailers to employ far fewer personnel and pass on the savings in labor costs to their customers; also, the large size of hypermarkets allowed for a far greater selection of goods and economies of scale, further driving down prices. Observers have conventionally viewed the rise and success of modern mass retailing as unsurprising. Impelled by the dual forces of economic scale and market deregulation, large-format suburban retailing has long been seen as the face of retail modernization.

One consequence of large-scale distribution was a transformation in the postwar built environment, as retail sites increased in size and moved from older urban centers to newer suburbs. The nation most closely associated with the twin phenomena of suburbanization and large-scale retailing is the United States. The United States was, with France, a leader in promulgating new mass retail distribution. By 1970, the United States boasted 14,000 suburban shopping centers.[4] Without question, traditional family retailers suffered from this growth. In many respects, though, the confrontation between traditional and modern mass retailers was never a fair fight in the United States. That is because suburban mass retailing in America was deeply linked to a *prior* surge in suburban housing. The growth of suburban mass retailing has often been explained as a side effect of the postwar growth in automobile ownership and highway construction. But these factors did not distinguish the United States from other advanced industrialized countries. More important in the U.S. case was the role of government housing support. The Federal Home Owner's Loan Association employed redlining practices that rationed loans for housing redevelopment in urban centers, especially areas with large black populations. Similarly, both the Federal Housing Authority and the U.S. Department of Veterans Affairs prioritized new construction over home renovation, which almost always meant buying in new suburban developments. With the exception of Walmart, which consciously targeted rural communities, the early mass retailers developed new suburban shopping formats because the customers were *already there.* Faced with this demographic shift, traditional retailers, who almost always owned their own (now depreciating) storefronts, were unable to raise sufficient capital to follow their customers into the suburbs. As urban geographers have noted, the flight from the inner city was led by middle-class residents, not by mass retailers.[5]

In France, by contrast, retailers tended to move to the suburbs *ahead* of their customers, hoping to avoid high real estate costs and municipal land use planning restrictions. Indeed, new protections for small retailers actively pushed the centers of larger modern retailing into the suburbs, and the consumers followed them out.[6] Even in their new suburban locations, though, large retailers were still vying with smaller downtown retailers for the same customers. The result was a hollowing out of the downtown areas in France—not to the extent seen in the United States, when urban residents as well as retailers fled town and urban centers—but enough to impoverish the city retail environment. One officer of Germany's land use planning ministry described the French situation: "What Germany fears is the experience of cities like Bordeaux, which has lost retail business to green field sites outside of town. All that is left is old buildings and monuments in the city center."[7]

Another dimension of the transformation in postwar retailing in both France and Germany was a dramatic shift in power between manufacturers and distributors. In the 1950s, manufacturers dictated to retailers what they would sell, at what price, and therefore at what margin. Margins offered by manufacturers typically conformed to norms in the manufacturing sector, i.e., roughly 25–30 percent. Because all retailers sold the same products at the same prices, competition focused on service and social connectedness. Politically, retailers were fiercely independent, typically relying on the sale of their stores to finance their own retirements. By the 1990s, this relationship had been inverted. Resale price maintenance was found to be anticompetitive and abolished: in 1960 in France, and in 1973 in Germany. Large retailers and purchasing organizations consolidating small retailers therefore negotiated with producers for volume price concessions. The largest retailers became such an important customer for some consumer-goods manufacturers that the retailers were in a position to influence the management of manufacturers. Because they either had access to their suppliers' balance sheets, or could piece together the components of their price structure, large retailers were increasingly in a position to propose cost-saving measures, and even occasionally to organize mergers among producers. They also brought to the table detailed knowledge about consumer preferences. The combination of market information and market dominance gave large retailers extraordinary bargaining power with producers. In many cases, they were in a position to dictate profit margins to producers. The problem for manufacturers was that retailers were accustomed to working with far narrower margins than they were. And they tended to force these narrow margins on their suppliers. Instead of 25–30 percent, suppliers to the large distributors were given a baseline of roughly 10–15 percent.

For the present argument, the most important consequence of retail modernization was the threat that large-format distributors posed to traditional small shopkeepers. This trend is graphically demonstrated by the decline in the number of stores over the postwar period, despite a rising population. This occurred nearly in parallel in both France and Germany, up to a turning point in the mid-1970s, when, as we will see, the policy environment in both countries dramatically shifted. France saw a decline from 750,000 stores in 1955 to less than 400,000 in 1975. Germany saw a similar decline, if from a lower starting point: from 620,000 in 1955 to 320,000 in 1975 (see Figure 4.1). By the mid-1960s, a rapid decline in the total number of retail sites combined with a growth in new large-format stores to leave little doubt that the livelihood of the traditional retail sector was under siege. Especially for small family-run stores, the situation in the two countries was similar, and dire.

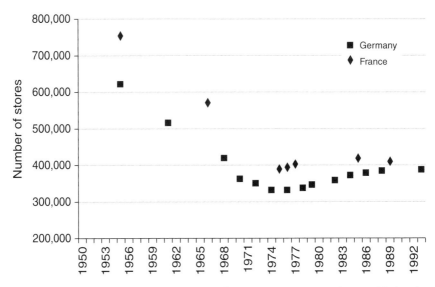

Figure 4.1. Retail businesses in France and Germany, 1955–1995. *Sources:* National Statistical Yearbooks, various years.

Although it may seem a foregone conclusion that mass retailing would dominate, traditional retailers enjoyed at least three advantages in their confrontation with the new mass retailers. First, they were incumbents. Unlike newly discovered diffuse interest groups that had to struggle to understand the interests they shared in common, traditional retailers already had profitable businesses, and clearly understood the threat that new mass retailing posed for their livelihoods. Second, incumbent manufacturers had good reasons to prefer distribution through traditional retailers over mass distribution channels. With traditional retailers, they could use either formal contractual restrictions or retaliatory distribution policies to control the prices at which their goods were sold. Until the legal practice was abolished as a vertical restriction on competition, resale price maintenance limited downward price pressure and created barriers for new product competitors. Thus traditional retailers should have had a powerful ally in the manufacturing sector. Third, large retail stores were not especially politically influential. Often social revolutionaries, their founders were not typically closely allied with the traditional political and economic elite in their countries. Many held deep, and often unconventional, religious convictions that kept them outside the inner circles of power. Although their interests were indeed concentrated—often among only a handful of large firms and individuals—they had few of the political or social ties that would have helped to insulate them from policies intended to protect traditional retailers. As the following case studies will show, these advantages, and others, served to allow shopkeepers to prevent concentrated hypermarket interests from systematically dominating policy.

Shopkeeper Success: Coalitions and Closing Hours in Germany

In Germany, traditional retailers defied the logic of collective action and obtained legislation that effectively restricted the growth of concentrated, large-format competitors. Their success had relatively little to do with their ability to organize their numerous members—indeed their mobilizations were unimpressive compared to those of France's energetic and visible shopkeeper-activists. Rather, Germany's shopkeepers successfully allied themselves with other interest groups whose interests overlapped with their own: trade unions resentful of long opening hours, and right-leaning religious groups suspicious of the hypermarkets' effects on traditional family life. Moreover, the German political system of proportional representation favored such coalitions of midsize interest groups. The political strength they represented more than compensated for the organizational weakness endemic to large groups of small retailers.

In Germany, store opening hours were the flashpoint of a decades-long struggle between large-format and traditional retailers. From the 1970s onward, hypermarkets could typically offer longer and more convenient shopping hours than smaller stores could manage. The dispute over store hours did not begin this way, however. The goal of the store hours legislation, as originally conceived, was to extend modern production techniques to the retail sector by promoting rational employment practices among shopkeepers. The goal was to ensure that larger stores with trained employees would not be at a competitive disadvantage to traditional retailers that could keep long hours with low family-based labor costs. German shop hour restrictions were imposed by the 1956 store closing law, or Ladenschlußgesetz, which was itself derived from the 1938 regulation of general working time (Arbeitzeitverordnung).[8] Until the store closing law was liberalized in 1996, it imposed a 6:30 P.M. closing time on weekdays, a 2 P.M. closing on Saturdays, and a strict interdiction on Sunday opening. Permitting a total of only 64.5 hours per week, the German law offered consumers the shortest shopping hours of any country in Europe.

The persistence of the store closing law was surprising given its lack of support in the general public. Surveys conducted from the early 1960s to the mid-1990s show that a majority of consumers had always favored store hour liberalization (see Table 4.1). Political support for the policy was instead based on what critics called an unholy alliance between supporters on the left and right.[9] The basis of this alliance shifted over time.

Early support for the store closing law coalesced around a bipartisan interest in modernizing the retail sector. Trade unions saw that short store hours had the advantage of placing retail employees on an equal footing with other industrial workers in negotiating wage contracts. The top retail trade union Gewerkschaft Handel, Banken, und Versicherung (HBV) recognized that retailers could only participate in patterned wage bargaining so long as work hours were limited and part-time labor kept

Table 4.1. Consumers favoring store hour liberalization in Germany, 1963–1996

Year	Favor liberalization
1963	52%
1964	55%
1969	74%
1972	62%
1985	77%
1995	74%
1996	60%

Sources: Jahrbuch der Öffentlichen Meinung: 1965–1967 (Allensbach: Verlag für Demoskopie, 1967), 126; Klaus Reichert, *Das Ladenschlußproblem in der Bundesrepublik Deutschland* (Vienna: Verlag Notring, 1971), 38; *Jahrbuch der Öffentlichen Meinung: 1968–1973* (Allensbach: Verlag für Demoskopie, 1973), 391; Monika Ketterer, "Die Diskussion um den ladenschluß—eine Diskussion der Theoretiker," *Verbraucher und Recht* 3 (1987): 143; "Kaufen ohne Ende," *Focus,* August 14, 1995; *Reuter European Business Report,* February 2, 1996.

to a minimum.[10] The law was also seen at the time to promote modern kinds of distribution by insulating them against owner-operated family stores. Whereas family stores could compete by extending their opening hours at little extra cost, larger stores were bound by wage contracts and faced high labor costs if they wished to stay open particularly late.[11] It was precisely to put larger stores on an equal competitive footing that the law was applied not only to store owners with paid employees but also to family stores without paid employees. Hence left-leaning and right-leaning early supporters of restrictive store hours shared an interest in extending the modern organization of labor relations into distribution. Germany's largest association of small retailers (Hauptverband Deutscher Einzelhandel, or HDE) recognized the negative impact that the law was likely to have on its members and strongly opposed the project.[12]

By the early 1970s, however, the original coalitions responsible for the store closing law had begun to fall apart. For one thing, it had become clear that large, self-service hypermarkets, with their lower ratios of staff to square footage, could afford far longer opening hours than even traditional retailers living above the family store. Shorter shopping hours no longer worked in favor of retail modernization. For another, many of the most traditional family shopkeepers had already been eradicated. In 1955, for example, Germany boasted 622,000 retail stores with an average of only three employees.[13] By 1972, Germany had only 350,000 stores with more than six employees per store.[14] Furthermore, the store closing law appeared increasingly to conflict with broader union priorities. An important reason was the growing female union membership. At the Ninth National Congress of Germany's top labor association (Deutscher Gewerkschaftbund, or DGB), two women from the metalworking industry called for union support of longer store hours. They argued that, given recent price increases, they required more time for comparative shopping.[15] Women's organizations such as the German Housewives' Association (Deutschen Hausfrauenbund) called traditional union opposition to longer store hours "unfriendly to women" ("*frauenfeindlich*").[16] They pointed out that Sweden, faced with similar pressures from women's groups in 1972, eliminated its store hour regulations as part of a broader economic rationalization program.[17] Among German consumers, 62 percent favored such a deregulation.

What saved the German store closing law was a reimagining, first by Germany's trade unions, then by the conservative Christian Democratic Union (CDU), of the function of small retailers in Germany's economy and of their contribution to consumers. On the political left, support came from the powerful retailing union HBV, which argued that longer work days would hurt the interests of women who worked in retailing as well as their families. They also warned that longer store hours would mean more part-time employment and a lower overall workforce skill level in the retail sector. In this way, the goal of store hour regulation was reconceived as a protection for retail workers against the social dislocation that modern distribution could cause.[18] The relevant interest of consumers was not convenient shopping times, but a professionalized and highly skilled retail staff.[19]

One of the surprises in Germany, certainly compared to the French case, is that the large distributors were not more active in forging alliances that would have given them greater influence in public policy. Germany's Association of Consumer Groups (Arbeitgemeinschaft der Verbraucherverbände, or AgV) was strongly opposed to the store closing law, which the association referred to regularly in its publications as "the worst legislation ever." Yet the AgV never collaborated with Germany's large distributors in any way. In 1973, amid concerns about price gouging in the context of higher inflation, the Social Democratic Party (Sozialdemokratische Partei Deutschlands, SPD) launched a campaign to identify stores that charged excessive prices. In the so-called yellow-dot campaign, these mainly small-format stores would be marked with a round yellow sticker so that consumers could be warned about their high prices. This effort could have provided the basis for collaboration with large-scale retailers, but again it never happened. The CDU accused the SPD of trying to impose price controls, and the SPD quickly stepped back from the project.

With the fall of the SPD/ Frei Demokratische Partei (FDP) coalition in 1981 and the formation of the CDU/FDP coalition, life became more difficult for small retailers. On the one hand, the CDU embraced retailers as a natural constituency. Shopkeepers were traditionally conservative, and short shopping hours were seen by the Catholic wing of the conservative party to offer needed protection for families. On the other hand, their liberal FDP coalition partner was pushing a strong deregulatory program, and the store closing law was high on its list of priorities. The first attempt to lengthen store hours came in 1984 when Helmut Kohl, who as recently as 1980 had proclaimed his support for the store closing law, called for liberalization.[20] He was supported in his liberalization effort by the FDP, by the AgV, and by the main industry association Bund Deutscher Industrie (BDI).[21] The response from retailers to this threat was swift and forceful. HDE, the association of small retailers, voted unanimously to reject store hour liberalization, arguing that this would increase product costs for consumers who would, in the end, bear the costs of additional operating expenses. They also argued that liberalization would hurt single-family stores, which would be forced to stay open longer to remain competitive.[22] The Association of Middle and Large Retailers (BAG) also opposed liberalization on the grounds that increased wage costs would be likely to push a number of shops out of business.[23] Larger stores located downtown feared that longer shopping hours would draw consumers to new shopping centers located outside of town. Kohl recognized the political importance of small retailers for the Right and backed down from his liberalization project.

The next challenge to the store closing law came in 1989, when, again under pressure from the FDP, the governing coalition proposed the creation of a "service evening" (*Dienstleistungsabend*) that would allow stores and other service providers to remain open until 8:30 P.M. on Thursdays. Though apparently small in scope, the new service evening proposal drew a line in the sand that mobilized forces on all sides of the store hour debate. The Ministry of Labor argued that the extended Thursday hours would be a boon to all, leading to a higher quality of life for consumers and new job opportunities for the unemployed.[24] The SPD raised vehement opposition, arguing that women working in retailing would have even less time with their families on Thursday evenings.[25] The retailer union, HBV, argued that the benefit of two extra shopping hours was negligible compared to the damage that the service evening would do to the families of shop workers.[26] Retail employees took to the streets in protest, with more than two hundred retail firms with thirty thousand employees participating in strikes during June 1989.[27]

When strikes failed to derail the legislation, retail unions across Germany renegotiated their labor contracts to include a mandatory closing time of 6:30. They also called for a 37.5 hour workweek, and for part-time workers to be hired for at least 4 hours per day and at least 20 hours per week.[28] In some of Germany's federal states (Rheinland-Pfalz and Saarland, for example), these new labor contracts specified that the stores could stay open late only if an early closing would place the store at a competitive disadvantage, or, stricter yet (as in Bremen), if longer hours were necessary to ensure the survival of the store.[29] And because these contracts were negotiated in sector-wide negotiations, they were binding on virtually all retailers in the state in which they were signed. Retail employers, who also generally opposed longer store hours, were content to assent to the restrictive wage agreements. The SPD, in support of the retail unions, also called on its constituency not to shop during the service evening.[30] Thus once again middle-class shopkeepers were shielded by the protection that labor union solidarity afforded.

Germany finally amended its store closing law to allow stores to remain open until 8 P.M. on all weeknights beginning in 1996. Looking at the preferences of consumers at the time, this change is difficult to explain. Only 60 percent of consumers reported favoring store hour liberalization at the time, fewer than in the past.[31] Among retailers, though, only 56 percent opposed liberalization in 1996,[32] compared to 79 percent who had opposed longer store hours in 1983.[33] This lower rate of retail opposition may have made store hour liberalization more politically palatable on the right. But the real pressure for change came from the growth in unemployment. In a study commissioned by the German government, the Ifo Institut estimated that lengthening store hours to 8 P.M. would increase retail employment by at least fifty thousand.[34] This argument was particularly persuasive given that Germany supported a low level of overall employment in the retail sector compared to other countries. Ironically, a subsequent study conducted by the Ifo Institut showed that the retailing sector had in fact shed six thousand jobs in the three years after liberalization. The study also found that 71 percent of retailers opposed longer opening hours on weekdays; 64 percent of consumers indicated that they did not need longer weekday shopping hours.[35]

The disappointing results of the Ifo Institut study made further liberalization politically contentious. Germany's two main political parties, the SPD and CDU, both opposed further liberalization. Even Germany's main retail employers' association, HDE, also opposed further liberalization. As HDE Director Holger Wenzel put it: "For culture and lifestyle, it is not so bad to have one day quieter than the others. A lot of retailers, politicians, unions, and churches share this view."[36] Rather than continue to confront the issue, the German federal government in 2006 handed over responsibility for store opening hours to the federal states, which could at their discretion opt for longer shop hours than provided in the national store closing law (Ladenschlußgesetz).[37]

Yet, even in states that liberalized opening times, large format retailers still did not prosper. The reason was a second critical limit on large-scale retailing that came in the form of Germany's zoning law, which had been amended in 1977 to make new greenfield retail construction virtually impossible. Up until that year, Germany had approximately two thousand large-surface-area green field retail sites, including hypermarkets, furniture stores, and home goods suppliers. In 1977, Germany enacted strict planning and zoning regulations (the Building Use Code) designed to protect traditional retailers.[38] With support from the burgeoning green movement, the planning legislation prohibited the construction of stores with more than 800 square meters sales area in locations not designated for retailing.[39] This resulted in large-store development being restricted to town or city centers. As one zoning official explained, "The objective is to locate retail close to the consumers and to the working areas of city centers."[40] Even within cities, where retail restrictions were less onerous, the approval process for a new store could require from one to four years.

Although opening a new large-surface-area store outside of an urban center was technically possible, it required clearing several difficult hurdles. First, a neighboring city or town was required to create a building use plan for the area being considered for development. The plan had to present a comprehensive development "concept" that would take into account environmental and conservation concerns, as well as potential private legal conflicts. For example, retailers in the new site could not sell products that would compete directly with stores located in nearby towns. Any failure to demonstrate that the project embodied this kind of "balanced approach to development" could be grounds for private legal challenges. Once a new plan passed these steps and was approved by the town or city council, it then came under review by regional planning boards at the state and national level.[41] Such regional plans rested on a system of retail categories for cities and towns that specified target levels of retailing based on population. The retail categories provided guidelines—without setting specific limits—for the numbers of new stores that could be approved. As one observer noted of large-surface-area retail sites outside of cities: "it is basically not allowed." Almost no new extraurban hypermarkets were opened in Germany after 1977.[42]

The one exception was in Germany's five new states immediately following reunification. With the fall of the Berlin Wall in 1989, West German retailers flocked to the East to meet pent-up demand for products from the West. As property rights within eastern cities were still disputed, and because new building codes imported from the West were not yet being enforced, retail development occurred primarily in the form of new suburban shopping centers. The retail experience of the five eastern states served as a reminder of what might happen in the absence of zoning policy. Downtown areas were left underdeveloped. One retail expert noted: "Cities in the East were hurt by this early development strategy. They are trying to change now, but it is already too late."[43] Behind this perceived failure was a distinctly German view of urban life, with cities organized around smaller neighborhoods that have their own retail centers. As the head of Germany's retail association explained: "Germany has a different urban culture than in the United States. Cities are arranged in concentric circles, not on the grid format of the Roman city. The concentric circles have created a culture of 'urbanity.' We value that."[44] It was toward this societal goal, rather than the purely material interests of consumers, that Germany's retail policies were oriented.

Consumers and Hypermarkets:
Shopkeeper Mobilization in France

Compared to their German counterparts, French shopkeepers were well-organized and effective activists despite their large numbers and diffuse nature. Yet they failed to halt the growth of large-scale distributors. Traditional retailers mounted dramatic and sustained public campaigns against regulatory measures that favored their large competitors, and there were times when legislation went against the hypermarkets. Large-format retailers ultimately prevailed in France, but their victory was neither easy nor inevitable. They won because they were able to position themselves successfully as the champions of a third, still broader group: the consuming public, for whom they claimed to provide a wider selection of goods, at lower prices and with more convenient shopping hours.

If store closing times were the leitmotif of retail protection in Germany, strict store-size restrictions served as a similar focal point for the politics of retail protection in France. In the immediate postwar period, retail policy in France—as in Germany—favored large retailers. A 1960 law to eliminate resale price maintenance in France was intended specifically to break the small-store stranglehold on the retail sector by allowing larger stores to negotiate lower prices. Similarly, a number of tax and lending policies were seen to favor modern over traditional forms of retailing. The French government had increased sales taxes in 1968 as part of an austerity plan to depress domestic consumption. However, in order to encourage investment and stimulate exports, large companies were given tax concessions. In retailing, this meant that large-surface-area and chain stores enjoyed a lower tax rate than small shopkeepers. The government also requested that banks not make loans to small store owners, in order to discourage further growth in what was considered to be a declining sector.[45] Finally, traditional retailers complained that a local business tax, the *patente,* was being used by the communities in which they worked to modernize distribution by financing the construction of new suburban shopping centers.[46]

Thus, when French retailers organized in the late 1960s, their grievances did not focus specifically on the economic threat from large stores, but on the political threat from government support for modern distribution. In 1969, French small shopkeepers mobilized around Gérard Nicoud, the charismatic 23-year-old café owner and founder of the Committee for the Information and Defense of Retailers, Artisans, and the Liberal Professions (CIDCAPL).[47] Their flamboyant and confrontational actions were focused not explicitly against large distributors, but against what they perceived to be discriminatory government policies. In their first protest rally, for example, CIDCAPL took over the tax office of Tour-du-Pin and threatened to dump all of their tax documents into the river. Nicoud's group quickly gained support among France's shopkeepers. He traveled throughout France to meet with groups of retailers and widen the membership of CIDCAPL. He called on retailers to remove all of their savings from nationalized banks, post office accounts, and savings banks because of the government restriction on granting loans to small retailers.[48] In March 1970, he organized Paris retailers to close their shops and drive around the peripheral motorway during morning rush hour at 3 miles per hour.[49]

When President Georges Pompidou refused to meet with Nicoud to discuss the government's policies, Nicoud widened his attack. In what became known as the April Fools protest, Nicoud's CIDCAPL blocked roads all over France during spring vacation, a peak travel time. Shop owners blockaded toll islands, scattering nails on highways, and in one case used chainsaws to fell trees across a road.[50] In Paris, five hundred retailers struggled with police from behind a flaming wall of tires.[51] Finally, in 1971, Nicoud launched a hunger strike in an effort to spur the government to release from prison two members of his organization who had been arrested during these protests.[52] Nicoud's creative mobilizations increased the membership and popularity of his group. CIDCAPL joined with another loose organization of retailers to form the Intersyndical Confederation for the Defense and National Unification of Independent Workers (CID-UNATI), and by 1971 CID-UNATI controlled 43 percent of the seats in local Artisanal Associations (Chambres de métiers).[53] Despite the disruptiveness of their tactics, Nicoud's group also gained significant public support. A 1970 Gallup poll found that 49 percent of the population sympathized with the shopkeepers' protest, and only 39 percent disapproved.[54] Consumer groups too began to endorse the goals of CID-UNATI.

The tide of government opinion began to turn in favor of small retailer interests in 1972 when Prime Minister Jacques Chaban-Delmas resigned under disclosures of personal tax fraud. Shopkeeper discontent over government tax policies appeared to have been vindicated. The National Assembly rallied to the support of shopkeepers, presenting a range of possible solutions to shopkeeper resentment. Proposed legislation included federally supported pension funds for small retailers, a new lending bank modeled on the Credit agricole that would be dedicated to retail development, and government compensation to shopkeepers whose property lost value due to the growth of new large-scale retailing. None of these measures were intended to support traditional retailing in the long term. Rather, all were strategies for cushioning the fall of a declining sector, and were modeled on agricultural subsidies intended to ease the decline of France's small farmers. The future of retailing was assumed to lie with large-scale distribution. A 1971 poll, for example, found that 83 percent of the French felt that the growth of large-surface-area stores was a necessity of modern life—only 15 percent thought their growth should be stopped.[55]

Prospects looked still brighter for shopkeepers the following year, when the newly appointed minister of commerce, Jean Royer, proposed more robust supports for traditional retailing. His 1973 Law for the Orientation of Trade and Artisans (*loi d'orientation pour le commerce et l'artisanat* or *loi Royer*) delegated licensing decisions for new stores with a sales area greater than 1,000 square meters to new decision-making bodies at the departmental level. As originally conceived, newly created Departmental Commissions of Commercial Town-Planning (CDUC), would bring together equal numbers of local businessmen and consumers to approve new store projects. Small shopkeepers, however, fearing the antagonism of consumer groups, lobbied to have consumer-group representatives banished entirely from the commissions. The consumer group UFC in turn lobbied hard for their reinstatement.[56] The result was that consumer advocacy groups would contribute two members per commission, which relied on majority voting and typically had twenty members.[57] Because local business interests were more strongly represented on these commissions, the *loi Royer* amounted to a moratorium on large store construction in most French cities and town. Rather than easing traditional shopkeepers out of business, the *loi Royer* would help to protect them.

This strategy of shopkeeper protection had two advantages for the political Right. First, by identifying modern mass distribution as the source of shopkeeper grievances, it was able to deflect criticism that would otherwise have fallen on the government. Second, by designating large retailers as a common enemy of all small retailers, the Right was able to create a set of common political interests for artisans and retailers who otherwise shared no common skills, workplace, consciousness, or culture.[58] Ironically, it had been the very antagonism of the previous government that, by mobilizing shopkeeper opposition to their tax policies, had revealed the potential for organizing retailers in support of the political Right.

France's consumer groups were initially supportive of the Royer law. The protections that the government created for small shopkeepers suggested that consumers and retailers shared an affinity as victims of big business. Both were revealed as pawns in a larger struggle between producers and large-scale distributors.[59] Indeed the *loi Royer* combined protections for small retailers with other provisions for consumer protection, including the first consumer class action lawsuits, that helped consumer groups to identify with the plight of small retailers. Josée Doyère, a political reporter on the consumer beat, recalled that ". . . curiously, consumers have benefited from the wave of electoral demagoguery that brought the members of parliament to the aid of small commerce. . . . They have made so many speeches in their defense—on the left and the right as well as the center—that it was difficult not to support a text in favor of consumers."[60] Following the Royer law, consumer groups increasingly emphasized the benefits of competition between small and large retailers. They also commonly supported policies that favored specialized retailers, which tended to be small shop owners. They opposed the distribution of pharmaceuticals by large chain stores, for example, favoring granting small pharmacies a monopoly on the sales of drugs.[61]

Although traditional retailers courted French consumers, consumer associations did not always see themselves as natural allies of the small shopkeepers. Price surveys, conducted frequently by consumer groups, emphasized the price advantage that large stores offered over the smaller traditional stores.[62] This concern came to a head as inflation began to mount with the first oil shock in 1973. That year, a survey by the UFC that compared prices of large-surface-area stores and small shops found that a standard basket of goods that cost 106.11 francs at the small shops cost only 94.87 francs at the large stores.[63] One coalition of regional consumer groups, the Associations populaires familiales (APF), launched a so-called Three-Six-Nine Boycott to protest the high prices of small retailers, in which consumers were asked to boycott meat for three days, fruit for six days, and mineral water for nine days.[64] When France's small food and vegetable sellers went on strike in protest of higher government taxes, consumer groups organized a punitive counter-boycott against these stores for having closed their doors to consumers.

Consumer groups also actively aided large distributors, including mass distributors like the Centres Leclerc and Centres Lemaire, in their attempts to secure business licenses to open new stores. In some cases, they rallied consumers in front of the licensing offices to encourage the CDUC to approve new hypermarket sites.[65] They also used their positions on the departmental committees to advocate for new large-scale retailers. Even France's trade union–affiliated consumer groups typically supported the hypermarkets. Pierre Marleix, head of the union-affiliated AFOC, describes the potential conflicts this could create: "We knew that we were advocating policies that could potentially hurt members of our own union. This put us in a difficult position, but we still supported the new projects."[66] Larger retailers for their part provided strong backing for the consumer movement. The FNAC, a cooperative music and book retailer, twice brought Ralph Nader to come speak in France. They offered the building for their new Montparnasse store as the site of a Consumer Salon in 1972, which an estimated 200,000 people attended.[67] And the new Printemps 2000 store that opened in Rennes in 1973 made room for a Maurice column at the center of the store on which consumer groups were encouraged to post product information and warnings.[68]

Not only did the alliance between hypermarkets and consumer groups contribute to the eclipse of France's small shops, but the regulatory measures intended to halt the spread of large-format retailers proved ineffective thanks to the structure of local government. As economic policy, the Royer law proved to be a significant failure. Cities that blocked the development of new large-area retail sites found that those stores would simply move to sites in the suburbs that lay outside of the city's administrative control. Sales by large-surface-area stores grew from 18.8 percent of total sales in 1976 to 34.4 percent in 1999. Meanwhile, traditional downtown retailers faced new local competition in the form of small-format hard discounters, often developed and owned by the large distributors.

But the alliance forged by the *loi Royer* between shopkeepers and the political Right nonetheless persisted in French politics, occasionally to the benefit of the small retailers. Conservative policymakers periodically proposed new laws to improve the functioning of the CDUCs. In an effort to address charges of corruption within the CDUC, a 1993 law (*loi Sapin*) reduced the size of the CDUCs by limiting the role of elected officials on the bodies. The newly renamed CDECs had only seven members instead of twenty.[69] Another major reform was launched in 1996. Frustrated by the ineffectiveness of efforts to control the growth of large-scale distribution, the shopkeeper association Committee for the Defense of Shopkeepers and Artisans (CDCA) in 1995 set fire to the tax offices of the city of Bordeaux. Commerce Minister Jean-Pierre Raffarin responded with legislation that extended CDEC authorization to stores larger than 300 square meters in area. The idea was to place a block on deep discounters that operated below the original 1,000-square-meter threshold. Similarly, Raffarin sought to protect traditional French bakers by reserving the name *boulangerie* exclusively for their use.[70] Employing a political rhetoric that had linked consumer and retail interests since the early 1970s, this new designation was justified as a form of consumer protection against the threat posed by industrial bread. Yet most of these measures were little more than crumbs tossed to the increasingly marginalized traditional retailers. Although the political Right had reasons for making periodic gestures to support small shopkeepers, they failed to implement a comprehensive policy to ensure that their sector could prosper.

Particularly interesting in the French case is that the failure of small shopkeepers to defend themselves against the rising tide of mass retailing did not stem from a failure to mobilize or organize their diffuse interests. As early as the monarchist-populist movement of General Georges Boulanger in 1889, French shopkeepers had shown a propensity to mobilize around activists and politicians who appealed to their conservative political agenda and antipathy to big business.[71] Gérard Nicoud became famous throughout France for his strident rhetoric, but also for the strong following he enjoyed from small shopkeepers. Rather, the problem for France's traditional shopkeepers was that large-format retailers had allied with consumer groups and politicians to endorse the broad advantages that modern retailing offered to consumers. Further, the majoritarian electoral logic of the presidential elections made consumers, rather than shopkeepers, a strategic voting bloc in French politics. Even labor unions, concerned about the declining purchasing power of workers, opted to support retail modernization as a means of achieving price restraint rather than supporting the jobs of unionized small retail businesses.

Shopkeeper Protectionism and Consumer Protection

The story of German and French retailers is in part a story of the failure of organization theory to explain differential national outcomes. German retailers were more successful at protecting themselves against the challenges of modern mass retailing, but not because they were better able to overcome the challenges of working collectively to pursue their common interests. If anything, the obstructionism and street theater of Gérard Nicoud and his allies suggest that the French shopkeepers were considerably better at rousing their base and organizing them for action. Instead, the two things that seem to have mattered were (1) institutional setting and (2) the ability of traditional retailers to link their own plight to other diffuse interests in society. Two features of the institutional setting were important. First, electoral systems seem to have played a central role. The French majoritarian system created a median-voter bias that favored broad consumer interests over narrower (and typically conservative) retail interests. German support for traditional retailers, by contrast, rested on cross-class alliances that were promoted by Germany's proportional parliamentary system. Second, production regimes mattered. German producers were especially concerned about the price pressure and lack of adequate consumer advice under mass retailing. French producers, by contrast, found a good fit between their strongly Fordist production strategies and the emergence of mass distribution channels.

If institutional context placed constraints on the strategies that traditional retailers could adopt, what also mattered was the way in which they portrayed their own interest in relation to broader consumer and societal interests. Small retailers in both countries were able to win political support by portraying themselves as defenders of the consumer interest. But the way in which that consumer interest was perceived differed significantly, and with different outcomes. In France, small retailers portrayed themselves as a barrier against the forces of monopoly capital, both in production and in distribution. Consumers, they argued, should always retain the choice of shopping at artisanal stores. Only in this way could the risks and disappointments inherent to mass distribution be countered. And, although consumers themselves did not always agree, small retailers did win some regulatory concessions with this argument. Large retailers, too, recognized the need to express their claims in terms of the consumer interest. They argued that only the collective purchasing power of large retailers was capable of negotiating on an even footing with large industry. Large retailers could thereby secure lower prices for consumers. On both sides, retailers portrayed their goals in terms of the consumer interest, and that interest was understood by small and large retailers as a form of opposition to the power of producers.

In Germany, small retailers found protection in the restriction of retail opening hours. As in France, the arguments deployed for restricting store hours implied a particular conception of the consumer identity. The basis of ongoing support for the Ladenschlußgesetz came from a combination of producer and labor union interests. Producers were concerned about the growing negotiating power of larger retailers, especially in so far as they could negotiate for lower batch prices on products. Labor unions too feared downward price pressure, as this would place limits on wage demands. But they also supported short store hours as a form of solidarity with the retail union. If manufacturing laborers enjoyed a short workweek and had their evenings free, then distribution workers should enjoy similar benefits. Undercutting the interests of the retail union could become the thin edge of the wedge of broader union concessions. The threat was especially poignant for bank and insurance workers, who shared the same labor union with retailers.

Ultimately, the story of the struggle between modern large-format retailers and traditional shopkeepers suggests that researchers seeking to understand and predict the outcomes of interest group conflicts must look beyond the simple variables of group size and individual material interest. Institutional contexts—such as those created by an electoral system or a national production strategy—have the power to shape and constrain a group's ability to translate its interests into policy. Those context in turn constrain the alliances groups makes with other interest groups, and the policy narrative they choose to explain their goals and tactics.

CHAPTER 5

Policy Narratives and Diffuse Interest Representation

O NE KEY FEATURE of interest group conflict that organizational theory tends to overlook is the power of policy narratives to affect outcomes. For one thing, compelling narratives offer organizational benefits that can allow diffuse groups to overcome the disorganization and lack of focus that often result from their large size. Promoting diffuse interests requires two kinds of coordination. First, the large numbers of disparate individuals who will benefit from public policies enacted in their interests must either actively or passively support those policies. They must see them as being in their interest, even if they do not specifically join activist groups dedicated to those interests. Because diffuse interests are potentially highly diverse, a single common narrative can focus the attention of the group, while coordinating the activities of activists, groups, businesses, politicians, and regulators around a single set of policies. The second requirement is a common set of principles and goals that help to coordinate regulatory responses across the diverse legal and administrative issues that typically confront any diffuse interest group. New diffuse interests may implicate regulators across existing bureaucratic boundaries; they may incorporate regulatory functions that bridge the state, business, and civil society; and they may touch on regulatory competencies of the administrative regulators and the courts in equal share. Serving a diffuse interest requires that responses be coordinated across this diverse regulatory environment. Legitimating narratives that specify the identity and common interests of a diffuse group in society serve that function.

In general, two model types of legitimating narratives dominate efforts to promote diffuse material interests: narratives of access, and narratives of protection. In debates on subjects ranging from the safety of genetically modified foods to access to firearms and abortions, the interests of the consuming public can be framed in terms of two broad categories: (1) access to markets and services, and (2) protection, from both uncertain risks and known dangers. The stakes in these apparently rhetorical battles are high because the dominant legitimating narrative in turn entails appropriate policy outcomes. For our purposes, what matters about the legitimating narratives that help to coordinate support around new or newly articulated diffuse interests is that they are initially up for grabs, and then subject to lock-in. Defining the legitimating narrative is part of the lure for activists, politicians, and business leaders who would attempt to organize and represent the diffuse group. Not only do these policy narratives help to coordinate diverse actors around a set of interests in society, they also provide coordination across very different kinds of policy issues in ways that can lead to significantly different regulatory outcomes.

The coordinating role of narratives has been an important driver in the regulation of consumer credit markets. Concerns about consumer over-indebtedness in the postwar period led to a recognition of household borrowers as a new group with distinct interests. Driven by falling interest rates, appreciating real estate values, and financial market liberalization during the 1990s and 2000s, consumers across the advanced industrialized economies dramatically increased their levels of borrowing. Both mortgage and nonmortgage lending grew sharply. For many countries, this shift occurred during a period of stagnant or even falling real wages. The consequence was a rapid growth in the number of over-indebted consumers, typically defined as persons whose debt service exceeds 35 percent of disposable income. In response, national governments set about revising their policies for protecting consumers who borrowed money. These protections included measures to ensure transparency in consumer credit contracts, to limit excessive or extortionate lending, and to provide a fresh start to household borrowers who became overly indebted. Beginning in the mid-1980s, for example, nearly every advanced industrialized country dramatically revised how it dealt with personal insolvency. At the same time, they were rethinking the ways in which they managed consumer credit rating and interest rate restrictions. Through a period of significant regulatory reform intended to help protect consumers, policymakers had to conceive what policies *would* protect the diffuse borrower interest, and how.

To focus the inquiry, this chapter offers a tale of two credit markets, France and the United Kingdom, where the borrowers' interest came to be defined in nearly opposite ways—with material consequences for policy, the structure of the consumer lending industry, and the nature of household borrowing. In both France and the United Kingdom, consumer lending was closely tied to issues of social and economic inclusion. Yet each saw the connection differently. For British policymakers, consumer credit was a tool for fighting exclusion. Exclusion there was understood as exclusion from modern credit markets and, by extension, from the goods and services that access to credit made possible. Around this idea emerged a legitimating narrative that focused on credit access as a core societal interest. For France, consumer credit was perceived as a useful tool of household finance, but one that risked aggravating rather than reducing social and economic exclusion. High interest rates charged to high-credit-risk consumers were perceived as potentially exploitative, as well as an additional financial burden on the lower-middle classes. Consumer protection was therefore understood at least in part as protection from credit itself. Around this idea emerged a legitimating narrative that focused on protection *from* debt as a primary societal interest. These different legitimating narratives—with their respective emphases on access and protection—became the basis for policy reforms in response to growing indebtedness.

In some areas of policy, the two narratives drove similar policy responses, although for very different reasons. In both the United Kingdom and France, for example, national governments legislated extra-legal remediation procedures for over-indebted borrowers that offered the promise of lower administration costs and higher repayment rates.

For cases in which creditors and debtors were unable to arrive at a solution, both countries moved to embrace the U.S. principle of the "fresh start." Both put in place procedures to provide a quick, automatic discharge after liquidation of assets, although the British system remained less restrictive than its French counterpart. Despite the similarity of institutional reforms, however, the motivating public logic of the reforms differed dramatically. In the United Kingdom, debtor discharge was designed to encourage individual risk-taking and economic inclusion. In France, debtor discharge emerged out of a concern for the inhumanity of leaving families to suffer under the extreme financial burden of excessive debt.

In other areas of public policy related to credit markets, these two competing narratives drove very different institutional outcomes. One of these was the collection and distribution of consumer credit histories. These data had the potential to increase competition in lending and thereby lower interest rates. But they also threatened the privacy of personal data, a principle that the European Union had designated as a basic human right. Consumer protection in credit markets required balancing these competing goals. For the United Kingdom, credit access prevailed over data privacy concerns. The United Kingdom embraced a privately run system of positive (so-called "white") data collection and distribution. The idea was that better credit data allowed lenders to price risk into individual debt contracts, so that whole classes of potential borrowers were not punished for the poor payment practices of a few. This kind of risk-based pricing also allowed creditors to offer low initial interest rates, then increase them if payment problems revealed heightened risk.

For France, data privacy won over credit data access. France embraced a state-run system of negative (so-called "black") data collection that recorded only cases of delayed payment and nonpayment. The idea was that the availability of positive data would allow creditors to target the most lucrative class of vulnerable borrowers, namely, those who were willing to pay high interests rates due to the higher default risk they represented. Borrowers who might not otherwise face credit problems could become stigmatized, as excess debt and late payments lowered their credit rating, and this in turn increased their interest burden.

The divergent interpretations of the consumer interest in France and the United Kingdom affected not only public policy, but even the very nature of the credit environment. In France, the higher number of restrictions made it extremely difficult for foreign lenders to make inroads into the French consumer lending market, and that in turn limited the sort of competition that would normally drive lenders to extend credit to higher-risk borrowers. As a result, certain classes of potential borrowers, including retirees, had virtually no access to credit in France. The broader consequence was one of the lowest rates of household indebtedness—68 percent of disposable household income, including mortgage and non-mortgage credit—among all of the advanced industrialized countries. The contrasting case for France was the United Kingdom. In 2007, U.K. households held debt, in the form of mortgages, installment credit, and revolving card-based credit, equal to 166 percent of their disposable income. The consumer debt burden in the United States at the time was 153 percent of household disposable income (see Table 5.1).

In many ways, the low debt burden of French households *was* attractive. Households faced lower interest payments, and lenders faced lower rates of late repayment. In 2005, French consumer credit defaults—payments more than ninety days late—affected just 2 percent of consumer loans, compared to 5 percent in the United Kingdom (and 6 percent in the United States).[1] Despite these advantages, critics of the French system were concerned that exclusion from credit markets was marginalizing already marginal populations. They also worried that this restrictiveness might be forcing borrowers to seek exploitative black market loans.

In addition to tracing the broad outlines of consumer credit markets in France and the United Kingdom, this chapter will address efforts at

Table 5.1. Mortgage and nonmortgage debt by country (share of disposable income)

	Nonmortgage debt		Mortgage debt		Total debt	
	1991	2005	1991	2005	1991	2005
US	22%	26%	76%	109%	98%	135%
UK	13%	26%	78%	131%	91%	159%
France	8%	18%	32%	46%	40%	64%

borrower protection in three areas of credit market regulation. The first section looks at efforts to protect borrowers as they enter credit contracts. It focuses on measures to promote transparency and limit exploitation. The second section discusses the regulation of national credit rating agencies. The third area of comparison is in bankruptcy reform, where tremendous changes were introduced in both countries. Although each of these policy areas is different in type and involves different government actors, a common legitimating narrative in each country has entailed outcomes that are highly coordinated around a core set of borrower interests.

Lending, Transparency, and Usury

In general, France's regulations regarding consumer debtors provided a higher level of protection than did those adopted in the United Kingdom. In a survey of European markets by the French lender Cofidis, France ranked uniformly high in consumer protections across four indicators: restrictions on credit advertising, rights of borrowers in contracting (including a cooling-off period and usury caps) and repayment, recourse in case of over-indebtedness, and protection of private financial data. On the same scales, the United Kingdom ranked low in all but one category: recourse for the over-indebted.[2] These scorings reflected different priorities of consumer protection in the two countries. In the trade-off between consumer access and consumer protection, the United Kingdom favored access whereas France favored protection. Although Britain moved to increase protections for consumers in the 1970s, as did France, the emphasis in the United Kingdom remained on increasing access to credit as a tool for bringing more of the population into the modern economy—credit was in part a tool of social and economic inclusion. In France, the perception was nearly the opposite. Although they at times worked to liberalize consumer credit markets, particularly during the 1980s, French policymakers tended to see consumer credit as a threat to social and economic cohesiveness. The policy implications of these different legitimating narratives can be seen particularly clearly in the two countries' respective legislation on transparency in consumer credit advertising and contracting.

Protection for borrowers in French credit markets had its roots in the early move to protect consumers more generally against product-related loss. Early legislation focused on transparency of consumer credit transactions. The basic consumer protection provisions for consumer lending in France were legislated in the Scrivener law of 1978.[3] The law applied to all forms of consumer credit, including lease-sale agreements. It set the terms for advertising credit, including direct mail campaigns. All offers had to include both the total repayment costs and the effective interest rate (TEG), taking into account all related fees. A variety of other stipulations applied, including a minimum font (8 point) in which the terms of credit could be printed, and a set of nine credit contract models to which any offers of credit had to conform. The law also provided a seven-day grace period for consumers to reconsider a credit contract.[4] The goal was to ensure that consumers were not pressured into accepting credit without sufficient time to read the terms and consider the implications.

Apart from these policies to promote transparency, the French government had a deep tradition of intervening in credit markets that continued to influence their approach to consumer lending even after financial deregulation in the early 1980s. In the immediate postwar period, concern that consumer credit would crowd out industrial investment had led the government to restrict access to consumer credit in various ways. Regulations limited the growth of consumer credit extension (to 3–5 percent per year), restricted the kinds of products for which credit could be used to finance purchases (primarily automobiles and household appliances), set a maximum duration (three years), a minimum required down payment (20 percent), and a maximum interest rate. The consumer credit law of 1966 set the maximum interest rate on consumer lending at twice the average industrial borrowing rate, although the economics ministry also commonly negotiated "voluntary" interest rate targets with the main consumer lending institutions that were somewhat below the statutory limit. From 1984 to 1987, French financial markets were progressively liberalized, and many of the restrictions on consumer credit were relaxed.

Despite liberalization, French politicians continued to view consumer credit as a potential cause of inflation. In 1984, as the Socialist government of François Mitterrand sought to rein in inflation, it passed a "law on the activity and control of credit institutions" that targeted offers of free credit by retailers. Retailers could no longer advertise free credit terms outside of the point of sale. More dramatically, when free credit terms were offered, retailers were required to provide a lower price for the same goods if they were purchased without credit. This lower price was set by a formula (based on the average interest rate plus 50 percent) and for average periods of credit it gave prices that were roughly 20 percent below the free credit price.[5] Most consumer groups supported the new law, as did small retailers, who did not have the financial means to compete with so-called free credit offered by large retail chains.[6] French politicians also saw consumer credit as a means to stimulate demand during periods of economic downturn. In 1996, President Jacques Chirac, faced with a potential recession, proposed a one-year tax incentive for consumer borrowing equal to one-quarter of all consumer interest payments. Facing a similar economic slowdown in the summer of 2004, President Nicolas Sarkozy replicated Chirac's policy, applicable through the end of 2005.[7]

French politicians were especially sensitive to the social consequences of high interest rates. A key piece of consumer credit legislation was the Neiertz law, enacted in 1989 and named for France's minister of consumption Véronique Neiertz, that liberalized France's usury law. The law redefined usury to accommodate different classes of consumer loans, while still limiting lending outside of a legally defined range. Each quarter, the Banque de France set interest rate caps for six classes of consumer credit and five classes of industrial credit, calculated at one-third above the average rate for each class in the previous quarter. This scheme was seen in France as market-based, because it allowed average rates to move with the market while limiting excessively high rates. One of the goals of the new legislation was to allow revolving credit accounts—a relatively new arrival in France—to charge higher interest rates that reflected the higher costs of managing such accounts. Since the mid-1990s, interest rate caps on revolving credit averaged 20 percent. One further protection added with the Neiertz law on consumer credit was a requirement that consumers be allowed to repay loans at any moment without additional fees.[8]

Public sensitivity about the social costs of high lending rates came to a head in 1996 when the United Kingdom–based Thorne group launched its first rent-to-sell store in Bobigny, France, followed quickly by a second site in Havre. Called Crazy George's, the store was based on the company's highly successful Rent-a-Center format launched in 1992 in the United States (and followed by an equally successful Crazy George chain in the United Kingdom). The store offered goods under a rental contract that would eventually lead to consumer ownership. Targeting communities with high concentrations of poor and elderly, where credit was not readily available, the stores sold only to customers within a 5-kilometer radius, and insisted that customers drop off their payments in person on a weekly basis. Because the rent-to-sell format was not formally a credit arrangement, it was not subject to France's usury restrictions. Indeed, the effective interest rate on rent-to-own products from the new stores reached as high as 56 percent per annum. A public poll found that 70 percent of French opposed the rent-to-sell format.[9] As one observer noted, "consumer lending . . . is to be condemned, and the old Christian tradition of usury, meaning a total prohibition on the charging of interest, not only abusive interest rates, should be retained."[10] Yet for Crazy George's customers, many of them retired, on a pension, and without access to traditional consumer credit, Crazy George's provided their only opportunity to purchase large household goods. Interestingly, Crazy George's forty outlets in the United Kingdom operated on far lower effective annual interest rates, ranging between 20 and 25 percent through its French stores. This was likely due to the more highly competitive consumer lending market in the United Kingdom, which gave Crazy George customers other borrowing options. Crazy George's eventually closed its French stores.

British consumers also gained new safety measures in credit contracts as part of a broad wave of consumer protection legislation instituted in the 1970s, but these regulations fell far short of France's sheltered credit environment. Most of Britain's basic protections were passed as part of the 1974 Consumer Credit Act. Transparency was a primary focus of the legislation. In general, the law required that consumer credit contracts specify the equivalent annual percentage rate (the legislation offered guidance in how to calculate this), the total cost of credit, and the cost of the product being purchased on credit. Unlike in France, not all financial institutions were required to disclose this information: building societies and insurance companies, for example, were exempt from these transparency requirements. All consumer credit providers, however, had to be formally licensed by a newly created Consumer Credit Licensing Bureau within the Office of Fair Trading. As in France, borrowers who contracted for a loan at their door or through the mail enjoyed a cooling-off period during which they might cancel a consumer loan contract. For installment credit, borrowers also received special protections against repossessions. Creditors were allowed to repossess without a court order only when the consumer had not yet paid for more than one-third of the product. In any case a seven-day notice was required.

Unlike in France, the 1974 legislation fully abolished usury limits. Conventional consumer loans in Britain regularly reached annual percentage rates of 45 percent. Small short-term doorstep loans reached up to 1,000 percent APR, although more typically they ranged from 75 to 175 percent.[11] One consequence was a significant growth in lending in the subprime sector. In 2003, a parliamentary commission considered the possibility of imposing interest rate restrictions on credit card companies operating in the United Kingdom, which triggered a debate on how to finance lending to risky segments of the population. Concern about access for working-class borrowers quickly undermined this proposal. Credit card companies emphasized that by charging higher fees and interest rates to customers who did not pay regularly, they were able to extend relatively inexpensive credit to reliable borrowers at all income levels.

In 2006, the Consumer Credit Act underwent its first major rewriting since its introduction in 1974. The legislation was a response to a government investigation into consumer lending, the results of which were published in 2003 and titled "Fair, Clear and Competitive."[12] Some of the provisions in the 2006 act were intended to increase transparency. Lenders were required to provide detailed printed annual statements, as well as printed notices of accounts in arrears. These provisions posed a specific challenge to doorstep lenders, who had not traditionally operated with high levels of disclosure. Consumers now also had more time to respond to notices of default—fourteen days rather than seven. Potentially more important were the new forms and standards of recourse the act created. First, consumers could take their grievances directly to the Financial Ombudsman Service, which could in turn order licensed lenders to provide aggrieved consumers compensation.[13] Second, the act replaced the legal standard of "extortionate" lending with a broader test for "unfair relationship" between creditor and debtor. If courts interpreted this standard broadly, it could have the effect of creating new norms for responsible lending among U.K. creditors. Creditors were quick to embrace the new legislation, with some relief that early proposals to impose hard interest rate caps were not included.

The consequences of differing interpretations of the consumer interest extended to significant differences in the structure of the lending sector as well as of policy. In France, nonmortgage lending was divided nearly evenly between conventional personal loans offered by banks and consumer loans offered by specialized consumer finance firms. The latter emerged in the early part of the twentieth century, spawned mainly from large retailers who needed to offer their consumers a credit facility. These included Cetelem, Cofidis, and Cofinoga, plus two large lenders specializing in automobile finance: Crédipar (PSA Peugeot-Citroen) and DIAC (Renault).[14] With financial liberalization in the early 1980s, France's large banks attempted to move further into the profitable consumer lending sectors. But high administrative costs and poor risk management typically led to failure. Credit Agricole opened the consumer finance group Unibanque, then had to close it. Citicorp France opened and then sold its Citifinancement group.[15] By the late 1990s, the big financial institutions began buying up the existing consumer finance groups. BNP Paribas bought Cetelem; Credit Agricole bought Sofinco; GE Capital bought Sovac. Of the big lenders, only Cofinoga remained majority-owned by its founding retailer, Galleries Lafayette. Revolving credit, offered by both kinds of institutions either via the *carte bancaire* payment card or as overdraft protection, accounted for approximately one-quarter of all consumer lending.

In the United Kingdom, banks and building societies accounted for two-thirds of all consumer credit. The remainder came from specialized lending institutions, including home credit providers. Half of all non-

mortgage credit took the form of personal loans; one-third was installment sales credit; roughly 20 percent was revolving card-based credit.
Unlike in France, where credit providers remained quite static following
deregulation, the United Kingdom saw the entrance of important new
players. Credit cards like Barclaycard and Visa, and newer card companies like Egg and Capital One, gradually began displacing traditional
store-based credit. By 2000, U.K. credit card transactions accounted for
30 percent of all such transactions in Europe, making the United Kingdom the most highly developed credit card market on the continent.
Traditional bank and building societies began losing market share to these
new lenders, although they still dominated the market. High-interest-rate
"subprime" lending, virtually unknown in France, accounted for about 10
percent of U.K. household debt (compared to 25 percent in the United
States).[16]

In sum, protections for consumer debtors in France remain considerably stronger than in the United Kingdom, reflecting differing interpretations of the consumer interest in the two countries. In the United
Kingdom, where personal credit was understood as a component of economic citizenship, legislation tended to privilege access over protection.
Although additional disclosure requirements for consumer credit contracts were instated in the 1970s, the same legislation fully abolished
usury limits, and certain financial institutions—building societies and
insurance companies—were exempted from full transparency requirements. In France, by contrast, usury limits remained in place despite a
measure of liberalization in lending in the 1980s, and all lenders were under stringent transparency requirements. The structure of the lending
sector in the two countries was also different. In France, a large portion of
consumer lending was in the hands of specialized consumer finance firms,
many sponsored by major retailers. In the United Kingdom, by contrast,
traditional store credit declined as credit cards and other forms of revolving credit grew in market share.

In both cases, the consumer interest prevailed. But the divergent
choice of narrative in each country produced significantly different results in policy, industry structure, and scale of household borrowing.

Credit Rating and Data Privacy

Money lenders have long found ways to share data on borrowers, both to assess the overall creditworthiness of new applicants and to avoid over-borrowing by a single borrower using credit lines from several sources. Because this sort of data could have a decisive impact on a consumer's access to credit, governments have frequently stepped in to regulate the credit rating sector in order to protect consumers. In Europe, such interventions have been shaped by deep concerns about consumers' rights to control the use of personal data. How countries balance these two goals—data privacy and credit access—can shape dramatically the credit environment consumers face. In France and the United Kingdom, the respective emphases on protection and access to credit produced significantly different data management regimes.

The generalized suspicion of credit and of lenders in France led to the instatement of a number of restrictions on the ability of consumer lenders to collect information on their customers. France's centralized credit rating system, managed by the country's central bank, recorded only negative credit episodes. Late payments were recorded once they reached ninety days, as well as any credit-related legal or administrative procedures (see below). The database, called the Fichier national des incidents de remboursement des credits aux particuliers (FICP), was accessible only to credit companies and to individual debtors who wished to view their own records.[17] Established in 1989, the FICP replaced a fully private list of negative payment incidents maintained by France's association of financial institutions for its member companies. In practice, the FICP database became a borrower blacklist against which lenders checked all applications before making a loan. In 2003, there were 2.3 million people registered in the FICP. Data were kept for a maximum of ten years.

Although some of France's lenders pushed for the ability to collect and distribute more extensive "positive" credit data—including information on outstanding loans, taxes, income, and assets—consumer groups successfully mobilized against it, citing the danger of a more commercialized credit environment. Lenders fearing competition from foreign firms adept with more liberal data-collection policies followed suit. In the latest proposal, which came before the National Assembly in 2005, the center-right Union for French Democracy (UDF) party argued that a positive registry would give financial institutions a better sense of total lending and help them to better assess a consumer's ability to repay. France's financial institutions were divided on the proposal. Some, including the consumer lending institution Cofinoga, argued that positive data on potential borrowers would help them to avoid adverse selection in selecting customers, thereby reducing both defaults and credit rationing. But many other financial institutions, supported by France's industry association for financial firms (Association des sociétés financiers, ASF), argued that a positive rating system would help foreign financial firms—like United Kingdom–based lender Egg—to identify and exploit new clients in France.[18] France's consumer groups generally agreed with this view, worrying that a positive list would become a tool for more aggressive commercialization of credit, leading to higher levels of consumer indebtedness.[19]

In the United Kingdom, by contrast, lenders enjoyed greater freedom to collect, analyze, and make judgments on consumer credit information. By using not just black but also positive white data—on income and outstanding credit, for example—lenders could better assess a prospective borrower's potential credit risk. This kind of risk modeling allowed them to extend loans to classes of borrowers that might otherwise have been considered too risky. Unlike in France, the United Kingdom had private credit reference agencies that gathered and stored the data. Through historical consolidation, three credit reference agencies eventually dominated the U.K. market: Experian, Equifax, and Callcredit.[20] Under the terms of the Consumer Credit Act of 1974, which governed the treatment of credit data, the credit reference agencies did not themselves make assessments about the creditworthiness of individuals. And, unlike France's FICP, the credit reference agencies were explicitly banned from creating a lending blacklist. They instead provided lenders with raw information, leaving the lenders to employ their own private data and scoring systems to determine the terms on which credit should be offered. Credit reference data were retained for a maximum of six years, and covered all jurisdictions in the United Kingdom.[21] The data compiled by credit reference agencies to create credit histories included electoral rolls (for proof of residency), county court judgments, payment of past debts, and recourse to any formal debt remediation procedures (such as bankruptcy), which remained on a credit history for six years. Each time a new form of credit was opened, data about the loan was recorded by the credit reference agencies. If an individual in the United Kingdom was refused credit, under the Data Protection Act the individual had the right to know the reasons for refusal. Reference agencies in the United Kingdom also allowed individuals to explain a period of poor credit on their record: consumers could attach a "notice of correction" to their credit report that explained missed payments.

The difference in consumer data protection regimes was all the more surprising given that regulatory freedom in both countries was limited by common European Union (EU) guidelines. Credit information activities in both France and the United Kingdom took place within the broader framework of the 1995 EU Data Protection Directive (EU Directive 95/46) governing the processing and movement of personal data. The directive came into force in 1998, and was transcribed into national law in the United Kingdom in 1998 and in France in 2004.[22] The goal of the EU directive was to harmonize national data protection policies so that member states with strong data protection regimes—especially Germany and France—would not block data flows with other EU members. The basic obligations imposed by the directive included consumer consent in the processing and transmission of personal data, consumer access to private data held by companies, and the creation of a national data protection authority to monitor the collection and use of private data and to enforce the data protection laws. Personal data were construed broadly in the directive to include such things as bank statements, credit card numbers, and criminal records. The term *processing* was also construed broadly as "any operation or set of operations which is performed upon personal data, whether or not by automatic means, such as collection, recording, organization, storage, adaptation or alteration, retrieval, consultation, use, disclosure by transmission, dissemination or otherwise making available, alignment or combination, blocking, erasure or destruction."[23] Finally, in a provision that continued to dominate trans-Atlantic economic negotiations, the directive banned companies from transmitting personal data to third countries that did not ensure "an adequate level of protection."

In practice, the requirement of consumer consent for data "processing" and "transfer" placed limits on the use of consumer credit data in more sophisticated credit direct marketing. Under the terms of the EU directive, only once consumers had made a request for a loan were they considered to have given consent, allowing the credit reference agencies to distribute private credit data. In the United Kingdom, credit card companies that relied on direct mailing reported that the data privacy protections doubled the cost of acquiring new customers compared to similar direct marketing campaigns in the United States. In France, the impact was even more dramatic. France's financial institutions had long proposed to enhance the country's publicly managed blacklist with a privately managed database of positive credit information. But France's powerful data privacy association, CNIL, acting under the terms of the EU directive, ruled out this approach, arguing that it infringed too heavily on consumer privacy. Moreover, although specific economic sectors were permitted to maintain private customer blacklists, CNIL found that these data must not be shared across sectors, a practice the association argued risked creating a permanent group of social and economic outsiders. Hence credit institutions were not allowed to consult data collected on rental fraud, even if these data were held within the same company.

With the exception of the borrower blacklist compiled by the centrally run FCIP, France's data protection regime placed much higher restrictions on lenders' ability to collect and use consumer data than did the U.K. regime. In France, the imperative to protect the borrower drove policy. The FCIP blacklist was thought to save the most vulnerable class of borrowers from themselves should they seek to take on debt; the prohibition on collecting other types of financial data was thought to protect the privacy of credit applicants. In the United Kingdom, the goal of maximizing access to credit led legislators to ban the keeping of an outright blacklist, but gave lenders greater freedom to compile and use personal financial data. The argument was that credit would be cheaper and more readily available if lenders could more accurately assess an individual's credit risk. Again, in both cases the diffuse consumer interest prevailed—just in different ways.

Consumer Insolvency

In the cases of truth in lending and personal financial data collection, the respective choices of narratives in France and the United Kingdom led to significantly different policy outcomes and impacts on the structure of the national credit industry. In the case of debt remediation, however, the imperatives to increase protection from debt and to increase access to credit led to similar results in both countries—the rise of more flexible, less stigmatized alternatives to formal bankruptcy procedures—though for very different reasons.

The household debt crisis that plagued Europe throughout the late 1980s and early 1990s served as a catalyst for change in consumer insolvency law across the continent. The deregulation of credit in the 1980s resulted in working-class and middle-class families taking on significant amounts of debt.[24] Alternative solutions to conventional contractual remediation were needed—not least because municipal court dockets were filling with consumer nonpayment cases. European politicians and policymakers looked to the U.S. model of bankruptcy that, since the nineteenth century, had included the discharge of debts. European countries increasingly adopted new laws that enabled consumers to submit a formal petition for adjustment of debt and partial discharge. In 1984, Denmark became the first European country to adopt a bankruptcy law that allowed for consumer debt adjustment and debt discharge. Denmark's bankruptcy legislation set a precedent for European bankruptcy law, though it was not widely copied outside of Scandinavia.[25] France and Germany were among the first to follow the Danish example. In 1989, France adopted a Law on Prevention and Regulation of Individual and Household Over-Indebtedness. In the United Kingdom, the 1988 Debt Administration Order provided for discharge in personal bankruptcy, but the procedure was onerous for indebted consumers.[26] It was reformed in 1990 to ease consumer access.

In many ways, the French and U.K. responses were similar. Both provided for a consolidated debt renegotiation procedure, with structured payment plans. Both established specialized consumer bankruptcy proceedings with a lower burden on applications. And both provided for a full discharge of debt in the most extreme cases. Yet the similarity of the reforms belies a very different view of the interests they were securing. In the United Kingdom, the idea was to promote individual risk-taking by lowering the cost of failure. This logic was an extension of the more general emphasis on giving consumers greater access to markets. In France, the idea was to prevent the over-indebted from becoming permanently marginalized in society. The emphasis was on protecting individuals from the consequences of market access. Such cases, in which similar regulatory outcomes are driven by divergent public logics, may be more common than we have previously suspected. It serves as a warning against the mechanical imputation of interests from regulatory outcomes.

Until 1989, France provided no useful recourse to over-indebted consumers. Creditors with defaulting borrowers brought their cases to the courts, which summoned the defaulting consumers, who often simply did not appear. Courts would then grant creditors the right to repossess property and attach salaries, typically leading to eviction.[27] For creditors, this ad hoc response created coordination problems, as creditors rushed to secure insufficient assets. With liberalization of consumer credit in 1987, a rising incidence of over-indebtedness led France's consumer and finance associations to negotiate a novel solution. The 1989 Neiertz law created a new administrative instrument that would work beside the legal system to help resolve cases of consumer over-indebtedness. The law was subsequently reformed several times, as the French government moved slowly toward a system of consumer debt discharge.

The core of the new system was a set of Departmental Commissions for Over-Indebted Individuals managed by France's central bank and to which any consumer could apply for debt restructuring or relief. The commissions could suspend payments for up to two years, restructure the payment period for loans, and modify interest rates. The new repayment schedule was based on a commission's assessment of the "minimum vital income" to meet the claimant's most basic needs. Repayment plans could last up to but not longer than ten years. Formally, commissions could only propose a repayment solution. If both parties did not voluntarily accept it, the case went before a judge, who, from 1995, had the right to enforce the recommendation of the commission on both parties, or, in rare cases, to design a new repayment scheme. A series of studies conducted in the 1990s showed that most cases went to the full ten years, that interest rates were reduced on average from 13 percent to 9 percent, and that average monthly payments were reduced from 6,000 francs to 3,800 francs.[28] Within certain limits—business-related debt was excluded, and consumers had to show "good faith" in presenting their case to the commission—nearly all cases were accepted. The number of cases filed with the commissions grew dramatically since their founding. From 90,000 cases in their first year, 1990, the number of cases rose to 190,000 in 2004.

Each commission had four members, representing the Banque de France, the treasury department, a consumer association, and a lender association. In 2003, two nonvoting members were added: a social worker and a lawyer.[29] Two features of the 1989 law were distinctive. First, the commissions included no formal requirement for credit counseling, although in practice consumer and family associations often helped indebted households to navigate the administrative procedures. Second, private credit intermediaries were banned in France, although credit consolidation remained legal.[30]

In assessing cases, the commissions distinguished first between "active" cases of over-indebtedness, in which consumers had simply taken on too much debt, and "passive" cases, in which external causes made it impossible for the borrower to continue paying. In 2001, active cases accounted for 36 percent of all cases. By 2004, active cases accounted for 27 percent of all cases. Because the total number of cases grew substantially, the number of active cases stayed nearly the same—approximately 50,000 cases per year. In 2004, the most important sources of passive cases were unemployment (30.8 percent), divorce or separation (14.7 percent), and sickness or accident (10.8 percent).[31]

Consumer creditors were initially highly skeptical of the Neiertz procedure. In 1990, only 45 percent of solutions proposed by the commissions were accepted by creditors. Paul Defourny, head of one of France's largest consumer lending groups, Cetelem, estimated in 1992 that 50,000 of the 160,000 cases heard up until that point represented instances of clear cheating by borrowers—borrowers who had gone from lender to lender in order to borrow as much as they could without intention of repaying. He estimated that the Neiertz law had cost the lending industry 1 billion francs in its first two years. As Defourny described it: "The [Neiertz] law . . . moralized our profession by creating a sort of deontological code."[32] Yet as cases of over-indebtedness rose, and as the commissions showed that they were able to produce workable solutions, industry acceptance of commission proposals rose, to 75 percent by the end of the 1990s.

Despite this success, a growing number of cases were coming back to the commissions. The Neiertz legislation had been intended for debtors who had simply fallen behind. Increasingly, however, the commissions were seeing cases in which the debtor did not have the means to repay at all, even at no interest over ten years. For these cases, debt restructuring was not enough. Increasingly, financial firms came to accept that, at least for the direst cases, a full discharge of debts might be necessary. There was a precedent for this in France, in the departments of Alsace and Moselle. These departments, while under German occupation between 1871 and 1945, had adopted the German law of 1877 providing for discharge in bankruptcy. With the region's reintegration into France, the German bankruptcy provisions were retained as a provision of local customary law.[33] Under this provision, courts in Alsace-Moselle could force creditors to accept partial repayment tied to a discharge of all remaining debt. In 2003, France introduced a version of this court-administered discharge at the national level. It applied only to debtors in good faith who had presented their cases before the commissions and were found to be "irremediably compromised" in their ability to pay. In such cases, which amounted to only 5 percent of all cases heard by the commissions in 2004, the judge could call for a liquidation of assets and a full discharge of remaining creditor claims.[34] Consumer group reactions to the civil bankruptcy procedure were mixed. Most family groups saw it as a positive step, but trade unions and other groups felt that it was overly harsh in its requirements to liquidate all property.[35]

In the United Kingdom, bankruptcy also moved toward a greater emphasis on negotiated settlements, but with important differences. In the context of Victorian ideals about morality and bankruptcy, and a tradition of debtor prisons that extended into the interwar period, Britain entered the postwar era with a legal system that continued to deal harshly with consumer debt default. Already by the mid-1960s, consumers who had purchased new household goods on credit in the postwar period were beginning to face payment problems. Over the course of the 1960s and 1970s, a series of government commissions, including the Payne Committee (1965–1970), the Crowther Committee (1968–1971), and the Cork Committee (1977–1982), proposed changes to the consumer bankruptcy regime that would make it less punitive for over-indebted households. The 1976 Insolvency Act brought some relief, for example, allowing bankrupts to apply for discharge after five years. The major reforms for noncommercial debtors were introduced in the 1986 Insolvency Act. Two reforms were most significant. The first was an automatic discharge in bankruptcy after three years. The second was an extrajudicial debt remediation procedure called the Individual Voluntary Agreement (IVA). The IVA had originally been intended for individual business proprietors, and was based loosely on the Company Voluntary Procedure designed to help larger companies restructure their debts outside of legal insolvency procedures. By the early 1990s, however, IVAs had become a popular alternative for over-indebted household consumers who hoped to avoid a formal bankruptcy proceeding. The effect was to create a second, private alternative to the harsh terms of formal bankruptcy in Britain. Although the 1986 law provided for debt discharge after three years, undischarged bankrupts were banned from public office, were forced to sell their homes and any luxury goods to pay creditors, and had their names published in the local newspaper. They were also legally required to tell any new creditors of their status as bankrupts. With the new IVA, the debtor was never formally bankrupt, could continue to gain access to credit, and, perhaps most important, could escape the social stigma still associated with bankruptcy.

In the IVA procedure, a private insolvency practitioner negotiated a new repayment schedule and contract between the debtor and creditors. The service had no up-front fee—instead, the agent took on some amount of the consumer's debt, up to 27 percent, as payment. The IVA required support by 75 percent of creditors, whereas the resulting agreement was binding on all creditors. This "cramdown" provision helped to avoid the problem of holdouts. In extreme cases, IVAs included the forgiving

of up to 75 percent of the consumers' debt. For creditors, the IVA ensured that some debt would be repaid, and studies found that repayment
rates for IVAs were higher than for traditional bankruptcy procedures.
One study of IVAs and bankruptcy proceedings in 1997–1998 found
IVAs repaid 46 percent of the outstanding debt, compared to 30 percent
for bankruptcies.[36] For debtors, the IVA was a private procedure that
avoided public embarrassment. Average repayment periods were five
years, compared to a three-year repayment under conventional bankruptcy proceedings. The details of the IVA remained on the debtor's
credit record for six years. If a debtor defaulted on an IVA, he or she
could pursue a legal bankruptcy proceeding.

Over the course of the 1990s, the number of IVAs for personal insolvencies rose at a slow rate. In 1990, the number of consumers with IVAs
was 1,927. In the mid-1990s, IVAs accounted for 17 percent of all personal
insolvencies in the United Kingdom. Surveys found that IVAs appealed
especially to young, married consumers and younger married families
who were eager to avoid bankruptcy and its emotional and financial consequences. In 2000, the number of consumers with IVAs was 7,978. Just
six years later, in 2006, Individual Voluntary Agreements reached 107,288,
representing an almost 60 percent increase just from 2005.[37]

U.K. consumer debt management companies, which arranged IVAs
for a percentage-based fee, experienced huge profits as the number of
IVA cases grew. Companies like Debt Free Direct promoted themselves
with fairly aggressive marketing campaigns including television and
newspaper ads, and operated huge call centers. Operators took thousands
of calls and typed in information on the type of debt, household income
and monthly payments (including rent, food, clothes, and utility bills).
Specialized computer software then calculated which option (IVAs, bankruptcy, or credit counseling) offered the least drastic solution for the caller.
So successful and profitable were the credit counseling services providing
IVA services that banks and other lenders began raising their expectations
of payout for distressed consumer loans, up from 20 pence on the pound
to 30–40 pence. Consumer advocates worried that the number of failed
IVAs would begin to grow as collections expectations became more
aggressive.

The Personal Insolvency Provisions of the 2002 Enterprise Act introduced a consideration of debtor intent into U.K. legal bankruptcy proceedings. Motivated by the U.S. experience, New Labour's goal was to encourage individuals to take risks without fear of overly burdensome bankruptcy costs. For debtors found to have been "honest but unlucky," discharge was accelerated, from a maximum of three years to a maximum of one year from the time of filing. Under certain conditions, discharge could be even faster. The new legislation met strong opposition from creditor groups. These pushed for special punitive conditions for debtors who were considered to have entered into excessive debt in bad faith, either without intent to repay or with no reasonable expectation of repayment. These "corrupt" debtors faced a so-called bankruptcy restriction order (BRO), lasting up to fifteen years after bankruptcy and discharge, that helped to protect potential future creditors. BRO restrictions included requirements that subjects disclose their status in order to apply for additional credit (and, in case they had changed their name, indicate the name under which they had filed for bankruptcy), and banned them from positions of financial responsibility, including company directorships and employment in credit consulting firms.

The new legislation also opened up the possibility for something akin to an IVA that could be filed within the bankruptcy procedure. Under the new fast-track voluntary agreement (FTVA), an undischarged debtor could make a written proposal to his or her creditors for a private settlement. The court-appointed receiver would act as the facilitator, no personal meeting was required, and, as with the IVA, the creditors could freely accept or decline subject to a three-quarters majority. For creditors, the absence of a private IVA practitioner meant that their returns could be higher. Fees for the receiver were fixed at 15 percent of funds collected.[38] From the government's perspective, it was hoped that the FTVA procedure would further lessen the burden on the court system, while also putting pressure on the margins of consumer debt counseling firms, for whom the IVA business was proving extremely profitable. A debtor could request an FTVA immediately following a bankruptcy order; once an agreement was accepted by creditors and the debtor, the bankruptcy proceeding was annulled.[39]

Common trends marked the French and British consumer insolvency reforms. Both moved toward easier access to discharge and toward an embrace of "voluntary" contract renegotiation. Both reforms were precipitated by a growth in consumer debt and defaults, with the goal of making over-indebtedness less punitive for consumers. The move toward a system of automatic discharge represented a direct borrowing from the American bankruptcy regime—ironically, at the very moment when the American system was moving away from universal automatic discharge. Perhaps surprisingly, both France and the United Kingdom (and France *more* than the United Kingdom) evinced a deep concern about abridging credit contracts, because of the foundational importance of contractual sovereignty and out of concern over its impact on "payment morale." The move to government-sponsored schemes for voluntary debt restructuring represented in both countries an attractive alternative to frequent state intervention in contracts. If private parties could be convinced to find a separate peace, then the sovereignty of the contract could remain intact. In cases where discharge was warranted, concerns over debtor abuse led both countries to make a distinction between "honest but unlucky" bankrupts and those that had taken out more debt than they either reasonably could or intended to repay. This distinction was a matter of judgment, but introducing it allowed both countries to accept the principle of automatic discharge without appearing to condone borrower opportunism.

Yet these similarities mask some very real differences. Despite their common emphases on the sanctity of contracts and the concern over the possibility that too-easy debt remediation might create perverse incentives for unscrupulous borrowers, the creation of negotiated alternatives to formal bankruptcy in France and Britain were motivated by very different accounts of the consumer interest. In the United Kingdom, legislators hoped to encourage individual risk-taking by lowering the cost of insolvency—part of the more general emphasis on giving consumers greater access to markets. In France, alternatives to bankruptcy were more a matter of clemency for the unfortunate than a measure for promoting economic growth. The emphasis there was on protecting individuals from the consequences of access to products and services that British legislators treated as goods in and of themselves.

Ideas and Interests

Behind all three policy areas—truth and transparency in lending, consumer data protection, and insolvency proceedings—lay different conceptions of the very purpose both of consumer credit and of borrower protection in credit markets. In the United Kingdom, access to credit markets was seen as a tool for greater economic and ultimately social inclusion. With access to credit came an equality of opportunity, giving even the poor a chance to be entrepreneurial. This view of credit as economically enabling for the poor had deep roots in liberal economic tradition, roots that it shared with the recent emphasis on bringing microfinance facilities and property titling to the poor in developing countries. From this perspective, the goal of consumer protections in credit markets was to enable entrepreneurship. This implied making bankruptcy proceedings less punitive so as to encourage risky innovation. This view also provided little rationale for imposing specific interest rate caps, because highly risky ventures necessarily implied higher interest rates. So long as consumers were not misled into exorbitant loans—and British law worked hard to avoid this—consumers should be able to contract for credit at any level of risk.

The conception of the borrower interest in French public discourse was different. Rather than emphasizing the possibilities of credit to encourage economic inclusion, French policy tended to emphasize the risk of persistent exclusion for consumers who became victims of excessive and persistent debt obligations. The motivation for a procedure leading to discharge was the view that it was patently unfair to allow families to live under persistent and degrading conditions of debt collection. The point was not to encourage risk-taking, but to ensure, for those consumers who had become over-indebted, that they would not be permanently excluded from the benefits of citizenship. This orientation helps to explain the broad support that usury limits enjoyed in France. For a country that retained an active commitment to a broad public interest in equality, redistributive goals related to opportunity and inclusion were expressed through political channels that emphasized government fiscal and labor policy, rather than access to credit. This approach rested in turn on France's underlying republican social ideal, which precluded a politics that emphasized the access or exclusion of particular groups from credit markets.

These two different views were embodied in the very different implementation of consumer credit rating practices, even under the common frame of the European Union Data Protection Directive. For France, data privacy was used as a rationale for blocking the collection of positive credit data on consumers. The fear was that such data, once assembled, would permanently exclude certain groups in society from access to credit through the logic of credit scoring technology. A public blacklist, by contrast, was limited in its scope to consumers who were clearly facing payment problems and thus could be plausibly construed as a protection for the economically vulnerable. French creditors embraced this logic out of concern that a public positive credit database would open their sector to excessive competition from foreign firms accustomed to integrating credit rating data into credit risk management. In the United Kingdom, the same principles of data privacy were followed, but with fewer constraints on data collection and use. Credit providers could still not use the full suite of data available from Britain's private credit reference agencies to design credit offers, because the consumer had not yet indicated consent. Once consumers applied for credit, however, credit reference data were seen to allow lenders to extend credit to individuals who might otherwise have been excluded based on simple geographical or demographic data. The public availability of such data was thought to promote competition. Even in Britain, however, credit rating remained a matter of competitive strategy as well as principle. New subprime credit card providers worked to force Britain's traditional doorstep lenders to include their privately recorded transactions in the publicly accessible credit registries.

The case of credit regulation has important implications for our understanding of diffuse interest representation. The first is that the austere logic of organizational theory fails to take into account the power of policy narratives in driving outcomes in cases of interest group conflict. Two competing narratives of consumer interest—one focused on market access and the other focused on protection from markets—have driven divergent policies that nonetheless are both intended to defend the practical interests of borrowers. To some extent, these narratives are trapped in the amber of their historical and national context. French policymakers have always been more skeptical of free markets, so there should be little surprise that they are inclined to protect borrowers from unregulated access to credit markets. It is also unsurprising that British regulators, with a deep tradition of liberal economic policy, have spurned interest rate caps as a means to limit creditor exploitation.

The second implication of this comparative analysis of credit regulation is that policy responses have not in either case been dictated primarily by the concentrated interests of incumbent lenders. To be sure, French domestic lenders may have benefited from regulatory restrictions that limited foreign access to the French market. Yet they also regularly were thwarted in their efforts to manipulate public policy. They systematically objected to bankruptcy reform, attempted to integrate their positive credit data into a common database, and objected to the interest rate caps they faced. These measures were not put in place because of the concentrated lobbying power of France's consumer lending sector. They were instituted because French politicians worked closely with industry and family groups to develop a regulatory framework that would promote greater economic and social inclusion in a way that fit with France's existing cultural tradition.

CHAPTER 6

The Limits of Regulatory Capture

IN THE PRECEDING four chapters, we considered cases in which diffuse interest groups defied the logic of collective action and prevailed
over concentrated industry lobbies. Again and again, compelling policy
narratives, interest group coalitions, and favorable institutional opportunity structures enabled broad groups to overcome the organizational
challenges inherent in their large size. Where these factors were absent,
diffuse interests could and did lose out to the concentrated resources
and tightly coordinated lobbying of narrow interests, though this sort of
industry capture was nothing like the foreordained result that organizational theory would predict.

In this and the following chapter, we show that not only is regulatory
capture far less common than social scientists tend to believe, but that
capture is typically contested and incomplete. We consider two cases in
which concentrated interests appear clearly to have dictated the terms of
public policy to the detriment of diffuse interests: farm supports and
pharmaceutical regulation. These chapters reveal the constraints on
narrow interest representation even in cases of apparently strong industry influence. Together, they suggest that narrow interests, even when
they are successful in influencing public policy, nonetheless must do so in
ways that credibly ally their own interests with broader group interests.

Once this sort of legitimacy coalition is forged, it places limits on the latitude that narrow interests subsequently enjoy to alter the kinds of policies they advocate. Narrow interests may indeed exert policy influence, but they do so with far less discretion over the direction of that influence than is commonly understood.

This chapter addresses the sustained public policy support for agricultural protections within the European Union (EU). The focus is on France, which was and remains the strongest advocate of a European farm support program. The case of farm supports emphasizes the importance of legitimating narratives in allowing concentrated interests to achieve their policy objectives by tying their own goals to those of a diffuse societal interest. What is fascinating about farm supports in the advanced industrialized countries is that they have been forced over time to change the public narratives by which they legitimate continued public financial supports for farmers. From a legitimating narrative that emphasized food self-sufficiency and high agricultural output, European farmers moved to adapt to a new narrative logic that linked farm supports to environmental protection and rural land management. This transition was exceedingly difficult, and it remained an open question whether the existing system of farm supports could survive the transition intact.

Despite extraordinary productivity growth in agricultural output in the postwar period, major agricultural countries in 2005 provided their farmers an estimated $200 billion in direct and indirect agricultural supports each year. One-third of this came from supports managed by the EU's Common Agricultural Policy (CAP). The United States accountd for another third, and Japan for one-sixth. For each of these support programs, government subsidies accounted for more than one-third of agricultural output. Tariffs on agricultural imports to the advanced industrialized countries averaged five times tariffs on manufactured goods.[1] These supports were also typically deployed selectively, so that staple crops like corn and beef received disproportionately high levels of support and protection. In France, one of the biggest recipients of CAP supports, a cereal farmer with 200 hectares under cultivation received (in 2005) on average 20,000 euros in revenue from grain sales and 60,000 euros from agricultural subsidies. The median French beef farm, with 50 cows grazing 78 hectares, received 12,000 euros in revenue from sales and 22,000 euros from agricultural subsidies. These supports sustained a large agricultural sector. France in 2005 produced 39 percent of all European beef (3.2 million tons in 2005) and 24 percent of all European cereals.[2] Perhaps unsurprisingly, France was among Europe's strongest supporters of the CAP program of farm supports.

The agricultural sector is a concentrated interest that has tied itself through a powerful legitimating narrative to a diffuse set of consumer interests in order to achieve its goal of sustained public financial support. Although Europe's farmers historically constituted the largest single sector of the economy, since the turn of the twentieth century their numbers declined significantly relative to the general population. Even in France, where the agricultural sector retained a particularly strong hold on public policy, there were in 2005 no more than 400,000 professional farms with 964,000 farmworkers in a nation of more than 60 million. Despite their declining proportion of the population, Europe's farmers had by the late twentieth century formed into one of the most politically powerful non-state actors in the European Union. French farmers in particular showed an extraordinary degree of coordination that helped them maintain a successful claim on public funds through dramatically changed circumstances.

Of particular interest for this account of regulatory capture is the challenge that the farm lobby in Europe faced in maintaining control of the narrative that it employed to tie its own concentrated interest to broader economic interests of the European public. Early price supports were grounded on the premise of public access to abundant food. In the early postwar context, in which hunger and starvation were a broadly shared experience, this narrative linkage was highly compelling. By the late 1970s, however, scarcity was a distant memory and the early logic of support had led to overproduction: simply warehousing the surplus was a strain on budgets, and export supports were taking up a growing share of the CAP budget. The need to solve the problem of overproduction would eventually lead EU administrators to force the farm lobby in Europe to embrace a legitimating narrative linked to issues of environmental protection and rural land management rather than consumer access. From the 1990s onward, the new idea was that farmers would be paid not for producing food, but for acting as stewards of an agricultural landscape. Farmers experienced the change as a negative development. Not only had the overall amount of support begun to decline, but farmers lost a cherished self-image as valued contributors to society. Moreover, it remained an open question whether the legitimating narrative that had traditionally provided public support for CAP could be changed without undermining the elaborate system of European subsidies itself. The leaders of France's powerful farming associations feared that paying farmers for not producing could brand farmers as welfare recipients and erode the public support for farm subsidies.

The case of EU farm supports suggests that even when concentrated interests prevail over more diffuse ones, their dependence on institutional opportunity structures and a public interest narrative tends to make it a qualified victory. To influence policy, narrow interests need backing from more diffuse—and hence more legitimate—interest groups. To get that backing, they need to be able to tell a compelling story about the way in which their narrow interest relates to the broader interest. This means that legitimating narratives are critically important to sustaining the influence of concentrated interests. Yet the choice of narrative is only partially within an interest group's control. Even relatively compact, efficient groups with considerable lobbying resources and lockstep organization cannot wholly dictate the terms of public support.

The Organization of Farm Interests in France

There are a variety of economic reasons for governments to participate in managing agricultural production.[3] This variety is due partly to the high volatility of supply conditions. Weather-related factors, diseases, and fluctuations in the costs of agricultural inputs can all lead to significant swings in product supply. Such supply shocks are typically symmetric across whole production regions, so that bad crops in one area are not necessarily offset by good crops in another. Consumer demand for foods, by contrast, tends to be sticky. Lower prices do not lead consumers to buy proportionally more. Most agricultural crops also cannot easily be stored from one growing season to the next. This means that excess production drives down market prices very rapidly, quickly lowering prices below even the cost of bringing products to market. The delay between sowing and reaping means that farmers cannot know what market conditions they will face at the time when they make investments in new animals and crops. Further, because agricultural shocks tend to hit many sectors and regions at the same time, private insurance schemes, including commercial crop insurance, have proved prohibitively expensive when it comes to managing seasonal downturns. Yet in Europe—and particularly in France, where the agricultural sector had historically exerted a strong pull on public policy—these reasons were only partly responsible for the long history of government involvement in agricultural production. The more important reasons had to do with taming the farmers, a large and potentially politically volatile societal group.

It is not a coincidence that France's continuous tradition of agricultural subsidies dates to the early years of the Third Republic: the political ascent of the farm sector, which employed more than 40 percent of the population as late as the First World War, coincided with the nation's first sustained experiment with democratic government. In 1881, France established the country's first Agriculture Ministry. Its goal was in large part to win over peasant farmers with royalist sympathies to the new parliamentary government. For much of France's history, peasant farmers had been a political wild card, wavering uncertainly between radicalism and royalism. In 1789, in the wake of a particularly bad harvest, French peasants rose up against the burden of taxes, tithes, and feudal obligations, setting off a wave of rural violence and destruction of property that became the backdrop of the French Revolution. But they were also behind the 1793 counterrevolutionary uprising in the Vendée. Through subsequent revolutions in 1830 and 1948, politically disorganized peasants continued to be torn between Bonapartist and republican identities. The sources of regional differences in the political response of rural farmers became one of the most vexed and heavily studied questions of French political economy. One scholar, André Siegfried, famously traced the political attitudes of French peasants to the underlying rock: according to him, granite areas bred royalist farmers, limestone areas bred republicans.[4] It was this mysterious incoherence of the French peasantry's political identity that would lead Marx to label them as a "sackful of potatoes."[5] As a political matter, however, the new Third Republic quickly realized it would have to neutralize the peasants as a potential political force. The last quarter of the nineteenth century saw a number of challenges to the livelihoods of French farmers. Sugar beet producers were increasingly threatened by cane producers in the new French colonies. Wine producers were losing their market share due to the phylloxera infestation that devastated domestic vineyards.[6] To shelter France's farmers from these discontents, the Third Republic began propping up the agricultural sector. The first measures took the form of import duties, first on wheat, in 1885, then on sugar and wine in the late 1880s. By 1914, the French government had begun a program of purchasing and storing wine and beet alcohols in order to stabilize market prices.[7]

In the wake of World War II, renewed concerns about the political orientation of French farmers became the basis for a dramatic increase in the influence of what would become France's dominant farm organization, the National Federation of Farm Worker Unions (FNSEA). During the period of German occupation, a large share of French farmers had played active roles in the French resistance, working alongside the French Communist Party to oppose the collaborationist Vichy government.[8] As the war came to a close, the left-center coalition worked to consolidate France's farmers into a corporatist structure, called the General Confederation of Farmers (CGA). Although the FNSEA was formally an entity established below the CGA to represent farmworkers, it staged a coup over the next seven years in which it took over most of the leadership functions intended for the CGA.[9] The FNSEA was able to consolidate its hold on French politicians in part because it helped them to solve three problems they faced. First, formerly communist farmers had been absorbed into the CGA, and conservative politicians worried that this would lead to a radicalized farmer's movement. The FNSEA, which was centrist-conservative, would block any potential radicalization. Second, the FNSEA would help to manage and control the inevitable decline in agricultural employment that would accompany modernization and growing productivity. Third, the FNSEA embraced the idea of a common agricultural policy at the European level. They backed the early proposal for a unified European agricultural authority laid out in the 1951 Charpentier Plan. They later embraced the integration project of President Charles de Gaulle, who feared that free trade without agriculture would generate a large balance of trade deficit with Germany.[10] In return, France's government granted increasing influence to the FNSEA in helping it to design agricultural policy both in France and, later, within CAP.

Mancur Olson's explanation of agricultural organization in the United States differs significantly from the government-activist partnership that promoted farmer mobilization in France during the early postwar decades. Whereas many of the diffuse material interests that clearly *did* manage to mobilize did so either while Olson was writing or immediately afterward, the highly diffuse group of American farmers unquestionably had organized in time for Olson to have noticed them. Olson's explanation for their political influence, in his account of the U.S. Farm Bureau organization, is that this group was primarily an organization of service groups that provided practical benefits to their own members. The considerable lobbying influence of the Farm Bureau was, he argues, "a by-product of its nonpolitical functions." His evidence, however, is purely deductive: "The theory of latent [diffuse] groups would suggest that the lobbying activities of an organization as large as the Farm Bureau would not provide an incentive that would lead rational individuals to join the organization, even if they were in complete agreement with its policies. Therefore, large pressure-group organizations must derive their strength as a by-product of some non-political functions."[11]

Whatever the merits of Olson's account of U.S. farmer organization, the "by-product" theory fits poorly with the French case. In France, we see a clear example of a state-activist coalition, in which farm mobilizers worked interactively with government officials interested in promoting agricultural interests. In this process, the FNSEA worked to consolidate and manage the modernization of French farming, while French politicians gave them increasing control over farm policy. The result was an enduring coordination of a previously highly diffuse set of interests. Although the French farmers' movement never managed to overcome the underlying fragmentation of the farm sector—with persistent divisions between left and right, small and large, and across classes of products— the FNSEA nonetheless sustained its dominance for nearly fifty years. At its peak in the early 1960s, the FNSEA represented 80 percent of French farmers. By the end of the century, it still represented 50 percent. Its broad membership gave the FNSEA tremendous political influence in matters of agricultural policy, including tariff levels and support policies. In 2006, Patrick Ferrère, the head of FNSEA, summarized that organization's ongoing relationship with France's political elite: "When the French Minister for Agriculture, whatever his political affiliation, wants to launch a reform or a new policy, he will meet with FNSEA's leaders and ask them their advice. We have a natural authority."[12]

Legitimating CAP—From Abundance to Overabundance

The history of the French farm movement was characteristic of the rest of the continent: though their numbers declined relative to population increase, most European farmers were well organized by the late 1950s. Their high degree of organization and coordination implies that we should think about the European agricultural sector in the post–World War II period as having transformed itself from a diffuse to a concentrated interest—and certainly it had when compared to the far broader classes of consumers who purchased their produce at prices propped up by tariff barriers, or taxpayers who funded their subsidies. True, farmers and farmworkers still represented 9 percent of economic output of the European Economic Community (EEC) and 17 percent of employment as late as 1960.[13] Yet they spoke with a coherent voice in national policymaking and deployed a formidable lobbying force to advocate their interests.

Still, if the shrinking of the European agricultural sector meant an increase in its organizational ability, it also meant a corresponding decrease in legitimacy. Given that they represented a relatively concentrated interest, how did Europe's farmers justify their claim to a disproportionate share of public goods and economic protection? The answer lay in the recent and visceral memory of scarcity during World War II and the immediate postwar period. The case for the farmers was easy to make through the mid-1970s: Europe needed to be able to feed itself. To arrive at this outcome, the new Common Agricultural Policy devised a combination of price fixing and direct supports to stabilize food prices at a high level relative to world markets. This account provided a narrative about agricultural supports that linked consumer needs for plentiful food with farmers' needs for stable and reasonable incomes. Yet this narrative was plausible only in the context of the early postwar years. By the early 1980s, the first set of policies had created a new problem—overproduction—that required its own solution and rendered the old narrative untenable.

The Common Agricultural Policy was conceived in the framework of the 1957 Treaty of Rome establishing the EEC. Article 39 of the treaty called for a common policy for agriculture that would increase productivity, ensure a fair standard of living for farmers, stabilize agricultural markets, and ensure availability of food at reasonable prices for consumers. In negotiations the following year, the six founding member states agreed upon three further principles for the CAP: a single market with common external tariffs, a "community preference" that explicitly favored products produced within the EEC, and "financial solidarity" that mandated a shared burden for funding agricultural supports.

Four more years of negotiations saw the final design for the CAP hammered out. It would be based on a system of price stabilization paired with rural development grants to assist poor farmers with restructuring and modernization. The bulk of CAP funding and administrative effort would go to stabilizing agricultural prices. To maintain stable prices that were also high enough to allow farmers a decent wage, the CAP provided tools to manipulate both supply and demand conditions. For each product category, a common EEC target price was chosen that was typically slightly above current (1962) market prices. If market prices within the EEC began to fall below the target price, national "intervention bodies" were paid to purchase and store products at an "intervention price" that was set slightly below the target price. Internal supply was also regulated through a program of refunds for exporters to cover the gap between internal and international market prices. Finally, to shield internal EEC prices from lower cost imports, a system of variable import levies raised the cost of imports to a "threshold price" set slightly above the target price.[14] Further complicating the system, each category of agricultural product within the CAP was managed by its own Common Market Organization (CMO). The first CMOs—including cereals, oilseeds, pork, poultry and eggs, fruits and vegetables, beef, dairy products, and wine—covered half of all EEC agricultural output. Over time, the CAP was extended to new classes of products with their own new CMOs, although the benefits to these later groups tended to be less generous than for the earlier "staple" product classes.[15] Each CMO worked with national agriculture ministers in the European Council of Agriculture to set target, intervention, and threshold prices for their product classes, and to allocate rural development grants. This system of indirect and direct subsidies was funded out of a common European Agricultural Guarantee and Guidance Fund (EAGGF), financed initially through customs duties and, from 1979, a 1 percent value-added tax.[16]

Initially, the CAP won wide support. For most EEC member states, the early postwar experience had been one of food scarcity and even starvation. By the early 1970s, Europe had become agriculturally self-sufficient. For consumers, the legitimating narrative for sustained CAP supports was self-evident: if consumers accepted slightly-higher-than-world prices for goods, farmers would produce enough for everyone, and more. Because most European consumers had no exposure to international food markets, they had little sense of how much more they were paying. By 1972, the EAGGF accounted for three-quarters of all community spending.[17] Had the OCMs allowed target prices to fall with increases in productivity, the system might have been sustainable. As it happened, broad public support for CAP led the farm lobby to push too hard for high prices, ultimately causing it to forfeit that support.

By the late 1970s, sustained high prices in the context of dramatically increased agricultural productivity were driving a wedge between European and international agricultural markets. High internal prices pushed farmers to seek ever increasing output, with costs for the European public. Environmentally, excessive fertilizing was causing high levels of agricultural pollution. Economically, the burden of maintaining high prices was also rising. By the mid-1980s, CAP was supporting the storage of 1.5 million tons of butter, 600,000 tons of beef, 1 million tons of skim milk powder, and 18 million tons of cereal.[18] The cost of storage alone in 1986 was 2 billion ECU (European currency unit, a precursor to the euro), or 10 percent of the entire CAP budget. It was also paying increasing premiums to agricultural exporters to compensate for the growing gap between European and world agricultural prices. In 1986, 34 percent of CAP expenditures went to export subsidies. EEC consumers were paying four times world prices for milk and sugar. The prospect of integrating new agricultural producers, especially Spain, into CAP only heightened concerns about the future costs of the program. If something was not done, the entire system risked losing public support. The first sign that this was a real risk came in 1984, when Margaret Thatcher negotiated a 300 million ECU rebate on the country's EEC contributions to make up for its loss in agricultural supports.

Already in the early 1980s, the EEC had begun to experiment with a variety of quotas and variable price supports that were meant to allow EEC members to maintain high market prices while limiting the costs of stockpiling. For some sectors with dramatic overproduction, quotas based on historical production levels placed administrative limits on individual farm output. In 1984, in a highly contentious move, milk production was placed under quota, with output set at just 1 percent above 1981 levels.[19] Milk producers took to the streets. A group of dairy farmers kidnapped the head of the French national milk board. For other sectors, the EEC began experimenting in 1988 with variable pricing schemes for non-quota products that were intended to limit the cost of stockpiling. When stockpiled wheat, for example, reached a preset volume, target prices were automatically reduced. The idea was to use these price reductions as automatic stabilizers, so that incentives for farmers to increase production decreased as stockpiles became too large. This experiment was a significant failure. Farmers responded by producing *even more* in order to meet their revenue goals given lower target prices.[20] The context of European farming had changed dramatically since the late 1950s: the old CAP programs, and the narrative that justified it, would have to adapt.

The MacSharry Reforms: From Production Subsidy to Income Support

With the failure to restrain the agricultural budget in the context of price fixing, and under increasing international pressure to do away with export subsidies in the context of early General Agreement on Tariffs and Trade (GATT) negotiations, CAP began looking at new options. The resulting MacSharry Reforms, launched in 1992, began moving European farm subsidies away from price supports that tied farmer income to output and toward income supports based on direct payments to farmers financed through tax revenues that covered most but not all of price-related losses. One of the goals was to limit production. Because direct payments were based on historic output levels, they created no new incentives to increase production. The reform also provided compensation for farmers who set aside land that would not be cultivated, as well as early retirement packages for small farmers.[21] Under this scheme, target prices would be allowed to decrease, with the lost incomes to farmers being made up through direct payments. The main targets were cereals, protein crops, oilseeds, beef, dairy products, tobacco, and sheep meat. Cereal prices were allowed to fall 30 percent; dairy fell 2.5 to 5 percent; oilseed prices were allowed to fluctuate freely. The target price for beef was reduced 15 percent, combined with a cap on intervention buying.[22] "It was quite a revolutionary step in those days," recalled Philippe Mangin, president of Coop de France, France's union of agricultural cooperatives. "There were demonstrations everywhere. Everyone foresaw the demise of the European farmer. We thought we were all dead."[23]

In economic terms, the impact on farmers was not dramatic. The new direct payments made up for 80 percent of revenues lost due to price reductions. But Europe's farmers understood that something more important was at stake. In moving from price supports to direct payments, the postwar narrative linking farmer support to consumer abundance was being undermined. The supports were also distributed unevenly, with 20 percent of French farmers receiving 80 percent of the benefits. For the European public, the CAP came increasingly to resemble a welfare policy, and one that favored the more secure large farmers over more vulnerable small producers.[24] Not only was it upsetting for many farmers to receive a check directly from the government, rather than to make their income through sales (admittedly at subsidized prices); farmers also understood that this risked undermining the very foundation of support for CAP in general. As Philippe Mangin describes it, "opened a debate on the legitimacy of state support." MacSharry struck at the core of their legitimating narrative. If popular support was to be maintained, CAP would need a new legitimating narrative that would serve to reestablish the link between farm supports, now in the form of direct payments, and the broader public interest. An early sign of that new strategy was rolled out in 1999. The idea would be to link farm supports to environmental protection.

In 1999, the EU implemented a second round of price cuts, called Agenda 2000, linked to an absolute limit in CAP expenditure in the EU budget. Like the prior MacSharry reform, income lost to lower prices was replaced—although, again, not completely—through increased direct payments to farmers. The price reductions targeted staple products: cereals, beef, dairy, and oilseeds. What was new in the Agenda 2000 reforms was an emphasis on environmental protection and rural land management. CAP supports were divided into two "pillars," with most conventional indirect (price) and direct supports falling into Pillar 1. Pillar 2 funding would encompass supports targeting rural development and the environment. This could include new investments in training programs to help farmers transition to other professions, rural village development programs to promote tourism, supports for farmers working in so-called disadvantaged areas, and supports for environmental protection programs. Initially, Pillar 2 funding was limited. But the 1999 reform included a provision, called "voluntary modulation," that allowed governments to transfer part of their Pillar 1 support to Pillar 2, often accompanied by matching member-state funds. The reform also allowed governments to withhold Pillar 1 funding from projects that did not meet strict environmental guidelines. Together, these provisions permitted national government to experiment with a new environmental orientation for their agricultural policies.

Critics warned that the provision for member-state cofinancing of Pillar 2 projects could be the beginning of a process of renationalizing agricultural support in Europe. Although such criticism was probably merited, Agenda 2000 was also the beginning of an experiment to see if the future of CAP could be secured to a new public logic of support. The idea was to test a new legitimating narrative, one in which farmers would receive direct payments from the government in return for undertaking what amounted to environmentally oriented land stewardship. If farm payments could be linked to a broader public interest in sustaining the rural countryside as a pastoral landscape, then direct payments to farmers could be tied to a sustained diffuse set of interests linked to the environment and regional development.

Immediately following the Agenda 2000 reforms, CAP faced two challenges that caused it to accelerate the reforms. The first challenge was the accession of ten new member states in 2004 that would place considerable pressure on CAP. Enlargement would increase the number of European farmers from 7 million to 11 million, and the land under cultivation from 130 million to 168 million hectares. For most major agricultural sectors, output was expected to increase from 10 percent to 20 percent.[25] As part of the accession agreement signed with the new member states, CAP payments would begin in 2004 at 25 percent of the final rate at which they would be distributed. Transfers would increase roughly 5 percent per year until they reached their full level in 2013. That still meant that the ten new states in 2005 would receive 18 percent of total CAP payments. (France, for comparison, received 22 percent of CAP outlays.) This growing bill would have to be fit in the limited CAP budget.

The second challenge facing CAP came from the ongoing Doha Round of World Trade Organization negotiations. For most of the postwar period, agriculture had been exempted from multilateral trade agreements. In 1993, signatories to GATT for the first time ratified the Uruguay Round Agreement on Agriculture (URAA) in which they agreed to reduce tariff and nontariff barriers significantly. Europe, which had committed to a 36 percent reduction over five years, was able to comply primarily thanks to the MacSharry reforms.[26] Signatories to the URAA also agreed to two further reforms that would have a major impact on European farm support policies. First, they agreed to negotiate reductions in export subsidies, which still played a significant role on the European Union's (EU) trade policy. By one estimate, Europe in 1996 accounted for 86 percent of all export subsidies in the world. Second, signatories agreed to negotiate reductions in the most distorting kinds of farm subsidies, with special attention given to price supports and output-based subsidies. These distorting policies—which in the arcane language of trade negotiation came to be known as "amber box" supports[27]— had long been core elements of the CAP, and still played an important role in the EU's overall subsidy regime. To have a chance of reaching a new agreement in the Doha Round, the EU had to figure out how to eliminate these supports. Progress in the Doha Round was particularly prized by Europe's manufacturers, who hoped that greater access to the EU market for especially Latin American agricultural producers could be exchanged for lower tariffs on manufactured goods from Europe into Latin America. Any reform effort was likely to look like a concession to manufacturing exporters at the cost of Europe's farmers.

From Farming to "Land Stewardship": The Move to Decoupled Direct Payments

In the shadow of the Doha trade round, the EU in 2003 launched another sweeping reform to the CAP. These so-called Luxembourg reforms began a process that would eventually lead to a full decoupling of farm payments from output. As under the MacSharry reforms, the new provisions granted farmers a direct payment based on historical production levels. Prices could then be allowed to float entirely freely. Unlike the MacSharry reforms, however, the Luxembourg reforms allowed farmers to grow whatever they wished. This decoupling of supports from decisions about output was seen as a way of introducing market efficiencies into agricultural production. The expectation was that farmers would take cues from the market, shifting crops to those that were more profitable or in greater demand. Most controversially, farmers could continue to receive subsidies without producing anything at all, so long as they maintained their land in a condition suitable for farming. The Luxembourg reforms applied to most products, with the exception of fruits, vegetables, and table potatoes. Decoupling of core products would begin in 2002 and be completed by 2007. Further reforms in 2004 extended decoupling to hops, cotton, tobacco, and olive oil. Sugar was to be the last crop for which supports would be decoupled, beginning in 2006. The goal was to have all agricultural supports unified into a single payment that was based on the historic support level per hectare based on 2000–2002 levels.

In practice, the transition proved far more complex. As with earlier CAP reforms, member states were given broad latitude to implement decoupling in ways that met local market (and political) priorities. In

Germany, for example, support payments to farmers would be based not on any individual farmer's former level of support, but instead on the average historical level of support for their entire region. In France, by contrast, payments would be calculated on a farm-by-farm basis. Further, individual countries were allowed to retain a limited number of output-based supports for specific crops that included beef, sheep, durum wheat, and cereals. After a brief early experiment with more extensive decoupling, France opted to return to the maximum level of output-based support that was allowed under the new reform. This included specific production premiums for the production of cereal (25 percent) and suckler cows (100 percent), veal slaughter (100 percent) and adult cow slaughter (40 percent), for ewe (100 percent), as well as specific supports to farmers in difficult regions. To a lesser extent, olive oil and tobacco and some specific seed premiums were kept linked to production as well. This meant that most farmers still received a combination of direct payments, including one calculated per hectare and based on historic support levels, and others based on current output. Farmers reported spending a full day each week filling out the required paperwork.

Even with these exceptions, however, the move to decoupled direct payments was expected to bring the EU into compliance with the expectations of the Doha Round of trade negotiations by eliminating its most distorting supports. It also helped to address growing criticisms that European export subsidies were hurting poor farmers in developing countries. One study found that sub-Saharan cotton growers, for example, had lost $305 million in revenue in 2001 due to low world prices caused by agricultural dumping. Sugar producers in Mozambique were found to have lost $38 million in potential sales in 2004 due to high tariffs in Europe, the United States, and Japan.[28] In 2004, CAP was spending 0.7 percent of its budget on stocking programs and 7.6 percent of its budget on export subsidies.[29] The elimination of these support programs would go a long way to addressing the perception that European farmers were profiting not just at the cost of European consumers and taxpayers, but at the even higher cost of poor African farmers.

The Luxembourg reforms also helped to solve the domestic fiscal problems facing the CAP. First, the reforms were tied to a cap on total CAP spending, with an agreement that the EAGGF budget would neither increase nor decrease until 2013. The savings would come from decreased export subsidies, as European agricultural prices fell, and lower storage fees based on new limits on stockpiling for products like rice and butter. The 2003 reforms also created a mechanism for funding CAP payments in the accession states. This was achieved by mandating the formerly voluntary practice of "modulation." For farmers receiving more than 5,000 euros per year in Pillar 1 supports, their level of support would be reduced by 3 percent in 2005, 4 percent in 2006, and 5 percent in each subsequent year. From this reduction, 80 percent would go to new Pillar 2 supports, tied to sustainability and rural development projects. The remaining 20 percent would fund the farm supports for the new member states.

In Brussels, however, the rationale for the Luxembourg reforms extended beyond Doha compliance or budget reform. Within the Directorate-General for Agriculture, the Luxembourg reforms represented a new way of thinking about European agriculture. As Pillar 2 supports increased, more and more of the CAP budget would be oriented toward maintaining the rural agricultural areas as sustainable economies. The goal, explained Hermanus Versteijlen of the European Commission, was to allow Europe to maintain a landscape of cultivated fields: "Farmers are no longer only in the business of food production; they are in the business of land stewardship. They don't know it yet, but they will have to accept it."[30] The gamble was that Europeans sufficiently prized cultivated landscapes that they would be willing to support rural farmers to preserve a pastoral countryside. By preserving traditional farming land, Europe would preserve areas that their populations prized as cultural legacies, but also as recreational and vacation destinations. As another EU official noted, the cost of the CAP, at about 400 euros per hectare per year, was significantly less than land conservancy groups charged for maintaining public preserves.[31]

The farm sector greeted decoupling, and the pastoral vision that accompanied it, with considerable apprehension. Farmers worried about a loss of social status. As one French agriculture official noted: "It is as if we are telling farmers: 'Whether you produce or do not produce doesn't matter. Here is your check.' This sounds like a denial of the contribution of agriculture to society."[32] Philippe Mangin, head of Coop de France, felt the reforms created an identity crisis for farmers: "Subsidies are not even linked to production. Farmers are losing the meaning of their job."[33] Even more, though, French farm representatives worried that it would undermine the basis for sustained political support for farmers. Said one representative: "Just imagine that prices increase through 2009. With the new CAP, farmers will benefit from direct payments *and* from price increases. Taxpayers will not understand that. One could thus question the legitimacy of CAP payments."[34]

Behind this skepticism was a perception that decoupling had been pushed onto the EU precisely to undermine political support for agricultural subsidies in general. The countries that advocated the reform most actively, especially Sweden and the United Kingdom, had long advocated cuts in CAP spending. Indeed the Swedish agriculture minister was reported to have made this case explicitly. These concerns led French agriculture officials and France's farm associations to drag their heels as much as possible in implementing the Luxembourg reforms. They were less worried about CAP funding being channeled through a new funding mechanism than they were that the Luxembourg reforms would undermine the consumer-producer link that had for so long sustained public support for CAP's large budget.

Regulatory Capture: Incomplete and Precarious

The case of European farm supports reveals that even one of the most apparently egregious examples of regulatory capture by industry is in fact a highly contingent and precarious affair, dependent on a legitimacy narrative linking farmers to broader societal goals. This narrative is in turn dependent on the broader institutional and economic context. Changing external conditions may threaten the plausibility of the legitimacy narrative and consequently imperil public support for farmers themselves. Initially European farmers had unparalleled success in translating their interests into public policy over the course of the postwar period. Through deals struck with national political parties and politicians in the immediate aftermath of World War II, they gained unprecedented leverage over agricultural support policy administered through the CAP. Memories of wartime and postwar scarcity made it easy for the agricultural sector to make a case for its claim on public funds and regulatory protections. Farmers made an essential contribution to society by providing a reliable and abundant food source for citizens in return for tariff barriers on imports, price fixing, and government buying of surpluses.

Yet changes in the international and domestic context rendered this narrative untenable. First, the programs of the CAP worked too well. In less than two decades, the nations of the EEC went from conditions of scarcity to conditions of overproduction. The costs of purchasing and stockpiling surplus produce rose to unsustainable levels. Second, the new ethos of environmentalism led to concerns about the effect of heavy fertilizer use on the European ecosystem. Third, the expansion of the EC and later the EU to include a number of less-developed nations in the 1980s and 1990s threatened to strain budgets further. And finally, the changing nature of global trade politics and international obligations made it difficult for the EU to retain tariff barriers to the agricultural produce of underdeveloped nations. Accordingly, EU administrators fashioned a new payment structure for farm subsidies that tied agricultural funding not to output, but to farmers' role as stewards of the environment. Since the late 1990s, European farmers have received the bulk of their support in the form of direct payments that compensate them not for producing, but for maintaining their land in a condition suitable for farming.

On the one hand, the story of European farmers in the postwar period is one of successful regulatory capture. Despite radical changes in the political and economic environment, the agricultural sector has tenaciously maintained its claim on public benefits, at the expense of the broader group of taxpayer-consumers. Yet theirs was at best a qualified and partial victory. The price fixing and import tariffs of the early decades of the CAP were sustainable only under the specific conditions of the immediate postwar period. Absent those conditions, farmers could no longer frame themselves as valued providers for the community, and demand the price supports that imperiled other national and regional objectives.

Though agriculturalists' share of the EU budget did not declined dramatically, farmers themselves experienced the changes as a threat. When CAP moved to direct payments under the MacSharry reforms, farmers rioted. When CAP decoupled payments from output with the Luxembourg reforms, farmers despaired. In part, these reforms changed the way that farmers thought about their role in society. Once productive contributors, they increasingly seemed to be welfare recipients. But this was not the main reason that farmers, and especially their national representatives, feared the move to decoupled direct payments. Rather, the shift in approach to farm supports undermined the narrative that had for so long given legitimacy both to the public benefits farmers received and to the policy influence they wielded. To justify the new system of direct payments, European officials attempted to draft a new legitimating narrative for European farmers. No longer viewed primarily as food producers, farmers were instead to be seen as maintainers of the traditional European cultivated landscape. Many farm representatives, however, viewed this new vision with deep skepticism. They doubted that a link to land stewardship would provide a sufficiently compelling new narrative to sustain political support for high levels of public funds that went to small farmers. They feared that the new approach was a Trojan horse by which public support for farm subsidies might be gradually eroded, and they worked hard to maintain at least some level of output-based subsidies for most crops. The case of European farm subsidies shows that regulatory capture exists. Yet even this most egregious of cases reveals, on closer examination, how contingent, partial, and insecure the power of concentrated groups may be.

CHAPTER 7

The Limits of Lobbying

T HE CASE of pharmaceutical regulation has all the signs of egregious industry capture. First, the sector clearly attempts to exert policy influence. Through generous contributions to electoral campaigns, political action committees, and issue advertisements, pharmaceutical lobbying added up to what one observer of the U.S. industry called "one of Washington's most elaborate advocacy strategies."[1] Second, these regulatory policies do not slip through legislatures unnoticed. Rather, the issues of drug pricing and development have high public salience. Press coverage of legislation affecting the pharmaceutical companies is extensive and often emotionally charged. Third, the pharmaceutical sector cannot plead indigence in its campaigns for favorable policies. High prices drive record profitability for the sector. In the U.S. case, pharmaceuticals had by the 1990s and 2000s become one of the most profitable sectors in the economy. In 2006, pharmaceutical firms enjoyed an average return on revenue of 19.6 percent, besting the Fortune 500 average (6.3 percent) by more than a factor of three.[2] It seems hard to avoid the conclusion that the pharmaceutical sector has invested in a campaign of regulatory influence and reaps the benefits of that investment at the cost of consumers.

Events during the presidency of George Bush seemed to confirm this assessment. Take, for example, the Medicare Prescription Drug Improvement and Modernization Act (MMA), which the U.S. Congress passed in 2003 to reduce drug costs for senior citizens. In negotiations for the bill, several proposals to curb the drug companies' freedom to set prices failed, and savings for the consumer were funded instead by government subsidies. A House-Senate committee suppressed a House of Representatives version of the bill that aimed to put downward pressure on U.S. prices by legalizing drug reimportation from other advanced industrialized countries where the same branded drugs cost a half to a third less.[3] The MMA also blocked the Medicare administration from negotiating drug prices directly with drug manufacturers—a practice that advocates believed resulted in a significant discount over the prices negotiated by private insurers, and which served as the baseline for Medicare drug pricing.[4] A subsequent 2007 Senate bill that would have legalized such direct price negotiations was also blocked.[5] Viewed as a self-contained incident, the 2003 legislation appears as an unmitigated defeat for diffuse consumer interests.

Yet an exclusive focus on pricing obscures the full scope of prescription drug policy and raises a risk of misinterpreting outcomes in pharmaceutical interest group conflicts. Struggles over the regulatory treatment of drugs have tended to be fought along two policy axes, not just one: consumers' concerns include quality *and* price. The first axis, spurred by a series of drug-related tragedies, has focused on drug quality, including safety, efficacy, and testing. The second axis of regulation has focused on pharmaceutical pricing, and was stimulated, as in the 2003 MMA, by the rapidly increasing costs of drugs and a growing concern about their share in national health budgets. Were the pharmaceutical industry to achieve rampant industry capture, as a strict application of the logic of collective action would predict, it would enjoy not just unrestricted drug pricing but also an unlimited freedom to develop new products. Yet, as this chapter shows, a comparative study of national price and quality regulation in four countries—the United States, Britain, France, and Germany—makes clear that nowhere has the pharmaceutical industry successfully blocked restrictions on quality *and* price.

In their respective national contexts, drug companies have been able to secure either freedom to set prices or a low threshold on drug safety and efficacy, or a limited degree of both. In the United States, the sector enjoys nearly unrestricted pricing, but must submit to an onerous and expensive regulatory regime in developing new products. In France, by contrast, the sector has a relatively high degree of freedom to develop new drugs, but must accept centrally set prices. Germany and the United Kingdom occupy middle positions on both continuums.

These findings raise questions about the constraints on regulatory capture by industry. If the U.S. pharmaceutical sector was able to restrict measures to impose lower prices, why was it not more successful in limiting the cost of the regulatory burden it faces? Conversely, why did pharmaceutical sectors in other countries fail to achieve higher prices, while successfully blocking the imposition of strict regulations on drug development? It is these questions that this chapter attempts to address.

Much of the answer lies in the policy narrative the industry has adopted in each country. As with other areas of diffuse material interest representation we have seen, the broad consumers' interest in drug policy is articulated either in terms of access or in terms of protection: low drug prices mean easy access for patients of limited means, while high regulatory hurdles force pharmaceutical producers to maintain rigorous product safety and efficacy regimes that protect patients from dangerous or ineffective drugs. France and the United States came to represent the two extremes of this spectrum. In the United States, where quality regulation preceded price regulation, the emphasis of drug policy was on a narrative of protection: the need to protect against unsafe drugs was understood as greater than the imperative to make drugs financially accessible. Further strengthening the U.S. pharmaceutical lobby's case against price restraints was the industry's success in associating high prices with increased investment in research and development (R&D), and hence with the discovery of new products for tomorrow's patients. In organizational terms, the diffuse material interests of today's consumers lose to the *even more* diffuse material interests of future drug consumers. In France, where regulation of price preceded the regulation of quality, the emphasis of drug policy was on a narrative of access for current patients.

Britain and Germany represent fascinating intermediate cases. Whereas the French and U.S. regulations were imposed on industry with little consultation, both the British and German regulations took the form of a negotiated outcome in which the dual goals of protection and access were reconciled in a complex set of negotiated outcomes. In Germany, new regulations emerged in the context of negotiations between the pharmaceutical sector and associations of doctors and medical insurers. In the United Kingdom, with its single-payer health system, new regulations emerged in the context of negotiations between the pharmaceutical sector and the government's National Health Services. The following sections describe the details of these early political contests that generated narratives of pharmaceutical access and protection that continued to persist in drug regulation in these countries through the turn of the millennium.

For each case, the chapter traces the broad trajectory of price and quality regulation governing the pharmaceutical sector during the formative period from the early 1960s to the mid-1990s. It explores the politics and institutional constraints that led some countries to emphasize short-term price restraints and others to favor high quality and high price. These case histories evoke the extent to which industry opportunities for capturing national regulatory policy are closely tied to national institutional legacies of diffuse interest representation. Successful policy manipulation by concentrated economic interests requires careful attention to the ways in which advocated policies fit with how diffuse interests have emerged and been represented in society. Narrow economic interests succeed not by ignoring diffuse material interests, but by pursuing their own narrow goals in ways that were consistent with those interests. Overall, the comparative development of pharmaceutical policy underlines the fact that even one of the most infamous cases of alleged industry capture is in fact far more contingent than the logic of collective action would predict.

Price versus Quality: The History of French and U.S. Drug Regulation

French and U.S. drug regulation represent opposite strategies in diffuse interest representation. In France, regulation focused first and foremost on price restraint. The French state stepped in to set drug prices beginning in 1948; drug safety and efficacy requirements were put in place first in 1976, and have remained relatively weak by international standards. The focus on pricing over quality was due in part to the role of the state as a single payer, but also due to the influence and autonomy of France's pharmacists, who were reluctant to give up their historic role in regulating the quality of drugs. In the United States, we observe exactly the opposite timing and emphasis of regulation. The turning point for drug safety and efficacy regulation came with the Kefauver-Harris amendment to the Food, Drug, and Cosmetic Act in 1962. These set an extremely high burden of safety and efficacy that was repeatedly criticized by industry for impeding new drug development. The first and only meaningful price regulation in the United States came with the 1990 Medicaid Prudent Pharmaceutical Purchasing Act (Prior Act) that set Medicaid drug pricing at 5 percent below the average discount accorded to private insurers.[6] From these two different regulatory histories emerged very different patterns of industry influence that persist today: U.S. pharmaceutical firms enjoy pricing freedom but face stringent quality regulation; French pharmaceutical firms enjoy broad freedom over drug quality but face stringent price regulation. In each country, pharmaceutical firms have been accused of exerting undue influence on regulators: on pricing in the United States, and on quality in France. A review of the emergence of drug regulation in these two countries reveals that these different emphases are less the result of regulatory capture, and more the outcome of a legitimate policy process in which policymakers felt they were defending the genuine interests of patients.

Quality Emphasis of the United States

Critical steps in U.S. drug safety regulation were driven by product tragedies. The history of the Food and Drug Administration (FDA) began in 1906 with the passage of the Pure Food and Drug Act in response to the advocacy of the U.S. Department of Agriculture's chief chemist, Harvey Washington Wiley, and muckraking journalists like Upton Sinclair, whose fictional account of the Chicago meatpacking industry in *The Jungle* (1906) raised awareness of dangerous and unsanitary conditions. Wiley's Bureau of Chemistry was initially charged with preventing the interstate transport of unsafe, adulterated, or fraudulent products, though the courts interpreted the act's powers narrowly until the newly founded FDA took over its responsibilities in 1927. The new bureau's primary effort was to impose accurate and standardized drug labeling. The FDA gained significant regulatory control over drugs only in 1938 following the death of 107 people from consuming an elixir of sulphanilamide. The 1938 Drug Act imposed drug labeling standards, or alternatively permitted drug companies to evade the labeling standards if they sold their drugs by prescription only. Under these early regulations, producers were required to register new drugs with the FDA, after which the FDA had ninety days in which to raise objections to commercializing the drug. In the absence of FDA notification, the company could proceed with marketing the drug. The process of drug testing was largely unregulated.[7]

The strict government oversight of pharmaceutical safety and efficacy that would eventually characterize the U.S. sector began with the 1962 Kefauver-Harris amendments. As with earlier reforms, these followed on the heels of a tragedy, in this case the revelation of birth defects caused by thalidomide, sometimes prescribed as a sedative or antinausea drug to pregnant women. The FDA had warned against this drug, but was at the time unable to block it for purposes of experimentation—a loophole employed by many physicians to administer drugs without formal approval. However if the thalidomide tragedy precipitated the reform, the strength of the regulatory response must be understood as a backlash against a pharmaceutical sector that was increasingly perceived as abusively monopolistic.

The 1950s had been a decade of consolidation for the U.S. pharmaceutical sector. Amendments to the Drug Act in 1951 that instituted a mandatory prescription-only class of drugs unexpectedly set the stage for an extraordinary consolidation of power by pharmaceutical manufacturers in the United States that allowed them to dominate the sector.[8]

The primary focus of this effort was on eliminating the generic drug industry, which amounted to nearly one-third of the drug market in 1950. The new National Pharmaceutical Council (NPC), created in 1954 by the large pharmaceutical manufacturers, proved so successful that generic sales fell to less than 5 percent by 1959. The NPC's strategy involved co-opting pharmaceutical service providers, namely drugstores and doctors. Drugstores in the United States, having received a boost during Prohibition thanks to their monopoly on the legal sale of alcohol and to the popularity of the soda fountain, had by the early 1950s become large and powerful retail chains.[9] This consolidation and the lively competition it generated worked to depress drug prices negotiated with pharmaceutical producers. Drug chains also increasingly favored generic drug producers for the price savings they offered. To undercut the power of the pharmacy, the NPC managed through intensive state-level lobbying to block drugstores in most states from advertising prices for prescription drugs. In many states a standard markup was provided for drugstores, typically 33 percent of the wholesale price, which helped to reduce competition over drug prices.[10] Finally, and critically, the NPC succeeded in making it illegal for pharmacies to substitute generic drugs for branded prescriptions. They achieved this by petitioning individual states' Boards of Pharmacy to change the legal definition of drug substitution.[11]

During the same period, the NPC launched a similarly effective campaign to promote branded drugs in the medical profession. In what appears to have been a quid pro quo agreement, the American Medical Association (AMA) in 1958 shifted its support away from generic drugs and toward branded drugs in exchange for greater drug advertising revenues in its medical journals.[12] The AMA-administered pharmacopoeia *Useful Drugs*, in which drugs were evaluated and categorized by generic name, was superseded by a new *Physician's Desk Reference (PDR)*. The PDR was compiled by brand name from manufacturer data and distributed by the newly created Pharmaceutical Manufacturers Association (Pharma), created in 1958. The AMA also began actively encouraging physicians to prescribe branded rather than generic drugs. When the drug industry came under increased government scrutiny in the 1960s, the AMA regularly argued *against* requiring a higher standard for drug efficacy. As Paul Hirsch has written, "it is clear that the medical profession was effectively co-opted by the drug industry."[13]

But if doctors had been paid for, legislators had not. In 1960, Senator Estes Kefauver (D-Tennessee) charged the pharmaceutical industry with monopolistic exploitation of consumers, and by that time the accusation carried broad popular resonance.[14] The resulting 1962 amendments to the Food and Drug Act required a positive approval from the FDA for a new drug to be marketed, and called on the FDA to establish good manufacturing practices.[15] They also required a preliminary FDA approval before undertaking clinical testing.[16] These new procedures set high standards not only for drug safety but also for efficacy—the extent to which a new drug improved on existing drugs. The Kefauver-Harris legislation fundamentally changed the U.S. pharmaceutical industry. The cost of creating a new chemical entity (NCE) rose by a factor of two over the decade following its enactment.[17] Development times grew from three to four years on average for each NCE before 1962, to seven to ten years after that date.[18] Moreover, a lag in U.S. pharmaceutical performance in the 1970s was seen as evidence that the more stringent FDA approval process called for in the 1962 amendments had hurt innovation in pharmaceuticals. Critics argued that the increased cost of innovation had pushed companies to lower their investment levels.[19] Pharmaceutical manufacturers aggressively lobbied their congressional representatives to intervene with the FDA on their behalf. In the years 1969 and 1970 alone, congressional hearings were held on thirty-eight separate FDA decisions that blocked the marketing of specific drugs.[20] Yet, surprisingly for a sector that is commonly accused of influencing regulatory outcomes, none of these efforts succeeded. The FDA was, and would remain, largely insulated from industry pressure to lower standards of safety and efficacy.

If high standards were perceived by pharmaceutical producers as a burden, they nonetheless provided an indirect benefit. That is because the case for U.S. drug pricing policy was built largely on this high burden of drug testing and safety measures. In a strategy that emerged in the 1980s, the U.S. pharmaceutical sector developed a legitimating narrative that justified current high prices as a necessary measure to fund research for new products for the future. The result was a set of policies that emphasized new drug development and protection from unsafe drugs over broad access to existing products at affordable prices. In organizational terms, the diffuse material interests of today's consumers lose to the *even more* diffuse material interests of future drug consumers.

The argument had two parts. The first part linked pricing to new drug development. This logic came to be broadly accepted by policy-makers, health researchers, and the medical profession. As one doctor writes of proposals to legalize reimportation as a means to restrain drug prices: "[A] more aggressive stance toward controlling today's drug prices must be considered in light of the effect of lower prices on the flow of new drugs that will be available to the next generation of consumer."[21] Critics of this claim have pointed out that U.S. pharmaceutical firms spend more on advertising than they do on R&D. But this obscures the novelty of the claim. The pharmaceutical sector may be the only major product sector that justifies high current prices in order to finance *future* product research. Their point is that pharmaceutical research provides a public good, and that other countries are free-riding on that public good by artificially lowering the prices of drugs in their countries. As John Calfee of the American Enterprise Institute explains: "[European] price controls prevent innovative pharmaceutical firms from reaping free-market rewards anywhere but in the United States."[22] Drug pricing was not a U.S. problem, in other words, but a European (and Canadian) problem.

The second part of the case for U.S. drug pricing policy related to the burden of drug testing and safety measures. On the one hand, reimports from other countries were generally objected to because of concerns about the safety of those drugs. On the other hand, higher prices were justified in part because of the high regulatory burden (i.e., stringent quality standards) imposed by the U.S. drug regulatory regime. As drug sector analyst Jacob Arfwedson has written: "New drugs cost, on average, $400–$800 million to develop. Their prices need to reflect that huge investment."[23] Government policies that enabled higher drug prices were not primarily a consequence of drug lobby influence over public policy, although they clearly had a keen interest in drug pricing policies. More important, it was a central element of the public policy agreement that was struck in the context of the Kefauver-Harris amendments: drug companies would be subject to rigorous standards throughout the life of a product, and in exchange higher prices would be permitted in order to support the necessary research and testing costs.

By the turn of the century, strict FDA oversight had increasingly come to be seen as an important comparative advantage for U.S. drug manufacturers. The standard of safety and efficacy set by the FDA remained unusually high by international standards. This meant that drugs originating in the U.S. market would meet a particularly high standard of safety and efficacy and should therefore be strong competitors for foreign sales. It also meant that many foreign drugs of questionable effectiveness were kept out of the U.S. market. Japan's top-selling drug in 1986, for example, an anticancer agent called Krestin, was never submitted for U.S. approval, in the understanding that it would not be likely to pass the FDA review.[24] Oddly, the high quality standards of the United States did not promote greater exports. Rather, they had the unexpected effect of encouraging U.S. drug exporters to move production overseas. Under the strict U.S. standards, drugs could not be exported if they had not previously received FDA approval, even if they *would* be acceptable in the receiving country. U.S. companies thus established foreign subsidiaries, operating under foreign safety and efficacy rules, to produce products for foreign consumption. In this way, the high safety and efficacy requirements of the United States exerted a strong pressure for globalization of drug development and manufacturing, and a corresponding reduction in the export of drugs produced in the United States. The U.S. prohibition against exporting unlicensed drugs was rescinded in the 1986 Drug Export Amendment Act, but by that time the strategy of overseas production by U.S. firms had been firmly established.[25] The phenomenon of overseas production was just one way in which the choice of policy narrative in national pharmaceutical policy had wide-ranging implications for the structure of the industry.

Price Emphasis of France

In France, an early decision to emphasize access to affordable drugs over protection from unsafe or ineffective ones had equally wide-ranging and lasting effects on the nation's pharmaceutical landscape. Because the French government pays an estimated 80 percent of that country's national drug bill, regulatory intervention on drug pricing has been correspondingly intensive, with the medical authorities acting aggressively to keep drug prices low. This strict price setting has been a decisive factor influencing the product market strategies of French producers, who have focused on low-cost, low-innovation products coupled with strong promotional campaigns to increase domestic demand. By contrast, the pharmaceutical industry has enjoyed far greater autonomy to police the quality of the drugs it produces. Hence government regulation of drug safety and efficacy has tended to be more lenient than in other advanced industrialized economies.

The French regulatory approach to the pharmaceutical industry is unusual in that it emerged directly from the regulation of apothecaries.[26] Drug safety and efficacy evaluations were, until the 1990s, carried out by industry experts paid for by pharmaceutical companies and employing data from the applying firm. Patricia Danzon estimated that only half of all drugs sold in France in the 1990s would meet U.S. Food and Drug Administration efficacy requirements.[27] Hence, while French pharmaceutical producers have enjoyed a high level of sales, the cost of this success has been borne directly by the French government, despite low drug prices, in the form of an unusually high domestic drug bill.

Price fixing has been a revered tradition in French product markets, dating back at least to the ordinances of 1945 (45-1483, 45-1484) that granted the government the right to intervene to set prices for any kind of product. Price setting in the pharmaceutical industry began in 1948 and can be usefully separated into four periods. Between 1948 and 1968, drug prices were set by the state based on a pricing framework (*cadre de prix*) calculated on a cost-plus basis from a combination of production costs and a predetermined margin of profit.[28] In 1968, drug pricing fell under the dual control of the old pricing administration and the new Commission de remboursement de la sécurité sociale (the Coudrier Commission), created in 1967. While drug prices were still set by the state pricing administration, the new social security commission worked with them to determine reimbursement levels for prescription drugs, and to decide which drugs should be included on the reimbursement list.[29] In 1980, drug prices for prescription drugs were "liberalized." This meant in practice that drug prices would be determined entirely by reimbursement levels set by the social security code. In order to decide on appropriate reimbursement levels, a new Commission de transparence, created in 1980, evaluated price applications from drug producers. The commission assessed production costs and compared applicant drugs with others on the market.[30] Under this system, a separate price was set by the government for each individual drug. When in 1986 the Plan Seguin attempted to reduce the financial burden of health care, its cost-cutting efforts included a reduction in state reimbursement for drugs and a cap on price increases for existing drugs to about 1 percent per year.

Concerned that this approach reduced industry incentives to innovate, and in particular that it was leading French drug companies to create false innovations in order to elude the cap on price increases for existing drugs, France imposed in 1994 a pricing system based on a so-called global envelope (*envelope globale*). The idea, first proposed in 1991, allowed the state to negotiate with each pharmaceutical producer an upper and lower level for its expected total drug sales for the year. Any sales exceeding the target level would be offset by a lower unit price on drugs so that the overall cost to the government would remain the same. The idea was to give producers the freedom to set prices as they wished among their portfolio of products. So as not to impede major innovations, breakthrough drugs were treated separately under the old price-setting scheme.[31] By mid-1995, 96 conventions had been signed under the *envelope globale* system, covering 81 percent of drug sales.[32] Failure by the industry to invest more research and development funds in new drug innovation led to a further reform, in 2003, that fully liberalized prices for drugs considered to be innovative by a commission of the ministries of health and social security.[33]

Although France's primary effort at reducing medical spending was focused on price control, it also attempted to create incentives on the demand side in order to keep down spending. Beginning in 1980, drugs were reimbursed under social security at different levels depending on effectiveness and need. Reimbursement was set at 100 percent for cases of severe sickness, 65 percent for regular drugs, and 35 percent for drugs with modest therapeutic value.[34] Most patients, however, had private insurance plans that covered the nonreimbursed cost of drugs. Only 10 percent of French patients were not covered in this way.[35] Later efforts focused on restraining doctor prescription levels. A 1990 *controle medicale* set nonbinding, indicative levels for doctors in order to keep them from overprescribing.[36] In 1994, a new set of negotiated good medical practice guidelines attempted to standardize prescription activities of doctors.[37] France also acted to reduce the level of drug advertising. As in the other European countries, advertising to the public for drugs covered by social security was prohibited in France.[38] Nearly 80 percent of promotional spending by French firms therefore focused on informational visits to medical practitioners.[39] As part of the 1994 framework agreement that implemented the global envelope pricing system, the top association of the drug industry, the Syndicat national de l'industrie pharmaceutique (SNIP), agreed to voluntary restraints on advertising spending in exchange for more liberal prices for innovative products.[40] French firms nonetheless still spend almost 13 percent of revenue on advertising and marketing, compared to only about 7 percent on research and development.[41]

Peculiarities of the French pricing scheme pushed companies to evade the effects of regulation. Three side effects were particularly formative for the drug industry. First, research costs under the cost-plus price setting scheme were fixed at 7 percent, so that in effect companies that did less research enjoyed higher profits. Second, because the prices of existing products were not systematically increased to adjust for inflation, producers commonly reintroduced existing drugs under new names in order to receive a higher price. Useful inexpensive drugs disappeared from the market and were replaced by a large number of copy drugs.[42] As Alan Afuad writes, "Price controls contribute to an increase in drug expenditure . . . because research and development is re-oriented towards developing non-innovative new products with contemporary price tags to replace older drugs with low controlled prices."[43] Third, because prices were calculated based on production costs, many French firms moved component production into their own subsidiary companies located in foreign countries. Through exclusive contracting with these subsidiaries, the firms could artificially elevate the prices of imported chemical components while extracting higher profits from their foreign firms.[44]

If French pharmaceutical producers had little success in sustaining high prices for their drugs, they were far more influential in fending off intrusive government regulation of product quality. Drug quality regulation in France began under the Vichy government in 1942 with the creation of the Service central de la pharmacie. Its primary emphasis was not on drug safety but instead on ensuring the quality of drug production, much of which occurred at individual pharmacies.[45] Under this system, drug producers applied for a visa that was granted based on the recommendation of experts from the industry. The visa required that any drug be both useful and new.[46] This novelty requirement permitted the visa to function as a kind of patent system before patents were applied to drugs, and newly registered drugs were granted a six-year window of monopoly sales. In 1959, a special patent was introduced for medicines and the novelty requirement was removed from the visa application process.[47] The visa system also required a manufacturing authorization (*autorization de débit*) from the French pharmaceutical inspectorate. This requirement effectively blocked the import of finished drugs into France.[48]

Under the influence of the European Economic Community (EEC) Pharmaceutical Directive of 1965, France enacted the 1967 ordinance that replaced the visa system with a new marketing authorization (*autorization de mise sur le marché,* or AMM) and drug test protocols. The system was overseen by the Commission on Marketing Authorizations (Commission d'autorisation de mise sur le marché des medicaments), which had a staff of only 28. These were primarily doctors, but also included two representatives from industry and one consumer representative. As under the visa system, industry experts played a central role in the approval process. Outside experts were paid by the company requesting an evaluation, and all information about the drug came from the applicant company itself.[49] The result was a system in which drug producers had a strong voice in decisions about product quality. In 1977, the Commission on Marketing Authorizations was replaced by the Direction de la pharmacie et du medicament (DPHM) within the Health Ministry.[50] This new centralized body was responsible for all aspects of drug regulation, but again had a staff of only thirty. As before, drug applications were assessed out-of-house by experts paid by the applying firm. In January 1993, the DPHM was restructured again and renamed the Agence français du medicament (AFM). The new agency was given responsibility for setting safety standards, for setting manufacturing policy, for deciding on product information and risk, and for assisting industry to further research and innovation. Unlike the previous DPHM, the AFM had its own internal experts that evaluated industry applications for marketing authorization. The AFM set labeling and dosage indications for new drugs. The AFM also determined whether a drug would be sold under prescription or over the counter. Modeled in part on the U.S. Food and Drug Administration, the AFM was intended to enjoy a high level of insulation from industry interference. In fact, industry still participated on important commissions, and the founding legislation included a loop-hole provision allowing "emergency procedures" in case of "serious menace to the public health."[51] In 1999, the AFM was once again restructured as the new Agence française de sécurite sanitaire des produits de santé (AFSSAPS).

This rapid succession of drug approval agencies in France was in part a response to a persistent perception that drug approval decisions were being influenced by the pharmaceutical industry. But, as with allegations of regulatory capture in the United States, the reality was more prosaic. French policy from the 1970s offered French pharmaceutical firms greater input into quality and safety decisions based on their claims to expertise in the field. Tacitly, it was understood that in exchange for far more rigorous state controls on price, industry had earned a place at the table in the drug approvals process. U.S. pharmaceutical politics conceded price regulation in favor of high standards of efficacy; French pharmaceutical politics led to exactly the reverse outcome.

Industry-State Alliances in Pharmaceutical Regulation: The British and German Cases

Britain and Germany offer examples of outcomes that managed to combine concerns about product quality and product pricing in ways that seemed to achieve both goals, at least to a degree. These solutions were negotiated over time, and tended to be administratively complex. But they offered more nuanced approaches to drug regulation and reimbursement that helped both countries to control their national pharmaceutical bill while also supporting innovative pharmaceutical sectors.

Germany's neocorporatist approach to economic governance led to policy solutions in which drug producers confronted the interests of two intermediate groups: doctors, who were seen to represent the interests of the patient, and the private health insurance funds, which became increasingly concerned about the bill for drug reimbursements. The result was a set of policy reforms in which prerogatives for the pharmaceutical industry were mainly justified in terms of their benefits as perceived by the medical profession and by the health insurance funds. Influence exerted by the pharmaceutical lobby was tightly constrained by a need to reinforce the more diffuse interests—for lower cost and effective drugs—represented by these groups. Within these limitations, however, drug companies were able to achieve important lobbying victories.

In Britain, pharmaceutical firms negotiated directly with the National Health Services. These negotiations resulted in agreements in which firms were allowed to sustain high profits in return for meeting government targets for both R&D intensity and restraint of the national drug bill. For both countries, these approaches suggest the potential social and private benefits of an industry-state coalitional approach to economic regulation.

Negotiated Outcomes in Germany

Early drug regulation in Germany granted pharmaceutical producers broad leeway in setting standards of drug quality. Regulatory intervention began with 1961 legislation. This was revised in 1964 in response to the Contergan (thalidomide) tragedies, which were most extensive in Germany where the drug was first patented. Remarkably, the thalidomide tragedies had little immediate impact. The first Drug Law (Arzneimittelgesetz, or AMG) of 1961 required only that all drugs in circulation be registered. The 1964 revision left testing unstandardized, and failed to require approval prior to prescribing. In a policy process in which doctors, industry, and the national health ministry dominated, patients themselves had virtually no direct voice.[52] Meaningful oversight of drug testing had to wait until 1976, when a revision of the AMG by the ruling Social Democratic Party–Liberal Democratic Party coalition imposed a system of mandatory certification for all drugs.[53] New drugs had to be certified by the Federal Health Office (Bundesgesundheitsamt, BGA) in Berlin, not merely registered as under the previous law. The new AMG also called for mandatory labeling of drugs, including instructions for use and side effects, restrictions on drug advertising, and mandatory patient consent for all clinical drug tests. Furthermore, section 84 of the 1976 AMG imposed a strict standard of product liability on drug companies, and required that they purchase liability insurance from a private insurer of their choice under a mandatory new pricing and risk-pooling system called PharmaPool.[54] This was the first instance in which strict product liability was applied to any product market in Germany.

The new AMG, which remained the foundation of drug safety in Germany, represented a clear victory for the Social Democratic Party (SPD), which favored a regulatory strategy based on government certification, and a failure for the pharmaceutical lobby, the Bundesverband der Pharmaceutischen Industrie (BPI). Both the Christian Democratic Union (CDU) and Germany's foremost employers' association (BDA) had sided with the BPI in favoring industry self-regulation. Rather than mandatory government certification, they had proposed a collaboration between drug manufacturers and the medical profession to establish a system of drug labeling that would help to increase market transparency. The SPD position also did not reflect the view of trade unions. The foremost German trade union association, Deutscher Gewerkschaftsbund (DGB), favored collaborative negotiations among drug companies, doctors, and insurers to evaluate not just the quality and efficacy of drugs, but also their price-performance, as well as to determine the kinds of information that should be included on drug packaging.[55]

Yet within the context of a government-regulated drug market, the details of how drug safety regulation would be implemented did reflect important industry priorities. First, as the registration requirement did not have to be met for all drugs until 1990, the cost of transition was spread over a period of ten years. Second, product liability damages were limited to 500,000 German marks (DM) for single cases and to a total of 200 million DM for total damages resulting from a single drug.[56] The cap on individual and firm liability meant that no single drug could put a large pharmaceutical firm out of business. Third, Germany resisted European efforts to create a formal system for reporting the harm caused by drugs.[57] The result was a strong mechanism for enforcing drug quality that nonetheless responded to core industry demands. As in the United States, Germany's more highly innovative pharmaceutical firms over time came to view the 1976 AMG, with its stricter policing of safety and efficacy, as a means to improve the marketability of their drugs abroad.[58]

At the same time as it was drafting the AMG, the German government was also attempting to restrain the cost of pharmaceuticals, but with little success. Germany's 1977 Federal Law on Cost Containment established a Concerted Action Committee to set spending ceilings for drugs paid for by the Sickness Funds (Kassen). It formed a Transparency Commission of industry, Sickness Funds, and health professional representatives, to publish "transparency lists" comparing drugs based on safety, efficacy, and treatment cost. These would be used as the basis for creating "negative lists" of drugs to be excluded from insurance reimbursement. Until the late 1980s, however, Germany's pharmaceutical industry had been highly successful at resisting price regulation. Under the 1976 AMG, questions of efficacy fell exclusively to the Health Department (Bundesgesundheitsamt). Industry used this provision to contest many of the criteria employed by the Transparency Commission to exempt drugs from insurance coverage. In 1985, the Supreme Court found in the industry's favor, arguing that a published transparency list infringed on the right of entrepreneurial activity, and that negative lists were illegal under current law. Only an amendment to the AMG the following year legalized the use of negative lists for reimbursement decisions.[59]

This reform led the way for the Health Care Reform Act of 1988, which deployed several parallel strategies for tackling the challenge of Germany's rising drug bill. The most dramatic reform was the introduction of reference pricing (*Festbeträge*) for therapeutic categories of drugs. Whereas other countries had experimented with reference pricing for chemically identical drugs, the German approach set a single level of reimbursement for all drugs that fell within pools defined in terms of specific common therapeutic targets. Producers were not formally bound by these price levels, but in practice manufacturers rarely exceeded them in expectation that consumers would be unwilling to pay the added cost. For drug innovators, this upward cap was a distinct disadvantage, and many simply stopped pursuing innovations within the therapeutic categories covered by reference pricing.[60] Below the reference price, pharmaceutical companies had little incentive to reduce their prices. This abetted an oligopolistic pricing environment in Germany that discouraged competition on price below the reference price. By 1993, under resistance from innovative export-oriented producers, reference pricing had been extended to only 30 percent of reimbursed drugs. To extend reference pricing further, the government froze prices on all drugs not covered by reference pricing at 5 percent below 1992 levels, then offered to extend reference pricing at a favorable price level to new therapeutic categories. To placate the innovative pharmaceutical firms, new on-patent medicines were exempted entirely from the reference pricing scheme in 1996. By 2000, reference pricing covered about half of drug expenditures.[61]

In addition to reference pricing, three other regulatory mechanisms were designed to hold down demand for drugs. The first was a negative or "black" list, including drugs thought to be of "questionable therapeutic value" that would therefore not be eligible from reimbursement by the Kassen. This list was drawn up and reviewed by the Ministry of Labor.[62] The blacklist initially covered about 20 percent of the drug market—leaving 13,000 drugs still eligible for reimbursement.[63] For the pharmaceutical industry this blacklist had the effect of concentrating competition in core therapeutic categories that had in any case been the focus of traditional German export success. A second element of the 1988 reform imposed volume controls on individual physicians based on recommended drug budgets for different categories of medical practice. This system was monitored by the professional association of physicians, and doctors who exceeded their recommended levels faced a professional audit from this group.[64] Finally, Germany introduced in 1994 a drug copayment fee intended to make patients more conscious of the costs of drugs they consumed. This move was strongly opposed by pharmacists, who experienced a 10 percent drop in profit when the copayment system was put in place.[65]

These cost containment efforts had been designed in close consultation with the pharmaceutical sector, and embodied important concessions to industry. They also eventually drove a wedge between Germany's highly innovative and less innovative firms. For sellers whose products were largely commodities, reference prices discouraged the entrance of generic competitors. This effect was reinforced by a 1989 law requiring that doctors specify whether or not a druggist can substitute a cheaper generic replacement for a prescribed name-brand product.[66] Reference pricing also helped to stem external competition, especially from inexpensive French drugs.[67] The remainder of the policies were targeted to benefit Germany's highly innovative firms. These firms supported the blacklist strategy, which they saw as weeding out the more frivolous kinds of drugs, even if they could pass regulatory safety and efficacy requirements. They also favored the system of volume controls on individual physicians on the grounds that decisions made by doctors were most likely to result in decisions that reflected the real qualities of drugs.

In 1993, Germany's innovative export-oriented drug companies broke away from the traditional top pharmaceutical association (Bundesverband der Pharmaceutischen Industrie, BPI) to form their own association, the Verband Forschender Arzneimittelherrsteller (VFA).[68] The result was a two-track market for drugs in Germany, with price protection for non-innovative products, and a strong quality emphasis reinforced by doctor-driven cost containment for innovative products.

Negotiated Outcomes in Britain

The most elaborate arrangements for pharmaceutical price and quality negotiations emerged in the immediate postwar period in Britain. As in France, the British National Health Service financed 90 percent of all drugs purchased. Its monopsony position gave it the incentive and purchasing power to set drug prices at any level. Yet what developed was something more interesting than mere price setting of the sort that took hold in France. Confronted with a dual concern over drug quality and drug price, British regulators pursued a strategy of negotiating with individual pharmaceutical manufacturers to form agreements in which the trade-off between quality and price was explicitly addressed and managed. Beginning in 1958, British pharmaceutical manufacturers negotiated directly with the government to set the sales price of drugs. But the British system did not focus either on therapeutic categories, as in Germany, or on individual product prices, as in France, but on firm-level profitability. Britain became the only country in Europe to set price controls based on the profits of pharmaceutical firms.[69] This approach required an extremely high level of government oversight and intensive government intervention in areas of basic producer strategy—features that might seem out of place in one of the world's most liberal market economies. But it offered the advantage of permitting British firms to pursue more risky products that could also be more lucrative.[70]

The history of postwar British pharmaceutical regulation can usefully be divided into two periods. From 1958 to 1978, the pharmaceutical industry negotiated with the government over voluntary price restraints. Until 1960, negotiations were carried out by the Association of British Pharmaceutical Industries (ABPI). After 1960, the government negotiated directly with many of the larger producers, in an approach called the Voluntary Price Regulation Scheme (VPRS). From 1969, price negotiations were based explicitly on return on capital for drugs purchased by the National Health Service.[71] A second period, beginning in 1978, was marked by the end of voluntary negotiations. The election of the Labour Party in 1974 carried with it the threat of nationalization, which put the pharmaceutical industry in a difficult negotiating position. The shift was made decisive when the 1977 Health Act granted the secretary of state for social services the right to impose drug prices.[72] Although Britain never fell back on this provision, the explicit right to intervene changed the nature of government-industry negotiations. In recognition of the involuntary character of later agreements, the price-setting scheme was renamed the Pharmaceutical Price Regulation Scheme (PPRS). The PPRS would remain at the core of British drug pricing for the next generation.

Under the PPRS, companies were compensated for higher investments and other desired activities, including export success.[73] Agreements were negotiated annually between the Medicines Control Agency

(MCA) of the Department of Health and individual manufacturers.[74] The price that the National Health Service (NHS) payed for drug products was set in these negotiations, based on the return on capital employed (ROCE) for those drugs that the NHS bought.[75] In the 1993–1998 period, allowed ROCE was between 17 percent and 21 percent. In the negotiation period spanning 2005–2009, ROCE was allowed to vary between 8.4 percent and 29.4 percent, depending on firm performance.[76] These levels were not guaranteed, but producers were permitted to increase drug prices in order to achieve their negotiated range.[77] In the case of excessive profits, producers were required to offer rebates directly to the government.[78] So long as they remained within their overall profitability cap, pharmaceutical firms were free to set the introductory prices of new products.[79] The result was to link policies that restrained the national drug bill with high profitability and high levels of pharmaceutical innovation. And although the PPRS did not cover unbranded generic drugs, it did nonetheless extend to 80 percent of the NHS total drug bill.

Apart from restraining the national drug bill, the way in which pharmaceutical pricing was set in Britain created strong incentives for industry to pursue safe and effective drugs. Basic safety and efficacy requirements were set first by the 1969 and 1971 British Medicines Acts. As in other European countries, the Medicines Acts required that drugs receive a market license certifying their safety, efficacy, and quality.[80] The new Committee on the Safety of Medicines (CSM), which began work in 1971, replaced the quasi-governmental Committee on the Safety of Drugs that had been formed in 1964 and operated with industry and academic experts. Within the new CSM, academics and representatives of the Association of the British Pharmaceutical Industry (ABPI) were still both highly influential. The academic culture led to a strong tradition of highly documented clinical trials.[81]

The formal drug review process that emerged in the United Kingdom tended to emphasize drug safety but focus less on efficacy. New drug evaluations were subcontracted to external expert committees rather than being evaluated by the MCA. Moreover, Britain relied more heavily than other countries on a postmarketing evaluation of a drug's performance in everyday use, and was more accepting of foreign trials than were other countries.[82] This permissive approach to quality regulation reflected not a diminished concern for drug safety, but instead a reliance on the incentives created by the PPRS to induce pharmaceutical companies to self-police the safety of their products. Thus the PPRS played a central role not only in restraining the government drug bill but also in creating incentives for industry to market safe and effective products.

Apart from controls on the profit of pharmaceutical manufacturers, Britain also implemented four projects to lower demand for pharmaceuticals. Many of these were similar to Germany's efforts to restrain demand. First, in 1985, the British government published a blacklist of six hundred drugs not to be prescribed by NHS doctors. Beginning in 1993 the list was progressively extended. Second, Britain had long imposed patient copayments on pharmaceutical prescriptions. These were gradually increased, from 0.45 pounds in 1979 to 5.50 pounds in 1996. However, 50 percent of the population was exempted from these fines, accounting for 80 percent of drug use.[83] Third, doctors were given indicative drug budgets beginning in 1991. Prescription levels of different categories of doctors were compared through the nationwide computerized Prescribing Analysis and Costs (PACT) system. Starting in 1991, in an effort to introduce market mechanism among prescribing doctors, some general practitioners became "fund holders," meaning that they were able to make their own decisions about dispensing a set pool of pharmaceutical funds for their patients. As in Germany, doctors who overprescribed were audited, in Britain by the Health Commissioner. And, as in Germany, this doctor-centered approach to drug sales restraint was supported by the pharmaceutical industry, because it placed the purchasing decision in the hands of expert consumers who were likely to emphasize high quality and innovative products.

Finally, beginning under the Labour government of 1974–1979, PPRS agreements included a 14 percent ceiling on promotional activities by the drug industry. This level was progressively lowered, to 9 percent in 1984, and to 6 percent by 2008. About half of this promotional spending went to paying medical representatives who visited individual practitioners to advocate specific products.[84] Indeed the high percentage of sales spent on R&D in Britain was due in part to the relatively low promotional spending mandated by national regulation.[85] Moreover, because the government kept permissible profit margins relatively high, and because these profit margins were not related to domestic sales levels, the drug industry accepted restraint on domestic promotional spending.

As in other countries, the U.K. pharmaceutical system was criticized for giving undue influence to the pharmaceutical sector. Because they focused on components of profitability, PPRS negotiations were necessarily confidential. This secrecy, combined with a high profitability for the most successful firms, led to concerns that drug prices were too high.[86] Others criticized the scheme as a tool for limiting competition in the pharmaceutical sector. Lacy Glenn Thomas described the PPRS as an "elitist collectivization of decision making on safety and efficacy levels, so that effectively the strongest and most sophisticated British pharmaceutical firms imposed their standards on all other market participants."[87] Yet these criticisms overlooked the degree to which the British government intervened in both pricing and drug development to generate one of the most innovative and successful national pharmaceutical sectors in Europe.

Narrative Legacies and the Limits of Industry Influence

The pharmaceutical sector has been particularly susceptible to charges of undue industry influence on public policy. It has a strong claim to providing a public good; the issues involved are highly technical; its regulators interact closely with industry, and many eventually find second careers with pharmaceutical firms. The sector is also regularly accused of manipulating the regulatory process. In the United States, these accusations have focused primarily on pricing policies. In France, concern has emphasized industry influence in drug approval. In the United Kingdom, the secretive PPRS negotiations are seen as the nexus of influence brokering. But this appearance of undue industry influence on regulation does not provide a complete picture. The patterns of regulation we observe today are also the result of a legacy of historical accommodations that emerged when the diffuse interests of drug prescribers and users first confronted the narrow interests of drug producers. How these early battles were resolved depended in important ways upon the institutional context in which they occurred. The results of these initial conflicts persisted in the patterns of industry influence a generation or more after they occurred.

The different patterns of industry influence corresponded to very different notions of the diffuse interests that the pharmaceutical sector was intended to serve. In France, the idea was to keep prices low in order to ensure access to current drugs for current patients. In the United States, the idea was to allow prices to stay high in order to protect patients from unsafe or ineffective products, and to promote the development of new high-quality drugs for future patients. Whereas the French approach led to strict price controls and more lenient efficacy standards, the U.S. approach was founded in strong efficacy standards and pricing freedom. In the United Kingdom and Germany, negotiated solutions—ones that mainly excluded input from patients' groups or the general public—found a middle ground between these two extremes. In Germany, a doctor-centered system of expenditure restraints created a bias toward effective drugs, while reference pricing restrained price competition on commodity drugs. In the United Kingdom, companies that achieved both R&D intensity and a low domestic drug burden were allowed higher returns on capital.

The choice of policy narrative in pharmaceutical regulation cast a long shadow in each country, shaping the very nature of the industry itself. Differences in national regulatory approaches to drug quality and pricing in turn drove different kinds of market strategy. British and American drug firms enjoyed high profitability relative to French and German firms (see Table 7.1). They also invested a correspondingly larger share of sales revenue in R&D. French firms enjoyed strong sales in their domestic market, and German firms were especially strong exporters. The United Kingdom was most effective at limiting its domestic drug bill. Yet it was still able to promote high profitability, high R&D spending, and strong success in globalizing innovative new drugs. Like the United Kingdom, the United States supported high levels of R&D spending, although this was made possible through high prices. One of the surprises of the U.S. industry was its relatively poor export performance—a direct result of its strict approach to regulating pharmaceutical safety and efficacy.

Table 7.1. Pharmaceutical sector summary statistics, 1997

	Profit margin (2000)	Price (1999)	Sales ($ per capita)	Trade balance ($bn)	Exports (% of sales)	R&D spending (%)	NCEs[a] (1975–1994)	Global NCEs[b] (1975–1994)
France	8	84	351	2.8	38	14	108	3
Germany	8	97	294	5.8	64	14	108	8
UK	20	100	233	4.0	54	20	59	30
US	18.6	184	319	–1.4	10	20	292	11

Sources: Martina Garau and Adrian Towse, "Pricing and Reimbursement Policies in the UK: Current and Future Trends," in *European Medicines Pricing and Reimbursement: Now and the Future,* eds. Martina Garau and Jorge Mestre-Ferrandiz (Oxford: Radcliffe Publishing, 2007), 40; Stan N. Finkelstein and Peter G. Bittinger, *Price Controls and the Competitiveness of Pharmaceutical Firms: A Preliminary Look at the Experience of Five Countries,* Program on the Pharmaceutical Industry, Sloan School of Management, Working Paper 8–93 (1993), 3.

a. New chemical entities (NCEs) are new therapeutic drugs that have been approved for use.

b. Global NCEs are innovative drugs that are sold in all seven major pharmaceutical markets.

For each of these countries, pharmaceuticals were an important economic sector that also served important public and social needs. Yet the regulatory environments in which they operated pushed their business models in very different directions. Although these directions were dictated in part by industry pressures, they were also shaped critically by the confrontation of organized industry interests with the diffuse interests of the patient community, as interpreted by politicians, doctors, and medical insurers.

These national outcomes were not predetermined. As the historical evolution of these policies shows clearly, national narratives about the purpose of the pharmaceutical sector emerged from periods of intensive negotiation and occasional conflict. Once national narratives emerged, however, they became deeply embedded in national expectations about the ways in which drug companies would be regulated to protect patient interests. This means that to understand national patterns of lobbying strength and weakness in the pharmaceutical sector we must look back at the critical junctures in which their narrow interests first confronted the diffuse interests of doctors, patients, and insurers. The legacy of these junctures constrained the subsequent regulatory influence of the pharmaceutical sector. U.S. pharmaceutical products are among the most expensive in the world. By contrast, the sector has drawn intensive regulatory scrutiny to issues of drug safety, efficacy, and quality. Taken together, these two components of U.S. drug policy—high price and high quality—constitute a social contract, one in which drug firms are allowed high prices on the understanding that they will develop useful drugs in the future. The result has combined a domestic market for expensive, highly innovative drugs with a low level of exports due primarily to the high costs associated with domestic certification. Conversely, European firms have had less influence on pricing policy but have enjoyed more control in setting the terms under which dimensions of product quality are regulated.

The reason for this protracted legacy of early regulatory debates is not that the institutions and regulations themselves were particularly sticky. Rather, the main source of stickiness was the common narrative that emerged regarding the interests of those who purchased, prescribed, and used pharmaceuticals. The surprise of the pharmaceutical sector is not the strength of its lobby, but how much its fate has been driven by historical compromises over which it had only limited control. It has not become one of the most heavily regulated industries in the world by choice. If the pharmaceutical industry has managed to maintain a fair degree of pricing independence within the United States, this is because it has almost entirely given up control over quality in drug design. In turn, the industry has engaged in a long-term lobbying strategy that has emphasized the importance of higher prices to enable research in new drug development. The case of drug regulation evokes the extent to which regulatory capture by concentrated industry interests is constrained, both by historical policy outcomes, and by the long time horizons needed to forge a broad consensus around the desired policy.

CHAPTER 8

Coalitions and Collective Action

RESEARCHERS IN PUBLIC POLICY have long assumed that diffuse
interests were therefore weak interests. Because large groups of individuals are difficult to organize, they are thought to go underrepresented in public policy. The problem is considered to be one of coordination. When groups of individuals share an interest in a common
policy, and the benefits of that policy cannot be excluded from any member of the group, then no single member has an interest to advocate for
that policy when advocacy requires any significant level of cost. As each
individual waits for others to act, their shared policy objectives remain
underprovided. The larger the interested group, the more challenging it
becomes to overcome these barriers to mobilization. The most diffuse
interests in society should therefore be least represented in public policy.
This conclusion, when it was first proposed by Mancur Olson in his
1965 book *The Logic of Collective Action,* was a direct attack on a school
of pluralism that assumed groups would influence policy in proportion
to their size. The Olson critique was profoundly influential on the social
sciences. It is not an exaggeration to say that an entire generation of political scientists learned from Olson—and a cohort of regulation theorists including George Stigler, Sam Peltzman, and Russell Hardin—that
concentrated interests enjoy the upper hand.

Yet this conclusion has rarely been tested through detailed empirical studies. The weakness in the Chicago School approach to regulation is highlighted by the success of national consumer protection policies. Consumer interests should, by their account, be among the most difficult to organize. Consumers as a group should suffer from high barriers to collective organization. Individual consumers have little incentive to contribute time or resources to a cause that may provide them only limited benefits. Diffuse benefits from consumer mobilization entail concentrated costs for business.[1] To succeed, consumers not only must organize but must do so more effectively than the businesses they confront. Moreover, consumers are themselves commonly also participants in production, as workers, managers, and shareholders. To the extent that new consumer protections impose a cost on producers, even those individuals who stand to benefit as consumers may choose to forego such benefits out of concern for the losses that new protections might impose on them via the impact of their actions on production. For all of these familiar reasons, the elaborate institutions of consumer protections that now suffuse the advanced industrialized countries pose a theoretical challenge. When and how do highly diffuse social and economic interests prevail over concentrated interests?

Through careful attention to the ways in which diffuse and concentrated interests confront each other in public policy, this book provides an account of political pluralism that offers a route to reintegrate theories of regulatory policy with research projects on national political and economic institutions in comparative politics. In the politics of interest representation that emerged from the Chicago School analysis, research necessarily focused on narrow points of access to policy influence. Regulatory studies therefore tended to emphasize bureaucratic institutions and the distortion of channels of democratic accountability. But these approaches also preclude the sorts of analysis that would link policy outcomes to broader national institutional and political frameworks. By focusing on policymaking as the product of legitimacy coalitions grounded in narratives about the public interest, this research opens up the possibility for meaningful macroinstitutional policy analysis. When different kinds of diffuse pragmatic interests are at stake, electoral institutions and national production regimes have the possibility to influence regulatory outcomes.

Comparative Case Studies

Research into diffuse interest representation has focused primarily on the U.S. case. One of the goals of this project has been to approach issues of diffuse interest representation employing comparative case studies from across the advanced industrialized democracies. By asking why and how diffuse interests come to be represented in some countries but not in others, we can start to isolate the underlying mechanisms of diffuse interest representation. This also means that we must confront tremendous institutional variation. For advanced industrialized countries, especially in Western Europe, formalized institutions of diffuse interest representation have a long legal and political tradition. Yet even in countries with strong and formalized interest mediation, observers have questioned whether these institutions help or hurt representation of entirely new diffuse interests.[2] In the cases I present, these countries are no better, but also no worse, at defending diffuse interests, although the kinds of interests they support appear to differ. The challenges and opportunities that diffuse interests face are surprisingly similar across countries.

A comparison of consumer protection across the Organisation for Economic Co-operation and Development (OECD) countries highlights the central role of coalitions to promote new consumer protection regulations as legitimate targets for government policy. These legitimacy coalitions take one of three forms: industry-activist coalitions in which consumer and producer groups work together to promote common consumer protection goals, state-activist coalitions in which consumer groups and regulators work together to promote new protection policies with relatively little influence from industry, or industry-state coalitions in which formal consumer groups play relatively little role in influencing the form of new consumer protections. Three lessons emerge from these cases. First, meaningful consumer protections emerged across a range of institutional and political contexts in a way that appears not to be consistent with the assumption that concentrated interests dictate public policy. Second, each of the main actors—industry, activists, and the state—had reasons to forge coalitions with other actors in order to promote their preferred policies. Common to these logics was a concern that their own interests be perceived as publicly legitimate. Finally, the legitimacy coalitions that came to dominate in each country established narratives about the consumer role in society that entailed specific kinds of regulatory responses. For example, in the cases where industry-state coalitions emerged, including Germany, Japan, and Austria, consumer complaints were interpreted primarily as problems of information asymmetry. Where state-activist coalitions came to dominate, as in the United States and Britain, consumers were understood to be deprived of protections that had the status of basic rights of citizenship.

A closer look at the development of consumer protection policies in France reveals the emergence of vibrant associations organized to protect consumers. This finding is especially surprising in the context of France, where intermediate associations have traditionally been viewed with skepticism. Part of their success was due to the French state, which actively promoted consumer associations in the hope that they might negotiate solutions directly with producers. Again, this sort of reticence to engage in direct economic regulation is unfamiliar in the French tradition of political economy. Ultimately, French industry associations were unable to negotiate a separate peace with France's consumer groups because they were unable to impose common standards on member firms. Hence the statist and relatively aggressive consumer protection stance that eventually emerged in France was the result both of highly successful social mobilization around the issue and of a relative organizational weakness by organized industry. This is a pattern of policy-making that turns the Olsonian organizational logic virtually on its head.

One of the weaknesses of organizational analysis based on group size is its limited ability to explain differences in policy outcomes where relative group sizes are the same. A comparison of retail policy in France and Germany illustrates this point. In each case, a very large number of traditional small retailers confronted a small number of large-surface-area retailers that threatened to undercut them on price and convenience. In France, where small retailers organized aggressively to block the new entrants, they nonetheless lost the battle against large retailers. In Germany, where small retailers were less organized, they nonetheless won. The difference in outcomes depended not on group size or challenges of coordination, but instead on the coalitions that small and large retailers were able to forge in their defense. At the core of each of these coalitions was a shared legitimating narrative that ultimately came to dictate the logic of state regulation of the sector. In France, an emerging coalition between new large retailers and existing consumer associations came to dominate the policy process. Both argued that larger scale in retailing led to lower prices and a welfare benefit for French families. In Germany, small retailers found a powerful ally in the service-sector trade union, which represented many retail employees. They argued that blocking new large-format stores helped to shield both retail workers and their families from the need to work during evening hours that were traditionally spent with the family. The case of retail regulation suggests that a focus on coalitional dynamics may offer a more promising framework for analyzing the policy process than does a static analysis of group size and underlying economic interest.

Similarly, size-based theories of interest influence fail to explain cases in which very different interpretations of the public good take hold. The case of consumer borrower protections in France and the United Kingdom shows that similar concerns about over-indebtedness of households led to systematically different policy responses. Those responses depended not on differences in lender goals or consumer organization, but on different narratives linking consumer credit to social welfare. In France, policies emphasized the risks of debt spirals and permanent economic and social exclusion. In the United Kingdom, policies emphasized the opportunities that accompanied credit access, and the need for unlucky borrowers to have access to a fresh start. In both cases, concerns about the diffuse interests of households dominated the policy process, but those concerns were understood in nearly opposing ways.

Finally, seemingly powerful concentrated interests face limits on their policy discretion. Small, powerful producer groups commonly craft narratives that link their narrow interests to broad public interests in order to legitimate their policy goals. And although they seem to enjoy discretion in designing that narrative, they also have to live with its implications. Hence, even for powerful concentrated interests, legitimating narratives impose constraints on their discretion in influencing policy. One kind of constraint is the lock-in effect that powerful narratives can create over time. One function of legitimating narratives is to link the narrow interests of producers with a broader set of diffuse interests embraced by the general public. In the case of European farm protections, that narrative link embraced price subsidies as a means to promote productivity at a time of food scarcity. By stabilizing prices, the Common Agricultural Policy gave farmers strong incentives to increase output, a goal shared by early postwar consumers. By the 1990s, however, the link between agricultural support and consumer welfare was breaking down. Under pressure from world trading partners and from the fiscal burden of farm supports to new member states, the European Union began to rewrite the narrative that had provided the legitimacy for farm supports. Working with national agricultural ministries, the Directorate General of Agriculture sought to reframe farm supports as a means to preserve traditional farmland rather than as a tool for promoting farm productivity. Interestingly, even farmers themselves expressed skepticism about this new narrative, because it was unclear whether it would provide an adequate coalition for legitimating future payments to farmers.

A second constraint is the need for narrative coherence, in particular when decisions about legitimating narratives embody trade-offs among policy priorities. The case of pharmaceutical regulation evokes the trade-offs that concentrated interests face when they work to influence public policy. U.S. pharmaceutical firms succeeded in defending high drug prices by convincing doctors and legislators that those prices helped to pay for research into new remedies that would help future patients. The problem is that this narrative—higher prices now for future cures—was inconsistent with lobbying efforts to reduce the efficacy standards and regulatory oversight of the Food and Drug Administration. In other countries, pharmaceutical firms made different narrative choices. French firms, for example, emphasized the expertise of pharmacists as a core feature of new drug development, but were forced to accept government price regulations that limited the kinds of innovations that were reimbursed.

Coalitions in Defense of Diffuse Interests

The obstacles that coordination problems pose for diffuse interest representation have been overstated for two reasons. First, diffuse interests can be represented without mobilization. On the one hand, policy entrepreneurs within the government may act to defend diffuse interests without those interests ever having been mobilized. This is especially true of more technical forms of regulation—including product liability reform and technical standard setting—for which mobilization may never have been a real possibility.[3] On the other hand, concentrated industry interests may step in to support the related interests of diffuse groups. Incumbent firms selling in competitive markets may support strong product regulations in order to block new entrants. In the context of globalization, domestic firms may advocate strong domestic standards to thwart import penetration.[4] Industry support for diffuse interest warrants skepticism, but the diffuse interests being defended are typically genuine. Second, the very obstacles to mobilization that Olson describes may become advantages, insofar as the ability to overcome them can signal the legitimacy of the interest that is being represented. In cases in which individuals *can* be induced to organize, the interest they are advocating is perceived to be both broadly and deeply held. In order to understand patterns of diffuse interest representation, we must shift our attention from the tactical challenge of interest coordination to the more fundamental, strategic problem of policy legitimacy.

Three sets of actors play a role in diffuse interest representation. Policymakers that are able to identify and defend a diffuse group can fend off potential challenges and solidify their own political support. Companies may benefit from larger markets or higher profits if they are able to define diffuse interests in ways that reinforce their competitiveness. Activists that successfully organize a previously unrepresented diffuse interest gain social standing and public influence. Yet none of these actors individually has a sufficiently strong claim on public legitimacy to pursue their policy goals alone. Companies face the greatest legitimacy deficit when it comes to drafting new policy. Their economic mandate pushes them toward a quid pro quo logic of political influence that is inconsistent with the democratic ideal. But policymakers and social activists also face legitimacy shortfalls. Policymakers may be seen to be beholden to narrow constituency interests, and the regulators who carry out their policy aspirations subject to capture by the actors they regulate. Social activists face different but important legitimacy concerns. Although success at mobilizing a diffuse group can confer added legitimacy to their interest, the tactics they used to attract membership may raise questions among the general public about the credibility of their message.[5] To overcome their legitimacy shortfalls, at least two of these three sets of actors must collaborate. The resulting legitimacy coalitions are grounded in a common conception of the diffuse interest and a shared narrative that defines the relevant interest of that group. Three such legitimacy coalitions are possible: between industry and activists, between industry and the state, and between activists and the state (see Table 8.1).

Even powerful concentrated interests that exert political effort to pursue their narrow interests therefore find they must express that interest in the form of a related diffuse interest. In doing so, they typically access one of two types of legitimating narratives. On the one hand, they may claim to defend market access for some broad group. Walmart, in its struggle against organized labor, vaunted the low prices it offered to the even more diffuse body of consumers. On the other hand, concentrated interest groups may pursue a narrative of protection. U.S. pharmaceutical firms lobbied to block drug reimportation primarily on the grounds that such drugs might be counterfeit and dangerous. Some of the most effective interest groups—the pro-choice abortion movement is an example—succeeded by combining narratives of access (to abortions) and protection (to safe medical care). In many cases, whether or not

Table 8.1. Sources of policy legitimacy in diffuse interest representation

Coalition	Narrative
State-industry	Access
Industry-activist	Protection
State-activist	

narrow interests achieve their own narrow goals depends on their ability to define and defend a parallel set of diffuse interests.

A Return to Pluralism

Given the considerable counterevidence, it is fascinating to consider why the Chicago School approach to public policy remained dominant for so long. Concentrated interests that were meant to dominate public policy typically failed; diffuse interests that were meant to go underrepresented regularly mobilized and gained representation. In the face of counterevidence, the persistence of the Olson analysis of economic regulation offers a fascinating case study in the sociology of knowledge. How do we explain the Lazarus-like qualities of the Olson thesis?

First, their durability is a testimony to the allure of game theory as a tractable model of social organization. Neither Mancur Olson nor George Stigler formalized their insights about the weakness of diffuse interests and the strength of concentrated interests, but both had disciples that did. Russell Hardin in particular pointed out that coordination in diffuse groups created payoffs that mirrored a prisoner's dilemma game. Given the move in political science at the during the 1970s and 1980s to adapt the insights of game theory, it was perhaps inevitable that the theories themselves would enjoy sustained influence. To be clear, my goal is not to denigrate this highly fruitful line of inquiry. The insights of a rational-choice approach help to define clearly the sort of obstacles to mobilization that have made diffuse-interest organization challenging. Rather, my goal has been to show that this is only half of the story, and that the incentives to overcome these challenges are frequently even greater.

A second reason for the persistence of the regulatory capture doctrine is that it was embraced in the United States by both the political Left and the political Right as a motivating policy insight. For the Left, the disproportionate influence of concentrated business interests defined a populist agenda that had its roots in the progressive movement. It lay at the core of the trust-busting policies of the 1930s, and of the leftist mobilizations of the 1960s. By the time Olson wrote *The Logic of Collective Action,* the Left had already embraced its core insight, although their proposed responses varied. John Kenneth Galbraith advocated a "countervailing force" to oppose the concentrated interests of business. Democratic theorists emphasized the role of new kinds of democratic institutions that could insulate policy formation from industry interests. Theorists of public policy studied new approaches to economic regulation that could contain the meretricious effects of policy capture.

For the political Right in the United States, the Olson/Stigler thesis had different implications. The difficulty of insulating economic policy from the influence of concentrated interests suggested that many areas of economic regulation, even those that had a sound economic basis, were likely to become distorted in practice and should therefore be foresworn. The way to remove policy capture was to eliminate the captured policy. This argument was commonly raised by opponents of strategic trade theory, of government technology subsidies, and of aggressive enforcement of competition policy. These public policy implications were the source of persistent tension within the Chicago School. On the one hand, the economics branch of the Chicago School argued that deregulation would permit markets to function unfettered, and therefore more efficiently. On the other hand, the implications of free markets for policy influence were potentially less benign. Rather than generating new efficiencies, they risked distorting producer incentives in ways that would generate less efficient outcomes. Given this fundamental tension, as well as their focus on policy, it is perhaps not surprising that the bulk of Chicago School public policy theorists moved closer to Washington, D.C.[6]

One consequence of this three-way consensus—among academic policy researchers, the Left, and the Right—has been the emergence of a restricted view of the role of business in regulation. Broadly, policy prescriptions have been contested between two extremes: either business must be insulated from regulation, or regulation must be insulated from business. This research suggests that such a policy framing is overly narrow. It opens the possibility for designing regulatory policy in which business is a collaborative partner rather than an opponent of regulators. Industry groups can support regulatory policies that they perceive as consolidating or expanding markets. And, increasingly, complex regulatory issues require more sophisticated interaction among government agencies, industry, and user groups.

The finding that diffuse interests commonly shape public policy outcomes represents a victory for pluralism, but it does not answer critical questions about *which* diffuse interests will come to dominate public policy outcomes that matter for the functioning of society. Some of the most crucial policy decisions of the postwar period have depended either upon the way in which a particular diffuse interest is interpreted, or upon whether moderately diffuse or highly diffuse interests dominate policy outcomes. For example, do consumers benefit more from hormone-treated beef that is less expensive per pound, or from nontreated beef that is perhaps less risky but also more expensive? Similarly, do genetically modified foods help or hurt consumers? Such questions raise natural disagreements between coalitions of concentrated industry groups and broader diffuse interests armed with legitimating narratives that stress the alternative virtues of access or protection. The winners of such battles are often described in terms of the concentrated industry interests that eventually profit from the outcomes. But any policy outcome is likely to have business interest winners, in addition to the diffuse interests it is intended to protect. Opposition to genetically modified organisms (GMOs) in Europe is commonly attributed to the strength of the farm unions; availability of GMO products in the United States is seen as a benefit to large agribusiness. But such accounts have a *post hoc ergo propter hoc* quality. Although both of these groups have undoubtedly benefited from the respective outcomes, their subsequent benefit cannot be read as a case for unmediated industry influence on public policy. Prior to the European Union ban on GMOs, for example, French agribusiness mainly *favored* GMO crops. In most cases, actual policy decisions have been based on evolving public discourse about the interests of diffuse groups in society, channeled through a democratically influenced policy process.

The point is not that business always works in the public interest; nor is it that business influence on public policy is necessarily benign. Business interest must be channeled into the public interest through functioning democratic and legal institutions. These include a free press with aggressive investigative journalism, freely contested elections, competitive economic markets, a right and an ability to mobilize interest groups, and an independent court system. One reason these institutions, where they exist, have been so effective in limiting industry capture of the regulatory process is that they do not have to create an insurmountable barrier to industry influence. They only need to make investments in regulatory manipulation *less* profitable than other investment opportunities that businesses face. This implies that the degree of necessary oversight will vary depending on the investment alternatives that different economic sectors perceive. Dedicated government contractors and declining industrial sectors, for example, may have few attractive options other than investing in policy influence. Sectors with poor nonregulatory options may therefore require closer public scrutiny—and they often receive it. Outside of these narrow cases, and in the context of functioning liberal democratic and market institutions, the threat of business capture is dramatically constrained.

There are important exceptions. First, the necessary institutional foundations of diffuse interest representation limit the applicability of this theory mainly to the advanced industrialized countries. Even among these, serious incursions into the freedom of the press, as in Italy under Sylvio Berlusconi, or limitations on party competition, as in Japan under Liberal Democratic Party rule, can limit the ability of diffuse interest groups to mobilize and defend their interests. In the Latin American countries for example, effective diffuse interest representation appears to have been limited to periods of genuine political contestation.[7] This implies that the Olson thesis may continue to characterize interest group organization in much of the developing world, much of the time. Second, the Olson thesis may continue to describe policy formation in certain narrow areas of foreign policy in the advanced industrialized economies for which a compelling diffuse interest does not exist within the domestic political constituency. The U.S. embargo of Cuba is an example of a policy driven by a concentrated interest group—the first generation of Cuban refugees to the United States—that has no compelling economic or security logic for the broader U.S. public. Yet no political, activist, or business group has mobilized to oppose the embargo because there is virtually no definable diffuse interest that is hurt in a meaningful way by the policy. Postcolonial economic policies of many of the European countries have a similar characteristic. They lack a set of diffuse domestic interests that might be organized to counter the concentrated interests of national industries. Without a countervailing diffuse interest to organize against it, policy capture in foreign economic policy faces little check.

In most cases in which concentrated interests have succeeded in achieving their narrow goals in the domestic realm, they have done so by allying themselves compellingly with more diffuse interests. This sort of coalition deserves more attention. It may be the key to understanding the political economy of liberalization in the late 1970s and 1980s. Whatever else was true about the neoliberal initiatives of this period, they represented a victory of a new coalition between the highly diffuse consumer interest and a set of concentrated industry interests.[8] The Reagan and Thatcher reforms in particular represented a reshifting of economic policy away from monopoly pricing and toward open, competitive markets. This process almost certainly hurt wages. But it also almost certainly lowered prices across a range of economic sectors. Neoliberal reforms flourished in those countries in which the business-consumer coalition prevailed over the competing diffuse interests of labor and welfare recipients. By studying how and under what circumstances concentrated interests were able to build coalitions with highly diffuse interests, we may better understand why neoliberal reforms took hold where and when they did. In particular, the role of electoral systems and varieties of capitalism appears to be central. Insofar as majoritarian electoral regimes and liberal market organization favor the highly diffuse consumer interest over the merely somewhat diffuse interests of labor, it is perhaps unsurprising that the United States and Britain led the neoliberal revolution.

The fact of effective diffuse interest representation should not be taken as a normative claim. As the cases above evoke, even an effective representation of weak interests requires that those interests be defined. It is precisely the need to define those interests that gives politicians, activists, and businesses strong incentives to act quickly to defend new diffuse interests. Olson was himself skeptical of the ability of states to govern effectively once diffuse factions in society had been effectively represented. The resulting "sclerosis" became a trope around which he and others built an entire historiography of American decline.[9] U.S. economic dynamism of the 1990s and the concurrent stagnation in Japan largely undermined these ideas. Nonetheless, the difficulty of accommodating a diversity of well-represented diffuse interests remains a basic challenge for the advanced industrialized democracies. Michael Piore has noted the particular challenge posed by the proliferation and growing influence of diffuse interests that are disconnected from the sources of economic production. Among other problems, they may create policy pressures that work to undermine the interests of workers and investors.[10] Managing such conflicts among highly diffuse interests arguably poses greater challenges for policymakers than does the existing preoccupation with capture of the regulatory process by narrow economic interests.

Exaggeration of the influence of business on public policy comes at a high cost. A deep skepticism of the possibility for regulation in the public interest has intensified interest in voluntary industry self-policing. The growth in interest in corporate social responsibility (CSR) can be attributed in part to skepticism about the efficacy of regulatory solutions. And although CSR clearly has benefits, it cannot overcome common problems of coordination that plague such nonregulatory solutions. The movement to encourage ethics training for future business leaders, though similarly laudable, suffers from the same obstacles to effective impact. One of the growing challenges to effective regulation is not that regulators are too close to industry, but that they are too far away. Important economic regulation, ranging from drug safety and monitoring to prudential regulation of financial institutions, has become so technically complex and evolves so quickly that it can be difficult for regulators to do their jobs in isolation. Recent regulatory experiments in Japan offer a cautionary example. In 2006, the Japanese parliament passed two reform laws that imposed strict new standards on building construction and consumer loans. Although the goals were laudable, the results proved traumatic. At a time when credit extension was becoming restricted, the new regulations forced a dramatic contraction in these markets. Housing starts in 2007 fell to a 40-year low. Lending by consumer credit companies had shrunk by 70 percent by the end of 2009. What was distinctive about both regulatory reforms was that industry was left almost entirely outside of the policy process. Regulatory strategies that accept greater input from diverse stakeholders can offer more effective solutions.

By diffusing the fear of regulatory capture, we open up the possibility for more responsive approaches to both the study and the practice of economic and social regulation. The benefits to research will be realized by setting aside unmerited preoccupation with regulatory capture and beginning to study more carefully the role of diffuse interests and legitimating narratives in setting national trajectories of public policy. The benefits to policy will come from paying more thoughtful attention to the institutions that have historically succeeded in constraining regulatory capture. With better tools to manage potential capture, we open up new possibilities for governments to deploy more responsive approaches to economic regulation. Taken together, an academic and policy emphasis on the power, rather than the weakness, of diffuse pragmatic interests may provide the necessary reorientation of policy toward practical, rather than ideological, preoccupations that will in turn make it possible to continue to regulate effectively the increasingly complex markets on which the advanced industrial societies now so critically rely.

Notes

1. THE POLITICAL POWER OF WEAK INTERESTS

1. Gabriel Kolko, *The Triumph of Conservatism: A Reinterpretation of American History, 1900–1916* (Glencoe, NY: The Free Press of Glencoe, 1963), For a critique see Richard H. K. Vietor, "Businessmen and the Political Economy: The Railroad Rate Controversy of 1905," *The Journal of American History* 64, no. 1 (1977): 47–66.

2. These included John Commons, *The Economics of Collective Action* (New York: Macmillan, 1950); Earl Latham, *The Group Basis of Politics* (Ithaca, NY: Cornell University Press, 1952); and David Truman, *The Governmental Process* (New York: Alfred A. Knopf, 1958). See especially Mancur Olson, *The Logic of Collective Action: Public Goods and the Theory of Groups* (Cambridge, MA: Harvard University Press, 1965), 113–125.

3. Charles E. Lindblom, *Politics and Markets* (New York: Basic Books, 1977).

4. James Q. Wilson, "The Politics of Regulation," in *Social Responsibility and the Business Predicament,* ed. James W. McKie (Washington, DC: Brookings Press, 1974): 86.

5. George Stigler, "The Theory of Economic Regulation," *Bell Journal of Economics and Management Science* (Spring 1971): 3.

6. Sam Peltzman, "Toward a More General Theory of Regulation," *The Journal of Law and Economics* 19, no. 2 (1976): 211–240.

7. Russell Hardin, *Collective Action* (Washington, DC: Resources for the Future, 1982).

8. Stigler and Wilson both received their degrees from the University of Chicago in the 1950s.

9. Richard A. Posner, "Social Costs of Monopoly and Regulation," *Journal of Political Economy* 83, no. 4 (1975): 807–828.

10. Research into "tunneling," the practice by which large shareholders or blockhold-ers manipulate stock values to extract resources from minority shareholders, is sur-prising in part because of findings that this practice occurs relatively infrequently in most countries. Simon Johnson, Rafael La Porta, Florencio Lopez de Silanes, An-drei Shleifer, "Tunnelling," NBER working paper 7523, February 2000.

11. Terry Moe, *The Organization of Interests: Incentives and the Internal Dynamics of Political Interest Groups* (Chicago: University of Chicago, 1980).

12. James Q. Wilson, "The Politics of Regulation," in *The Politics of Regulation*, ed. James Q. Wilson (New York: Basic Books, 1980): 370–372.

13. John Kingdon, *Agendas, Alternatives, and Public Policies* (Boston: Little, Brown, 1984); Nelson Polsby, *Political Innovation in America: The Politics of Policy Ini-tiation* (New Haven, CT: Yale University Press, 1985); Frank R. Baumgartner and Bryan D. Jones, *Agendas and Instability in American Politics* (Chicago: Chicago University Press, 1993); Michael Minstrom, "Policy Entrepreneurs and the Diffu-sion of Innovation," *American Journal of Political Science* 41, no. 3 (1997): 738–770.

14. Robert Axelrod, *The Evolution of Cooperation* (New York: Basic Books, 1984).

15. Kenneth A. Oye, *Cooperation under Anarchy* (Princeton, NJ: Princeton University Press, 1986); Joseph M. Grieco, *Cooperation among Nations: Europe, America, and Non-Tariff Barriers to Trade* (Ithaca, NY: Cornell University Press, 1990).

16. Eleanor Ostrom, *Governing the Commons* (New York: Cambridge University Press, 1990).

17. Suzanne Berger, ed., *Organizing Interests in Western Europe: Pluralism, Corporat-ism and the Transformation of Politics* (Cambridge, UK: Cambridge University Press, 1984).

18. David Vogel, "Political Science and the Study of Corporate Power: A Dissent from the New Conventional Wisdom," *British Journal of Political Science* 17, no. 4 (1987): 385–408.

19. Sam Peltzman, Michael E. Levine, and Roger G. Noll, "The Economic Theory of Regulation after a Decade of Deregulation," *Brookings Papers on Economic Activity: Microeconomics* (Washington, DC: Brookings Press, 1989), 38.

20. David Vogel, "Why Businessmen Distrust Their State: The Political Consciousness of Corporate Executives," *British Journal of Political Science* 8, no. 1 (1978): 45–78.

21. Stephen Ansolabehere, John M. de Figueiredo, and James M. Schnyder, "Why Is There So Little Money in U.S. Politics," *Journal of Economic Perspectives* 17, no. 1 (2003): 105–130.

22. Alex Dyck, David Moss, and Louigi Zingales, "Media versus Special Interests" (working paper, National Bureau of Economic Research, Cambridge, Mass., 2005).

23. John D. MacCarthy and Mayer N. Zald, "Resource Mobilization and Social Move-ments: A Partial Theory," *American Journal of Sociology* 82, no. 6 (1977); Sidney Tarrow, *Power in Movement* (Cambridge, UK: Cambridge University Press, 1994).

24. Alain Tourraine, *The Post-Industrial Society* (New York: Random House, 1971).

25. This definition is broadly consistent with our perception of the sporting fanatic. The fan is a person who bothers friends and family with a sporting obsession without claiming that they should also share the obsession.

26. The findings of their initial experiment have been reproduced in a variety of forms by subsequent researchers. Gerald Marwell and Ruth E. Ames, "Experiments on the Provision of Public Goods. I. Resources, Interest, Group Size, and the Free Rider Problem," *The American Journal of Sociology* 84, no. 6 (1979): 1335–1360.

27. The only significant difference was driven by rules about how the returns from the collective investment would be distributed.

28. Marwell and Ames, "Experiments on the Provision of Public Goods," 1350.

29. Martha Kropf and Stephen Knack, "Viewers Like You: Community Norms and Contributions to Public Broadcasting," *Political Research Quarterly* 56, no. 2 (2003): 187–197.

30. My thanks to Noel Maurer for his suggestions about the functioning of government during wartime.

31. Meghan Sweeney, "Regulating Mercury with the Clean Air Act" (master's thesis, Massachusetts Institute of Technology, 2006).

32. Erik Stokstad, "Inspector General Blasts EPA Mercury Analysis," *Science* 307, no. 5711 (February 2005): 829–831.

33. Shankar Vedantam, "New EPA Mercury Rule Omits Conflicting Data," *Washington Post,* March 22, 2005.

34. Union of Concerned Scientists, *Scientific Integrity in Policymaking* (Washington, DC: Union of Concerned Scientists, 2004).

35. Bridget Kuehn, "Medical Groups Sue EPA over Mercury Rule," *Journal of the American Medical Association* 294 (2005): 415–416.

36. Joe Truini, "16 States Attempt to Block Mercury Rule," *Waste News,* July 3, 2006.

37. Another report in the *Washington Post* revealed that whole paragraphs of the EPA rule were lifted from a document prepared by Latham & Watkins, a law firm employed by the electricity-generating sector.

38. Gordon Tullock, "The Purchase of Politicians," *Western Economic Journal* 10 (1972): 354–355.

39. Stephen Ansolabehere, John de Figueiredo, and James Snyder, "Why Is There So Little Money in Politics?" *Journal of Economic Perspectives* 17 (2003): 111.

40. Norman Frohlich and Joe A. Oppenheimer, "I Get By with a Little Help from My Friends," *World Politics* 22 (1970): 104–121.

41. If one assumes that a population exists that may have noneconomic reasons for mobilizing around a particular issue, then selective incentives can help to target this group. The more valuable the selective incentive is, the less excess value it yields. But it also serves a less useful function in sorting out potential movement members who are susceptible to noneconomic inducements. On the noneconomic motivations for the provision of common goods, see Eleanor Ostrom, "Collective Action and the Evolution of Social Norms," *Journal of Economic Perspectives* 14, no. 3 (2000): 137–158.

42. Erika Meins, *Politics and Public Outrage: Explaining Transatlantic and Intra-European Diversity of Regulations on Food Irradiation and Genetically Modified Food* (Muenster, Germany: LIT, 2003), 32.

43. Roy Kiesling, "Report to Those Most Concerned" (unpublished book manuscript recounting the emergence and evolution of consumer movements in the United States in the 1960s and 1970s, Roy Kiesling Papers, Kansas State University, 1981), 44.

44. Louis Hyman, "Debtor Nation" (PhD dissertation, Harvard University History Department, 2007).

45. Éduard Leclerc, *Ma vie pour un combat* (Paris: Pierre Belfond, 1974), 103–104.

46. Staffan Jacobsson and Volkman Lauber, "The Politics and Policy of Energy System Transformation," *Energy Policy* 34, no. 3 (2006): 256–276.

47. Howard K. Gruenspecht and Lester B. Lave, "The Economics of Health, Safety, and Environmental Regulation," in *Handbook of Industrial Organization,* ed. Richard Schmalensee and Robert D. Willig, vol. 2 (Amsterdam: North-Holland, 1989), 1530–1531.

48. David Vogel, *Trading Up: Consumer and Environmental Regulation in a Global Economy* (Cambridge: Harvard University Press, 1995).

49. Ibid., 5–8.

50. Benjamin Cashore, Graeme Auld, and Deanna Newsom, *Governing through Markets: Forest Certification and the Emergences of Non-State Authority* (New Haven, CT: Yale University Press, 2004).

51. Anthony Downs, *An Economic Theory of Democracy* (New York: Harper Collins, 1957); William Riker, *The Theory of Political Coalitions* (New Haven, CT: Yale University Press, 1962).

52. John Kingdon, *Congressmen's Voting Decision* (New York: Wiley and Sons, 1973); R. Douglas Arnold, *The Logic of Congressional Action* (New Haven, CT: Yale University Press, 1990); Michael Bailey, "Quiet Influence: The Representation of Diffuse Interests on Trade Policy, 1983–1994," *Legislative Studies Quarterly* 26, no. 1 (2001): 45–80; Victoria Murillo and Cecilia Martinez-Gallardo, "Political Competition and Policy Adoption: Market Reforms in Latin American Public Utilities," *American Journal of Political Science* 51, no. 1 (2007): 121.

53. Giandomenico Majone, "From the Positive to the Regulatory State: Causes and Consequences of Changes in the Mode of Governance," *Journal of Public Policy* 17, no. 2 (1997): 161; Daniel Carpenter, *Reputation and Power: Organizational Image and Pharmaceutical Regulation at the FDA* (Princeton: Princeton University Press, 2010).

54. Marver Bernstein, *Regulating Business by Independent Commission* (Princeton: Princeton University Press, 1955); Paul Sabatier, "Social Movements and Regulatory Agencies: Toward a More Adequate—and Less Pessimistic—Theory of 'Clientele Capture,'" *Policy Studies* 6, no. 3 (1975): 301–342.

55. Harvey M. Sapolsky, "The Politics of Product Controversies," in *Consuming Fears: The Politics of Product Risk*, ed. Harvey Sapolsky (New York: Basic Books, 1987), 183.

56. Annemarie Bopp-Schmehl, Uwe Heibült, and Ulrich Kypke, *Technische Normung und Verbraucherinteressen im gesellschaftlichen Wandel* (Frankfurt am Main: Haag & Herchen Verlag, 1984), 101; Christian Joerges, Josef Falke, Hans-Wolfgang Micklitz, and Gert Brüggemeier, *Die Sicherheit von Konsumgütern und die Entwicklung der Europäischen Gemeinschaft* (Baden-Baden: Nomos, 1989), 187.

57. Geoffrey Garrett and Barry Weingast, "Ideas, Interests, and Institutions: Constructing the European Community's Internal Market," in *Ideas and Foreign Policy*, ed. Judith Goldstein and Robert O. Keohane (Ithaca, NY: Cornell University Press, 1993); Mark Blyth, *Great Transformations: Economic Ideas and Institutional Change in the Twentieth Century* (Cambridge, UK: Cambridge University Press, 2002), 45; Pepper Culpepper, "Institutional Change in Contemporary Capitalism: Coordinated Financial Systems since 1990," *World Politics* 57, no. 2 (2005): 173–199.

58. Luc Boltanski and Laurent Thévenot, *De la justification: Les économies de la grandeur* (Paris: Gallimard, 1991); Pierre Muller, "Les politiques publiques comme construction d'un rapport au monde," in *La construction du sens dans les politiques publiques: Débats autour de la notion de référentiel,* ed. Alain Faure, Gilles Pollet, and Philippe Warin (Paris: Éditions L'Harmattan, 1995); Erik Bleich, *Race Politics in Britain and France* (Cambridge, UK: Cambridge University Press, 2003).

59. Fritz Scharpf, *Governing in Europe: Effective and Democratic?* (Oxford: Oxford University Press, 1999), 6–8.

60. Peter Hall and David Soskice, *Varieties of Capitalism* (Cambridge: Harvard University Press, 2001).

61. Their account relies on the greater seat-vote elasticity of majoritarian electoral regimes. See Ronald Rogowski and Mark Andreas Kayser, "Majoritarian Electoral Systems and Consumer Power: Price-Level Evidence from the OECD Countries," *American Political Science Review* 46, no. 3 (2002): 527.

62. Thomas Cusack, Torben Iversen, and David Soskice, "Coevolution of Capitalism and Political Representation: The Choice of Electoral Systems," *American Political Science Review* 104, no. 2 (2010): 393–403.

63. John Kingdon, *Agendas, Alternatives, and Public Policies* (Boston: Little, Brown, 1984).

64. Robert H. Bates, Avner Greif, Margaret Levi, and Jean-Laurent Rosenthal, *Analytic Narratives* (Princeton: Princeton University Press, 1998).

2. THREE WORLDS OF CONSUMER PROTECTION

1. Olson, *Logic of Collective Action* , 132

2. Wilson, "The Politics of Regulation."

3. Vogel, *Trading Up*; Patricia L. Maclachlan, *Consumer Politics in Postwar Japan: The Institutional Boundaries of Citizen Activism* (New York: Columbia University Press, 2002).

4. Gunnar Trumbull, *Consumer Capitalism: Politics, Product Markets and Firm Strategy in France and Germany* (Ithaca, NY: Cornell University Press, 2006).

5. Alfred Hirschman, *Shifting Involvements: Private Interest and Public Action* (Princeton: Princeton University Press, 1982); Matthew Hilton, *Consumerism in*

Twentieth-Century Britain: The Search for a Historical Movement (Cambridge, UK: Cambridge University Press, 2003); Trumbull, *Consumer Capitalism*.

6. No comprehensive comparative study has been written on the postwar consumer movements. The best detailed study is a series of volumes by Hans and Sarah Thorelli written in the 1970s, including *Consumer Information Handbook* (1974), *Information Seekers* (1975), and *Consumer Information Systems and Consumer Policy* (1977). For the best recent comparative account, see Matthew Hilton, "Consumers and the State since World War II," *Annals of the American Academy of Political and Social Science* 611, no. 1 (2007): 61–88.

7. Organisation for Economic Co-operation and Development (OECD), Committee on Consumer Policy (CCP) (72)1 (1st Revision), Annex. This chapter draws on the records of the OECD's Committee on Consumer Policy, formed in 1974. The archive consists primarily of annual reports on consumer policy developments of member state, and is available for public consultation at the OECD in Paris. The citation convention for these records changed over time. In general, the format includes the last two digits of the year and a number designating the member state.

8. Michel Génin and Bernard Suzanne, "Les rapports de l'industrie de consommation en Suède et aux Etats-Unis," *Les Cahiers de l'ILEC* 7 (1963): 48.

9. Iselin Theien, "From Information to Protection," *Economic History Yearbook* 1 (2006): 34.

10. OECD, Directorate for Financial and Enterprise Affairs (DAF)/CCP, 73.20/18.

11. In practice its focus was primarily on chemicals and imported goods.

12. Interview with Anders Stalheim, Former head of Norwegian Consumer Council, April 2008.

13. OECD, Folder 212674, *Information on Consumer Policy in Denmark*, February 1968.

14. OECD, CCP (72)1 (1st Revision) Annex.

15. OECD, Folder 212674, *Information on Consumer Policy in Denmark*, February 1968.

16. OECD, DAF/CCP 73.20/05.

17. OECD, DAF/CCP 75.48/05.

18. OECD, CCP (76)5, *Annual Reports on Developments in the Field of Consumer Policy*.

19. Ibid., (82)1/05.

20. Ibid., (78)2/05.

21. Ibid., (84)1/05

22. Ibid., (72)1 (1st Revision), Annex.

23. OECD, DAF/CCP 74.33/05; CCP (76)5, *Annual Reports on Developments in the Field of Consumer Policy*.

24. Bernd-Dieter Pioch, "Verbraucherschutz in Japan," *Mitteilungen des Instituts für Asienkunde* 112 (1980): 21.

25. Sheldon Garon, "Japan's Post-War 'Consumer Revolution', or Striking a 'Balance' between Consumption and Savings," in *Consuming Cultures, Global Perspectives*, ed. John Brewer and Frank Trentmann (New York: Berg, 2006), 208; Steven K. Vogel,

"When Interests Are Not Preferences: The Cautionary Tale of Japanese Consumers," *Comparative Politics* 31, no. 1 (1999): 189.

26. Patricia Maclachlan and Frank Trentman, "Civilizing Markets: Traditions of Consumer Politics in Twentieth-Century Britain, Japan and the United States," in *Markets in Historical Contexts: Ideas and Politics in the Modern World*, ed. Mark Bevir and Frank Trentman (Cambridge, UK: Cambridge University Press, 2004), 193.

27. OECD, CCP (72)1 (1st Revision), Annex.

28. The 1962 legislation on advertising and rebates was called the Law to Prevent Unjustifiable Premiums and Misleading Advertising.

29. Maclachlan, *Consumer Politics in Postwar Japan,* 90. For an overview of the different movements, see pages 89–102.

30. Ibid., 88–89.

31. Two types of centers catered to consumers: the Better Living Information Centers, whose activities were coordinated by MITI, and Local Consumer Life Centers. OECD, CCP, compiled by author from various years.

32. OECD, CCP (82)1/21.

33. Jay Tate, "National Varieties of Standardization," in *Varieties of Capitalism*, ed. Peter Hall and David Soskice (Oxford, UK: Oxford University Press, 2001), 458.

34. OECD, CCP (85)1/21; Good Design Award, "Award General Info," accessed May 11, 2011, (http://www.g-mark.org/english/aginfo/info/generalinfo.html).

35. OECD, CCP (77)3/21.

36. United Nations Industrial Development Organisation, *International Product Standards: Trends and Issues* (New York: United Nations, 1991), 24.

37. Later legislation, in 1995, created a different "S-mark" that ensured that a product had been tested and found safe by a private testing lab.

38. Charles Smith, "Just Under the Wire: Japan's Cabinet Clears Product Liability Bill," *Far Eastern Economic Review* 157, no. 16 (1994): 37.

39. Takahashi Fumitoshi, "Japan's Product Liability Law: Issues and Implications," *Journal of Japanese Studies* 22, no. 1 (1996): 115.

40. *Product Liability Rules in OECD Countries* (Paris: OECD, 1995), 32.

41. The Vienna Chamber of Commerce formed the Verein für Einkaufsberatung in 1953; the Austrian Trade Union Federation formed the Verband Österreichischer Konsumentenorganisationen (VOKO) in 1958.

42. Hans Peter Lehofer, "Minimum Implementation of Minimum Directives? Consumer Protection in Austria in the Context of European Integration," *Journal of Consumer Policy* 17, no. 1 (1994): 5.

43. OECD, CCP (81)1/2.

44. Hans Thorelli and Sarah Thorelli, *Consumer Information Handbook: Europe and North America* (New York: Praeger, 1974), 77.

45. OECD, CCP (83)1/02.

46. Ibid., (81)1/2.

47. This event was modeled on Germany's annual consumer film festival, hosted in Berlin by that country's main consumer association beginning in 1971.

48. Roland von Falckenstein, *Die Bekaempfung unlauterer Geschaeftspraktiken durch Verbraucherverbaende* (Köln: Bundesanzeiger, 1977).

49. Ewoud H. Hondius, "Unfair Contract Terms: New Control Systems," *The American Journal of Comparative Law* 26, no. 4 (1978): 535.

50. OECD, DAF/CCP 73.20/02.

51. OECD, CCP (84)1/02.

52. Ibid., (83)1/02.

53. Ibid., (79)1/03.

54. Matthew Hilton, *Consumerism in 20th-Century Britain* (Cambridge, UK: Cambridge University Press, 2003), 188–189. Hilton's work provides the most authoritative and complete account of the British consumer movement, and I rely heavily on it for the description that follows.

55. The Kitemark symbol was indicated by the letters *B* and *S* arranged to look vaguely like a kite. United Nations Industrial Development Organisation, *International Product Standards: Trends and Issues* (New York: United Nations, 1991), 37.

56. Dorothy Goodman, an American graduate student at the London School of Economics, imported the idea to the United Kingdom. See Lawrence Black, "Which? Craft in Post-War Britain: The Consumers' Association and the Politics of Affluence," *Albion* 63, no. 1 (2004): 55.

57. Thorelli and Thorelli, *Consumer Information Handbook*, 29.

58. Yiannis Gabriel and Tim Lang, *The Unmanageable Consumer: Contemporary Consumption and its Fragmentation* (London: Sage Publications, 1995), 181.

59. Hilton, *Consumerism,* 214–215.

60. Ibid., 215–216.

61. Barrister J. T. Molony, who oversaw the commission, reportedly prided himself on having no professional knowledge of consumer issues.

62. Hilton, *Consumerism,* 228–233.

63. Roberta Sassatelli, "Power Balance in the Consumption Sphere: Reconsidering Consumer Protection Organizations," EUI Working Paper SPS No. 95/5 (Florence, Italy: European University Institute, 1995): 27.

64. Lizabeth Cohen, *A Consumer's Republic: The Politics of Mass Consumption in Postwar America* (New York: Vintage, 2004); Mark V. Nadel, *The Politics of Consumer Protection* (Indianapolis: Bobbs-Merrill, 1971).

65. For an extensive account of these committees, see Jeanine Gilmartin, "An Historical Analysis of the Growth of the National Consumer Movement in the United States, 1947–1967" (PhD dissertation, Georgetown University, 1969).

66. Gary Bryner, "La Protection du consommateur aux Etats Unis," *Revue française d'administration publique* 56 (1990): 596.

67. Ibid., 591–603. Bryner notes that the entire New Deal encompassed only forty legislative projects.

68. Cohen, *Consumer's Republic,* 348.

69. This sort of simplified content analysis does not provide a perfect indicator. As consumer policies are increasingly adopted, published articles capture both aspirations for consumer protection as well as successful projects to secure consumer protection.

70. Louis Bader and J. P. Wernette, "Consumer Movements and Business," *The Journal of Marketing* 3, no. 1 (1938): 8–9; Hayagreeva Rao, "The Construction of Non-profit Consumer Watchdog Organizations," *American Journal of Sociology* 103, no. 4 (1998): 940–941; Cohen, *Consumer's Republic,* 59–60.

71. Eugene R. Beem and John S. Ewing, "Business Appraises Consumer Testing Agencies," *Harvard Business Review* 32 (March–April 1954): 121.

72. Lawrence Glickman, *Buying Power: A History of Consumer Activism in America* (Chicago: University of Chicago Press, 2009), 285.

3. CONSUMER MOBILIZATION IN POSTWAR FRANCE

1. Michel Crozier, *The Bureaucratic Phenomenon* (Chicago: University of Chicago Press, 1964), 316–317; Jonah D. Levy, *Tocqueville's Revenge: State, Society, and Economy in Contemporary France* (Cambridge, MA: Harvard University Press, 1999), 13.

2. Peter A. Hall, *Governing the Economy: The Politics of State Intervention in Britain and France* (New York: Oxford University Press, 1986), 165.

3. Dominique Pons, *Consomme et tais-toi* (Paris: Epi, 1972), 97.

4. G. H. Gallup, *The International Gallup Polls: Public Opinion 1978* (Wilmington, DE: Scholarly Resources, 1979), 365; *Le Nouveau Journal,* 28 September 1979.

5. *Liberation,* 7 April 1983, 14.

6. Olson, *Logic of Collective Action,* 157.

7. "Une enquête de l'Union fédérale des consommateurs," *Le Monde,* 12 December 1979.

8. Louis Pinto, "Le Consommateur: Agent économique et acteur politique," *Revue Française de Sociologie* 31, no. 2 (1990): 190.

9. From an internal document of the UFC, cited in François Daujam, "Information et pouvoir des consommateurs: Le rôle de l'union fédérale des consommateurs," (thèse, présentée a la faculté des sciences économiques et sociales de l'Université de Toulouse, 1980), 23. (Sadly, nearly all of the archives of the early period of the UFC were lost in the 1996 Crédit Lyonnais fire.)

10. "La naissance de l'U.F.C.," *Bulletin D'Information de L'UFC,* September–October 1973, 6–7.

11. Frank Cochoy, "A Brief History of 'Customers,' or the Gradual Standardization of Markets and Organizations," supplement, *Sociologie du Travail* 47, no. Sl (2005): 40.

12. Daujam, "Information et pouvoir des consommateurs," 26.

13. Gunnar Trumbull, "Strategies of Consumer-Group Mobilization," in *The Politics of Consumption,* ed. Martin Daunton and Matthew Hilton (Oxford, UK: Berg, 2001), 269.

14. Daujam, "Information et pouvoir des consommateurs," 44–63.

15. Ibid., 33; *Que Choisir?* 42, February 1970.

16. National Assembly, Second Session, 1 December 1966, 5151.

17. He uses the term *complexe*, a psychological diagnosis that implies an irrational response. I translate this as "hysteria" to capture the pejorative and specifically misogynistic tone.

18. Sénat, Second Session, 13 December 1966, 2431–2433.

19. *Que Choisir?* 70, December 1972.

20. Archives of the National Consumer Institute (INC), Paris, France. Speech by Michel Debré, Ministere de l'Economie et de Finance, 18 January 1968, at the first meeting of the Administrative Council of the INC.

21. Alain Ancelot, "Henri Estingoy: Changer la vie, c'est changer la manière de consommer," *Telerama*, 10–16 January 1976 (no. 817).

22. Jean Calvo, "L'affaire Beaufour et le problème de la résponsabilité des associations de consommateurs," *Le Moniteur des Pharmacies et des Laboratories*, 20 October 1984, 4371–4374.

23. Cited in Jean-Claude Fourgoux, "Halte aux apprentis sorciers du boycott!," *LSA*, 10 November 1978 (no. 689), 34–35.

24. "Nouveau Visage pour l'INC," *COCLICO—Consommateurs, Clients, Consommateurs* 41, 23 June 1978.

25. *Agra Alimentation* 668, 21 June 1978, 1.

26. "INC version 1979: A la recherché de l'efficacite," *LSA* 689, 10 November 1978, 36.

27. *Le Quotidien,* 13 January 1983.

28. *La Croix,* 23 June 1984, 16.

29. Helene Crie, "Guerre des virgules et grève anti-chef a '50 millions de consommateurs,'" *Libération,* 25 May 1984.

30. Archives of the UFC, accessed at the offices of the UFC, Paris, France. Letter from Marie-José Nicoli to the secretary of state for consumption and competition, 11 March 1988.

31. These groups included la Confédération syndicale des familles (CSF—1946); la Confédération nationale de la famille rurale (CNFR—1944); l'Union des associations familiales (UNAF—1945); la Fédération des familles de France (FFF—1948); and la Confédération nationale des associations populaires familiales (CNAPF).

32. This excludes funding for the government-sponsored group INC.

33. Marie-Elisabeth Bordes and Sylvie George, *Politique de la consommation dans la communauté Européene,* Memoire (Paris: Université de Droit et de Sciences Sociales de Paris, 1982), 101; Noëlle Marotte, *Bilan et perspectives de la politique française a l'égard des consommateurs* (Paris: Conseil Economique et Social, 1984), 20; Michel Bernard and Jacqueline Quentin, *L'avant-garde des consommateurs: Luttes et organisations en France et a l'étranger* (Paris: Editions Ouvrières, 1975), 87–91.

34. *Un monde en mouvement: les organisations de consommation* (Paris: Ministère de l'économie—comité national de la consommation, September 1980), 79.

35. "Six organisations de consommateurs contre les 'Boîtes postales 5000,'" *Le Monde,* 26 November 1976.

36. Michel Bernard and Jacqueline Quentin, *L'avant-garde des consommateurs: Luttes et organisations en France et a l'étranger* (Paris: Editions Ouvrières, 1975), 87–91.

37. "Les Français ne font pas confiance aux fabricants pour défendre les consommateurs," *La Croix,* 2 October 1976.

38. "Le Consumerisme," *Libre Service Actualités* 632 (30 June 1977): 135–136.

39. Ibid., 134.

40. "Les contestataires amoureux," *Le Monde Dimanche,* 25 November 1979.

41. "Le Service consommateurs prend peu à peu figure dans l'entreprise," *Les Echos,* 3 May 1979; Christiane Scrivener, "Pour un 'service consommateurs' dans les entreprises," *Les Notes Bleues du Service de l'information du Ministére de l'économie et des finances,* 6 April 1977; Jean-Marc Biais, "L'État dépense pour les consommateurs," *La Vie Française* 30, January 1978, 6.

42. AFEI was eliminated in 1984. Pierre Frybourg (president of AFEI), "L'Étiquetage d'information," *Revue de la concurrence et de la consommation* 12 (1980): 14–16; "L'Étiquetage informatif vous aide dans vos achats," *Information Consommation Or-Ge-Co* 27 (March–April 1978): 3–4; Jacques Dubois "L'affichage des prix . . . ne doit être qu'un premier pas." *Information Consommateur* 72, no. 1 (1972): 3–4.

43. Dominique Pons, *Consomme et tais-toi* (Paris: Epi, 1972), 98.

44. Marcel Garrigou, *L'Assaut des consommateurs pour changer les rapports producteurs—vendeurs—consommateurs* (Paris: Aubier-Montaigne, 1981), 53–54.

45. "Que la protection des consommateurs est un objectif essentiel des producteurs et des distributeurs et que l'intervention de l'état n'est pas toujours indispensable pour resoudre leurs problemes d'information et de défense." Chambre de commerce et d'industrie de Paris, "Problèmes de la consommation," rapport présenté au nom de la Commission du Commerce Intérieur par H. Ehrsam. Adopted May 24, 1973, p. 15.

46. Garrigou, *L'Assaut des consommateurs,* 53–54.

47. Gérard Lavergne, "Eux, les clients," *CNPF Patronat* 429 (November 1981): 22.

48. ". . . nous sommes tres ouverts a toute forme de concertation, plus particulierement dans le domaine de l'information . . ."; "Opinions sur la fonction consommation et la libre entreprise," *Humanisme et Entreprise* 102 (April 1977): 16.

49. *"Je voudrais affirmer qu'une concertation est indispensable"*; Jean-Georges Marais, "Le consommateur, cet inconnu?" *Humanisme et Entreprise* 102 (April 1977): 69.

50. Garrigou, *L'Assaut des consommateurs,* 161–162.

51. Commisariat General du Plan, *Rapport du comité consommation: Préparation du 7e plan* (Paris: Documentation Française, 1976), 16; Jacques Dubois, "Les consommateurs dans le 7ème plan," *Information Consommation OR-GE-CO* 15 (March–April 1976): 1–2.

52. René Monory, *Inauguration des locaux de l'institut national de la consommation* (Paris: Ministre de l'économie, Service de l'information, March 1979), 3.

53. Gisèle Prevost, "Consommation: 'l'Agressivité' de l'INC préoccupe de plus en plus le CNPF," *Les Echos,* 28 May 1979.

54. Jean Marchand, "M. Monory veut des consommateurs puissants," *La Croix,* 28 September 1979.

55. "René Monory: D'avantage de moyens pour informer les consommateurs," *Démocratie Moderne* 22 (November 1979).

56. Formerly the *Direction de la concurrence et des prix*. Jean Marchand, "Une 'mission consommation' au ministère de l'economie," *La Croix,* 17 June 1978.

57. Gérard Lavergne, "Eux, les clients," *CNPF Patronat* 429 (November 1981): 22.

58. "Accords négociés entre associations de consommateurs et professionels," *INC Hebdo* 624 (3 February 1989): 14.

59. "La guerre est finie," *CNPF Patronat* 447 (July 1983): 71–72.

60. "La charte 92," *50 Millions de Consommateurs* 122 (February 1981).

61. *Consommateurs Actualité* 282 (3 April 1981).

62. Garrigou, *L'Assaut des consommateurs,* 70–71.

63. Noëlle Marotte, *Bilan et perspectives de la politique francaise a l'egard des consommateurs* (Paris: Conseil Economique et Social, 1984), 98–99.

64. Elisabeth Rochard, "Pour informer les consommateurs: Un 'certificat de qualification,'" *Le Matin,* 27 Jun 1979.

65. Didier Ferrier, *La Protection des Consommateurs* (Paris: Dalloz, 1996), 80–81.

66. Created by decree 81–704 of 16 July 1981.

67. Josée Doyère, "Un entretien avec le ministre de la consommation," *Le Monde,* 17 September 1981.

68. Gérard Lavergne, "Eux, les clients," *CNPF Patronat* 429 (November 1981): 22.

69. "Négociation collective: Le point de vue des juristes," *Que Savoir* 43–44 (June–July 1982): 53.

70. Chambre de commerce et d'industrie de Paris, "La Politique de la Consommation," rapport présenté au nom de la Commission du Commerce Intérieur par Messieurs Lefebvre et Blat, adopted 14 January and 11 March 1982.

71. Jean Calais-Auloy, *Droit de la Consommation,* 3rd ed. (Paris: Dalloz, 1992), 49–50.

72. "Contrats d'amélioration de la qualité," *Consommateurs Actualités* 501 (21 March 1986): 19.

73. "Contrats de qualité," *Consommateurs Actualités* 498 (28 February 1986): 17.

74. Calais-Auloy, *Droit de la Consommation,* 49–50; Ferrier, *La Protection des Consommateurs,* 83.

75. "Contrats d'amélioration de la qualité," *Consommateurs Actualités* 501 (21 March 1986): 17–19.

76. "Qualité: Les consommateurs veulent un label unique européen," *Consommateurs Actualités* 604 (9 September 1988): 20.

77. Josée Doyère, "Des 'conventions collectives' de la consommation rendront obligatoires les engagements des professionnels," *Le Monde,* 5 December 1981.

78. Chambre de commerce et d'industrie de Paris, "La Creation du Conseil National de la Consommation," rapport présenté au nom de la Commission du Commerce Intérieur par M. Gaucher, adopted 19 May 1983, 10.

79. Elisabeth Rochard, "Le CNPF ne veut pas de conventions collectives de la consommation," *Le Matin,* 19 February 1982.

80. Ministère de la Justice, "Observations sur l'eventualité de conventions collectives entre les organisations de consommateurs et les professionnels" (Paris: Ministère de la Justice, 14 March 1980), 2.

81. The "Aprouvé" contracts remained a feature of the French product quality system, but were in limited use (only twenty-four such agreements were in use 2003) and were applied mainly in services, especially the life insurance sector.

82. Françoise Vaysse, "Les anges gardiens de la sécurité," *Le Monde,* 14 April 1992.

83. Thomas Bernauer and Ladina Caduff, "In Whose Interest? Pressure Group Politics, Economic Competition and Environmental Regulation," *Journal of Public Policy* 24, no. 1 (2004): 99–126.

4. INTEREST GROUP COALITIONS AND INSTITUTIONAL STRUCTURES

1. Emilia Titan, Vergil Voineagu, Gheorghe Epuran, Simona Ghita, Christina Boboc, and Daniela Todose, "Retail Commerce in Large European Store Chains," *Revista Romana de Statistica* 2007, no. 2 (2007): 1–11.

2. Rachel Poole, Graham P. Clarke, and David B. Clarke, "Growth, Concentration, and Regulation in European Food Retailing," *European Urban and Regional Studies* 9, no. 2 (2002): 172.

3. Clifford M. Gay, "Controlling New Retail Spaces: The Impress of Planning Policies in Western Europe," *Urban Studies* 35, no. 5–6 (1998): 206. Germany compensated for the efficiency of large suburban retail sites in part by the efficiency of its downtown deep discount sector.

4. Michael H. Ebner, "Re-reading Suburban America: Urban Population Deconcentration, 1810–1980," *American Quarterly* 37, no. 3 (1985): 379–380.

5. See, for example, John Stilgoe, *Borderland: Origins of the American Suburb, 1820–1939* (New Haven, CT: Yale University Press, 1988); Lewis Mumford, "Suburbia: The End of a Dream," in *The End of Innocence: A Suburban Reader,* ed. Charles M. Haar (New York: Free Press, 1968); Edwin Banfield, *The Unheavenly City: The Nature and Future of Our Urban Crisis* (Boston: Little, Brown, 1970); Anthony Downs, *Opening Up the Suburbs* (New Haven, CT: Yale University Press, 1973).

6. Kristin Ross, *Fast Cars, Clean Bodies: Decolonization and Reordering of French Society* (Cambridge, MA: MIT Press, 1995).

7. Interview with Wilhelm Söfker, Bundesministerium für Verkehr, Bau- und Wohnungswesen, Berlin, Germany, 3 February 2004.

8. Bruno Tietz, *Konsument und Einzelhandel: Strukturwandlungen in der Bundesrepublik Deutschland von 1970 bis 1995* (Frankfurt: Lorch, 1983), 79.

9. Sighart Nehring, "Ladenschlussgesetz: Deregulierung auch im Einzelhandel?" *Wirtschaftsdienst* 1 (1984): 41.

10. HBV was later integrated into the larger union organization Ver.di.

11. *Ladenschluß in Europa: Erfahrungen der Nachbarn—Konsequenzen für die Bundesrepublik?* (Königswinter: Friedrich Naumann Stiftung, October 1985), 6; Christian Uwe Täger, Kurt Vogler-Ludwig, and Sophia Munz, *Das deutsche Ladenschlußgesetz auf dem Prüfstand: Binnenhandels- und wettbewerbspolitische sowie beschäftigungspolitische und arbeitsrechtliche Überlegungen* (Berlin: Duncker & Humblot, 1995), 75.

12. *Bundestagdrucksache* 10, no. 517 (1955), question 23.

13. James B. Jefferys and Derek Knee, *Retailing in Europe: Present Structure and Future Trends* (London: Macmillan & Co., 1962).

14. Patrick Molle, *Le Commerce et la Distribution en Europe* (Paris: Editions Liaisons, 1992).

15. Andreas Fischer, *DGB-Verbraucherpolitik zwischen Anspruch und politischer Praxis* (Frankfurt: Peter Lang, 1991), 165.

16. Ibid., 171.

17. Jean J. Boddewyn and Stanley C. Hollander, *Public Policy Toward Retailing: An International Symposium* (Lexington, MA: Lexington Books, 1972), 264.

18. Interview with Sonia Hein, Bundesministerium für Wirtschaft und Arbeit, Bonn, Germany, 2 February 2004.

19. Interview with Ingeborg Erdmann, Bundesministerium für Wirtschaft und Arbeit, Berlin, 3 February 2004.

20. Günter Triesch, "Mehr Sachlichkeit in der Ladenschlußdiskussion," *BAG-Nachtrichten* 5 (1984): 4.

21. "Eine liberalere Ladenschlußregelung ist überfällig," *Verbraucherpolitische Korrespondenz* 21 (22 May 1984): 3.

22. "Das Ladenschlußgesetz: Die Argumente des Einzelhandels," *Hauptgemeinschaft des Deutschen Einzelhandels,* Press Release, 3/4 November 1983.

23. "BAG für sachliche Argumentation in der Ladenschlußdiskussion," *Press-Information: Bundesarbeitsgemeinschaft der Mittel- und Großbetriebe des Einzelhandels*, 22 May 1984.

24. "Blüm: Dienstleistungsabend ein Gewinn für alle," *Süddeutsche Zeitung,* 23 June 1988.

25. "Gesetz über Dienstleistungsabend gebilligt," *Süddeutsche Zeitung,* 3 June 1989.

26. "Ladenschluß: Die Stimmung ist geladen," *Der Spiegel,* 29 May 1989, 105.

27. Hans Jürgensen, "'Langer Donnerstag' auch in Warenhäusern?" *Frankfurter Allgemeine,* 29 June 1989.

28. "'Langer Donnerstag' nur bei Konkurrenz," *Frankfurter Allgemeine,* 12 July 1989.

29. Jürgensen, "'Langer Donnerstag' auch in Warenhäusern?"

30. Peter Gillies, "Die SPD im Kampf gegen den abendlich Einkauf," *Die Welt,* 5 October 1989.

31. *The Reuter European Business Report*, February 2, 1996.

32. Ifo Institut für Wirtschaftsforschung, *Überprüfung des Ladenschlußgesetzes vor dem Hintergrund der Erfahrungen im In- und Ausland* (Munich: Ifo Institut, 1995), 10.

33. Wilfred Paulus, *Ladenschluß* (Königswinter: Friedrich Naumann Stiftung, 1985), 140.

34. Ifo Institut, *Überprüfung des Ladenschlußgesetzes*, 18.

35. Interview with Sonia Hein, Bundesministerium für Wirtschaft und Arbeit, 2 February 2004.

36. Interview with Holger Wenzel (director, HDE) 4 February 2004.

37. Sunday openings were the exception to this devolved power, as they were blocked along with all other noncritical Sunday jobs by the German Constitution.

38. Peter McGoldrick and Gary Davies, eds., *International Retailing: Trends and Strategies* (London: Pitman Publishing, 1995), 90.

39. Cliff Guy, "Internationlisation of Large-Format Retailers and Leisure Providers in Western Europe: Planning and Property Impacts," *International Journal of Retail & Distribution Management* 29, no. 10 (2001): 452–461.

40. Söfker interview.

41. The legal basis for state planning is provided in another piece of legislation, the Raumordnungsgesetz.

42. McGoldrick and Davies, *International Retailing*, 23.

43. Interview with Ulrich Martinius, BAG, Berlin, Germany, February 2004.

44. Wenzel interview.

45. Robert Lagre, "Giscard contre Nicoud ou la dernière galéjade de Valéry," *Rivarol*, 2 April 1970.

46. Roger Eatwell, "Poujadism and Neo-Poujadism: From Revolt to Reconciliation," in *Social Movements and Protest in France*, ed. Philip G. Cerny (London: Frances Pinter, 1982), 81–82.

47. "Entretien avec Gérard Nicoud," *L'Express*, 1 June 1970.

48. Lagre, "Giscard contre Nicoud."

49. "Militant Shopkeepers," *The Times*, 11 March 1970.

50. "Barrages de routes et manifestations de commerçants hier dans tout le pays," *Humanité*, 24 March 1970.

51. François Mirallès, "Revendications legitimes et actions injustifiées," *Le Figaro*, 24 March 1970.

52. "Le carême de M. Nicoud," *L'Express*, 22 March 1971.

53. Suzanne Berger, "Regime and Interest Representation: The French Traditional Middle Class," in *Organizing Interests in Western Europe: Pluralism, Corporatism, and the Transformation of Politics*, ed. Suzanne Berger (New York: Cambridge University Press, 1981), 94.

54. Eatwell, "Poujadism and Neo-Poujadism," 83.

55. Eric Langeard and Robert Malsagne, *Les Magasins de grande surface* (Paris: Dunod, 1971), 12–13.

56. Daujam, "Information et pouvoir des consommateurs," 41.

57. Claude Romec, "Organisations de consommateurs," *Reforme*, 15 December 1975.

58. Berger, "Regime and Interest Representation," 95.

59. Luc Bihl, *Consommateur, Défends-toi!* (Paris: Denoël, 1976), pp. 23–24.

60. Josée Doyère, *Le Combat des consommateurs* (Paris: Éditions du Cerf, 1975), 69–70.

61. Michel Wieviorka, *L'Etat, le Patronat, et les Consommateurs: Etude des mouvements de consommateurs* (Paris: Presses Universitaires de France, 1977), 53–54.

62. Pierre Combris, J. Hossenlopp, and Elise Zitt, "Evolution des associations de consommateurs et leurs impact sur les industriels," *Problèmes Économiques* (11 January 1978): 10.

63. "La Naissance de l'U.F.C," *Bulletin D'Information de L'UFC*, September–October 1973.

64. Roger-Xavier Lanteri, "Prix: Que peuvent faire les consommateurs?" *L'Express,* 20 September 1976.

65. Pons, *Consomme et tais-toi!,* 98.

66. Interview with Pierre Marleix (former president of AFOC), 2004.

67. Wieviorka, *L'Etat, le Patronat, et les Consommateurs,* 131.

68. Maurice columns, still used in France, are a traditional public forum for the posting of information. Wieviorka, *L'Etat, le Patronat, et les Consommateurs,* 53–54.

69. Gérard Cliquet, Véronique des Garets, Guy Basset, and Rozen Perrigot, "50 ans de grandes surfaces en France: Entre croissance débridée et contraintes légales," paper presented at the 7th International Congress on Marketing Trends, January 2008 (http://www.escp-eap.net/conferences/marketing/2008_cp/Materiali/Paper/Fr/Cliquet_DesGarets_Basset_Perrigot.pdf).

70. Emmanuelle Réju, "Commerce 'défendre le pain artisanal contre le pain industriel,'" *La Croix,* 4 January 1997.

71. Philip Nord, *Paris Shopkeepers and the Politics of Resentment* (Princeton, NJ: Princeton University Press, 1986).

5. POLICY NARRATIVES AND DIFFUSE INTEREST REPRESENTATION

1. Cédric Houdré, "L'Endettement des ménages début 2004," *Insee Première* 1131 (April 2007): 2.

2. One might question Cofidis's objectivity. Their conclusion from the survey was that the European Union should step in to impose uniform consumer protection standards across European credit markets. Cécile Desjardins, "Cofidis appelle à une réglementation européenne du crédit à la consommation," *Les Echos,* 29 May 2001.

3. Law 78–22, transcribed as articles 311–313 of the Consumer Code.

4. Hubert Balaguy, *Le crédit à la consommation en France* (Paris: Presses Universitaires de Paris, 1996), 88–89.

5. François Renard, "Le crédit gratuity va pratiquement disparaître," *Le Monde,* 25 July 1984, 19.

6. Laurent Chavane, "L'Enterrement discret du 'crédit gratuit,'" *Le Figaro,* 23 July 1984.

7. Marie-Emilie Morel, *L'Evolution du crédit renouvelable: La consolidation du regime de protection de l'emprunteur,* Mémoire (Montpellier: Université de Montpellier, 2006), 34–35.

8. Michel Gaudin, *Le crédit au particulier: Aspects économiques, techniques, juridiques et fiscaux* (Paris: SÉFI, 1996), 77–83.

9. *Le Monde,* 25 November 1996.

10. Hugues Puel, "Crazy George's met l'éthique au défi," *La Croix,* 11 December 1996.

11. Jan Evers and Udo Reifner, *The Social Responsibility of Credit Institutions in the EU* (Baden-Baden: Nomos Verlagsgesellschaft, 1998) 133.

12. 2003 White Paper: "Fair, Clear and Competitive: The Consumer Credit Market in the 21st Century."

13. John Willman, "Shake-Up of Credit Rights to Protect Borrower," *Financial Times,* 7 April 2007.

14. Cécile Desjardins, "La guerre ouverte des professionnels," *Les Echos,* 29 March 2000, 63.

15. Renaud de la Baume, "Les banques peinent sur le marché du crédit à la consommation," *La Tribune de L'Expansion,* 26 March 1992.

16. Kerry Capell, "Britain's Coming Credit Crisis," *Business Week,* 17 September 2007, 68.

17. Pierre-Laurent Chatain and Frédéric Ferrière, *Surendettement des particuliers* (Paris: Editions Dalloz, 2000), 188.

18. Catherine Maussion, "Crédit: Tout le monde dans le même fichier?" *Libération,* 5 October 2002.

19. Bertrand Bissuel and Anne Michel, "Les établissements de crédit accusés de favoriser le surendettement, *Le Monde,* 28 April 2005; Sylvie Ramadier, "La bataille du crédit à la consommation," *Les Echos,* 21–22 January 2005, 8.

20. CreditCall was established 2001 in close collaboration with its U.S. counterpart TransUnion.

21. Hence the term *credit reference agency* rather than *credit rating agency.*

22. The European Commission brought a case against France before the European Court of Justice for delaying implementation of the directive. France responded slowly in part due to the challenges of modifying its own strong data protection policies established in its own data privacy regime dating to 1978 legislation.

23. EU Directive 95/46/EC Article 2.d.

24. Niemi-Kiesilainen, "Changing Directions in Consumer Bankruptcy Law and Practice in Europe and the USA," *Journal of Consumer Policy* 20, no. 1 (1997): 133–142.

25. Ibid.

26. Civil Justice Review, *Report of the Review Body on Civil Justice* 394 (London: Her Majesty's Stationery Office, 1988); J. E. Davies, "Delegalisation of debt recovery proceedings: A socio-legal study of money advice centres and administration orders," *Debtors and Creditors: A Socio-legal Perspective*, ed. I. Ramsay (Abingdon: Butterworth, 1986), 191–192, 182–207.

27. "Un peu d'oxygène pour les familles surendettées," *Nous* 103, March–April 1990, 9.

28. Balaguy, *Le crédit à la consommation*, 106–107.

29. INC, *Le dispositif juridique* (internal publication).

30. *Familles de France* 664 (September 2000).

31. INC, *Le surendettement en chiffres* (internal publication).

32. Renaud de la Baume, "Surendettement: Un banquier dénonce les 'tricheurs,'" *La Tribune a l'Expansion,* 19 March 1992.

33. Dominique Dagorne, "La faillite civile en Alsace et en Moselle," in *Le surendettement des particuliers*, ed. Michel Gardaz (Paris: Economica, 1997).

34. INC, *Le dispositif juridique.*

35. INC, "Les débats sur le surendettement continuent," *INC Hebdo,* 28 March 2003, 2.

36. "Reinventing the Wheel: The Government Is Looking at the US Model in its Plans to Reform UK Insolvency Law," *Financial Times,* 15 July 1999, 26.

37. Jane Croft, "Personal Insolvency Hits Record 107, 288," *Financial Times*, 3 February 2007, 13.
38. The Enterprise Act 2002," in *Credit Management*, March 2004, 30.
39. Vernon Dennis and Alexander Fox, *The New Law of Insolvency: Insolvency Act 1986 to Enterprise Act 2002* (London: Law Society, 2003), 215.

6. THE LIMITS OF REGULATORY CAPTURE

1. U.S. Congressional Budget Office, "Agricultural Trade Liberalization" (Economic and Budget Issue Brief), November 20, 2006, 3–5.
2. European Commission, *Agriculture in the European Union: Statistical and Economic Information 2005* (Luxembourg: European Commission, February 2006), 211–223.
3. Australia and New Zealand were notable exceptions, with previously generous agricultural subsidies having been virtually eliminated in the late 1980s.
4. André Siegfried, *Tableau politique de la France de l'ouest sous la Troisième République* (Paris: A. Colin, 1913); Charles Tilly, *The Vendée: A Sociological Analysis of the Counter-Revolution of 1793* (Cambridge, MA: Harvard University Press, 1963).
5. Karl Marx, "The Eighteenth Brumaire of Louis Bonaparte," in *The Mark-Engels Reader,* ed. Robert C. Tucker (New York: W. W. Norton, 1978), 594.
6. Phylloxera is a fungus that produces galls on the leaves and roots of grape vines; it is considered to be a serious disease in wine-producing regions.
7. R. D. Anderson, *France 1870–1914: Politics and Society* (Boston: Routledge, 1984), 31.
8. Henry W. Ehrman, "The French Peasant and Communism," *American Political Science Review* 49, no. 1 (1952): 27.
9. For a fuller account, see Gordon Wright, "Agrarian Socialism in Postwar France," *American Political Studies Review* 47, no. 2 (1953): 402–416.
10. Agriculture's influence was also written into the electoral institutions of the Fourth and Fifth Republics. French senators are appointed by an electoral college composed of electors drawn from France's 36,000 municipalities. Ninety-five percent of these municipalities were rural. As one official noted: "A French politician needs to be grounded in a local community and to be sure that he has enough political support there if he wants to be appointed to the National Assembly, the Senate, the local council [. . .]. That means French politicians need the support of farmers. Even if today things are changing, there still is a strong link between French politicians and the agricultural world." Interview with Patrick Ferrère, President of the Fédération nationale des syndicats d'expoitants agricoles (FNSEA), June 2006.
11. Olson, *Logic of Collective Action*, 157.
12. Interview with Patrick Ferrère, June 2006.
13. Markus F. Hofreither, "The Treaties of Rome and the Development of the Common Agricultural Policy" (Discussion Paper DP-23-2007), Vienna, Institut für nachhältige Wirtschaftsentwicklung, 2007.

14. CAP import tariffs had numerous exemptions that were often politically motivated. Former European colonies in Africa and among the Caribbean and Pacific islands (ACP countries) were also granted preferential access to European agricultural markets within specific quotas.

15. By 2005, the CAP was covering 90 percent of European agricultural production: only potatoes for human consumption and spirits were excluded.

16. The EAGGF was made of two different sections: the Guarantee section, which financed the CMOs, and the Guidance section for farm restructuring and modernization investments and rural development policies. The Guarantee section of the EAGGF is commonly referred to as the CAP budget; the Guidance section is usually associated with EU regional development policies (structural funds). In the 1960s, the Guidance section mainly financed modernization investments and farm restructuring. In the 1970s and especially after the launch of the European Structural Funds, the fund started focusing more on rural development in poor regions (called Objective 1 Regions).

17. Allan M. Williams, *The European Community* (Oxford, UK: Blackwell, 1991), 46. Member states could also provide additional direct supports to their own farm sectors, so long as these met general European Commission requirements for the provision of state aid.

18. The stockpile of wheat alone was sufficient to feed all of France for two years, at an average consumption rate of 200 kilos of wheat per person per year.

19. Italy and Ireland both received dispensations allowing them to use 1983 as a reference year.

20. Interview with Hermanus Versteijlen (director of direct support, EU Agriculture Directorate-General), Brussels, June 2004.

21. Jean-Christophe Bureau and Alan Mathews, "EU Agricultural Policy: What Developing Countries Need to Know," Institute for International Integration Studies (IIS) Discussion Paper No. 91, Dublin, Ireland, October 2005.

22. Cereals and beef markets are closely linked. In particular, beef farmers benefit from lower prices for cereals used as animal feed. Bureau and Mathews, "EU Agricultural Policy."

23. Interview with Philippe Mangin, June 2004.

24. Aggravating this perception, agricultural prices remained high for several years after the 1992 reform. This meant that farmers were benefiting both from high prices *and* from direct supports.

25. Bureau and Mathews, "EU Agricultural Policy," 200.

26. The reforms were to be launched in five years for developed countries, or nine years for developing countries.

27. Under the URAA, amber box supports were to be eliminated entirely. Less distorting "blue box" supports, which included output-based payments that were linked to specific output limits, were accepted as a means of transitioning away from amber box supports. A third group of "green box" supports were fully acceptable. These included decoupled payments—supports that were not linked in any way to specific output.

28. Oxfam, "A Recipe for Disaster: Will the Doha Round Fail to Deliver for Development?" Oxfam Briefing Paper 87, Boston, Mass., April 2006, 8.

29. European Commission, *Agriculture in the European Union,* 122.

30. Versteijlen interview.

31. Interview with CAP official (anonymous), June 2006.

32. Interview with French agriculture official (anonymous), June 2006.

33. Budget outlays for market price support measures decreased while those for direct support to farmers increased. In 2004, 66.63 percent of the Guarantee section of EAGGF was allocated to direct aids. European Commission, *Agriculture in the European Union,* 122.

34. Ferrère interview, June 2006.

7. THE LIMITS OF LOBBYING

1. John K. Inglehart, "The New Medicare Prescription Drug Benefit: A Pure Power Play," *New England Journal of Medicine* 350, no. 8 (2004): 832.

2. *Fortune* 155, no. 8 (2007): F-32.

3. At the time, drug reimporting was only allowed with safety approval by the Department of Health and Human Services, and that was unlikely to occur. For a more detailed account of the legislative process, see Inglehart, "The New Medicare Prescription Drug Benefit, 826–833.

4. The 1990 Prior Act (Medicaid Prudent Pharmaceutical Purchasing Act, Public Law 101–508) had set Medicare drug purchase prices at 5 percent below the average discount of private insurance companies. The size of this discount is disputed. A Congressional Budget Office study found little advantage. Another study by U.S. Department of Veterans Affairs (VA) doctors found that the VA receives a 55 percent discount over the most favorable available prescription discount card program. John Kerry, John M. Hayes, Heather Walczak, and Allan Prochazka, "Comparison of Drug Regimen Costs between the Medicare Prescription Discount Program and Other Purchasing Systems," *Journal of the American Medical Association* 294, no. 4 (2005): 428.

5. Richard G. Frank, "Prescription Drug Prices," *New England Journal of Medicine* 351, no. 13 (2004): 1375.

6. Public Law 101–508.

7. Peter Davis, *Managing Medicines: Public Policy and Therapeutic Drugs* (Buckingham, UK: Open University Press, 1997), 15.

8. William C. Bogner, *Drugs to Market: Creating Value and Advantage in the Pharmaceutical Industry* (Oxford, UK: Pergamon 1996), 76.

9. Jane Mobley, *Prescription for Success: The Chain Drug Store* (Kansas City, MO: Lowell Press, 1990).

10. Bogner, *Drugs to Market,* 77–78.

11. Paul M. Hirsch, "Organizational Effectiveness and the Institutional Environment," *Administrative Science Quarterly* 20, no. 3 (1975): 333.

12. Bogner, *Drugs to Market,* 77.

13. Hirsch, "Organizational Effectiveness," 338–339.

14. David Schwartzman, *Innovation in the Pharmaceutical Industry* (Baltimore: Johns Hopkins University Press, 1976): 325.

15. Charles C. Edwards and Lacy Glenn Thomas, *The Competitive Status of the U.S. Pharmaceutical Industry: The Influences of Technology in Determining International Industrial Competitive Advantage* (Washington, DC: National Academy Press, 1983), 58–59.

16. Henry G. Grabowski, "Regulation and the International Diffusion of Pharmaceuticals," in *The International Supply of Medicines: Implications of U.S. Regulatory Reform,* ed. Robert B. Helms (Washington, DC: American Enterprise Institute, 1981), 7.

17. Henry G. Grabowski, John M. Vernon, and Lacy Glenn Thomas, "Estimating the Effects of Regulation on Innovation: An International Comparative Analysis of the Pharmaceutical Industry," *Journal of Law and Economics* 21, no. 1 (1978): 157.

18. Grabowski, "Regulation and International Diffusion of Pharmaceuticals," 8.

19. Edwards and Glenn Thomas, *Competitive Status of the U.S. Pharmaceutical Industry,* 62, 66–67.

20. Grabowski, Vernon, and Glenn Thomas, "Estimating the Effects of Regulation," 137.

21. Frank, "Prescription Drug Prices," 1377.

22. John Calfee, "The High Price of Cheap Drugs," *AEI Online,* July 1, 2003.

23. Jacob Arfwedson, "The High Cost of Cheap Drugs," *AEI-Brookings Joint Center Policy Matters,* December 2004

24. Michael R. Reich, "Why the Japanese Don't Export More Pharmaceuticals: Health Policy as Industrial Policy," *California Management Review* 32, no. 2 (1990): 140.

25. Casadio C. Tarabusi and Graham Vickery, "La mondialisation de l'industrie pharmaceutique," in *La Mondalisation de l'industrie: vue d'ensemble et rapports sectoriels* (Paris: OECD, 1996), 101–102.

26. Monique Plat, *Droit pharmaceutique industriel* (Paris: Centre de Documentation Universitaire, 1970), 7.

27. Patricia M. Danzon, *Pharmaceutical Price Regulation: National Policies versus Global Interests* (Washington, DC: American Enterprise Institute Press, 1997), 44.

28. Leigh Hancher, *Regulating for Competition: Government, Law, and the Pharmaceutical Industry in the United Kingdom and France* (Oxford, UK: Clarendon Press, 1990), 76.

29. Ibid., 92–93.

30. Jean-Paul Juès, *L'Industrie pharmaceutique* (Paris: Presses Universitaires de France, 1998), 70.

31. Stan N. Finkelstein and Peter G. Bittinger, "Price Controls and the Competitiveness of Pharmaceutical Firms: A Preliminary Look at the Experience of Five Countries." Working Paper 8–93, Sloan School of Management, Program on the Pharmaceutical Industry, Massachusetts Institute of Technology, Cambridge, MA, 1993, 12–13; Danzon, *Pharmaceutical Price Regulation,* 18–19.

32. Sandrine Hofstetter, "Les restructurations dans l'industrie pharmaceutique dans les années 1990," (PhD diss., University of Paris, Pantheon Sorbonne, 1996), 15.

33. Different levels of innovativeness were distinguished, ranging from 1 to 5, with different levels of reimbursement. Monique Mrazek and Elias Mossialos, "Regulating Pharmaceutical Prices in the European Union," in *Regulating Pharmaceuticals in Europe: Striving for Efficiency, Equity and Quality,* eds. Elias Mossialos, Monique Mrazek, and Tom Walley (London: McGraw-Hill, 2004), 117.

34. Juès, *L'Industrie pharmaceutique,* 77.

35. Albert Wertheimer, W. Michael Dickson, and Becky A. Briesacher, "Pharmacy in the Western World Health Care Systems," in *Contested Ground: Public Purpose and Private Interest in the Regulation of Prescription Drugs,* ed. P. Davis (New York: Oxford University Press, 1996), 162–163.

36. Finkelstein and Bittinger, "Price Controls," 12.

37. Wertheimer, Dickson, and Briesacher, "Pharmacy in the Western World," 162–163.

38. Juès, *L'Industrie pharmaceutique,* 70.

39. Syndicat National de l'Industrie Pharmaceutique (SNIP) data, 1996.

40. "L'industrie pharmaceutique," *Economie Géographie* 321–322, no. 1–2 (1995): 4; Danzon, *Pharmaceutical Price Regulation,* 18–19.

41. SNIP data, various years.

42. Hancher, *Regulating for Competition,* 89–90.

43. Alan Afuad, "Public Policy and Pharmaceutical Innovation: A Literature Review and Critique." Working Paper 14–93, Sloan School of Management, Program on the Pharmaceutical Industry, Massachusetts Institute of Technology, Cambridge, MA, 1993, 9–10.

44. Laurent Faibis, *Les laboratoires pharmaceutiques* (Paris: DAFSA Kompass, 1984), 23; Hancher, *Regulating for Competition,* 115.

45. Jean-Philippe Buisson and Dominique Giorgi, *La politique du médicament* (Paris: Montchrestien, 1997), 20.

46. Jean Brudon and Georges Viala, "France," in *International Pharmaceutical Services: The Drug Industry and Pharmacy Practice in Twenty-Three Major Countries of the World,* ed. Richard N. Spivey, Albert I. Wertheimer, and T. Donald Rucker (New York: Pharmaceutical Products Press, 1992), 215.

47. Buisson and Giorgi, *La politique du médicament,* 19.

48. Hancher, *Regulating for Competition,* 115.

49. Ibid., 124–127.

50. Buisson and Giorgi, *La politique du médicament,* 20–21.

51. Georges Viala and Daniel Vion, "La loi no. 94–43 du janvier 1994 et la pharmacie," *Revue de Droit Sanitaire et Social* 30, no. 2 (1994): 246–248; Valérie Paris, "Pharmaceutical Regulation in France: 1980–2003," *International Journal of Health Planning and Management* 20, no. 4 (2005): 308.

52. Arthur A Daemmrich, *Pharmacopolitics: Drug Regulation in the United States and Germany* (Chapel Hill: University of North Carolina Press, 2004), 39.

53. Günter Borchert, "Artzneimittelgesetz und Verbraucherschutz," *Zeitschrift Für Rechtspolitik* 8 (1983): 195.

54. H. Jaeger and R. Kaukewitsch, "Le droit pharmaceutique en République fédérale d'Allemagne," in *Droit Pharmaceutique*, ed. Jean-Marie Auby and Frank Coustou (Paris: Litec, 1998), 9.

55. Gerhard Wilhelm Bruck, *Perspektiven der Sozialpolitik: Synopse sozialpolitischer Vorstellung der Bundesregierung, SPD, FDP, CDU, CSU, DAG, des DGB und der Bundesvereinigung der Deutschen Arbeitgeberverbande* (Goettingen: Otto Schwartz, 1974), 136–139.

56. G. Rambow, "Verbraucherschutz in der 7. Legislaturperiode (1972–76) der Bundesrepublik Deutschland," *Zeitschrift für Verbraucherpolitik* 1, no. 2 (1977): 163.

57. Stiftung Warentest, *Test* 3 (1983), 2.

58. Heribert Schatz, "Consumer Interests in the Process of Political Decision-Making: A Study of Some Consumer Policy Decisions in the Federal Republic of Germany," *Journal of Consumer Policy* 6, no. 4 (1983): 386.

59. Leigh Hancher, "Regulating Drug Prices: The West German and British Experiences," in *Capitalism, Culture, and Economic Regulation*, ed. Leigh Hancher and Michael Moran (Oxford, UK: Clarendon Press, 1989), 90–91.

60. Finkelstein and Bittinger, "Price Controls," 18.

61. Patricia M. Danzon and Jonathan D. Ketchum, "Reference Pricing of Pharmaceuticals for Medicare: Evidence from Germany, the Netherlands, and New Zealand," in *Frontiers in Health Policy Research*, ed. David Cutler and Alan Garber (Cambridge, MA: MIT Press, 2004), 7.

62. Jaeger and Kaukewitch, "Le droit pharmaceutique," 10.

63. Finkelstein and Bittinger, "Price Controls," 17.

64. Wertheimer, Dickson, and Briesacher, "Pharmacy in the Western World," 166.

65. Jaeger and Kaukewitch, "Le droit pharmaceutique," 11.

66. Hennelore Sitzius-Zehender, Bertram Dervenilch, Frank Diener, and Gerd M. Foh, "Federal Republic of Germany," in *International Pharmaceutical Services: The Drug Industry and Pharmacy Practice in Twenty-Three Major Countries of the World*, ed. Richard Spivey (New York: Pharmaceutical Products Press, 1992), 244–245.

67. Danzon, *Pharmaceutical Price Regulation*, 19–20.

68. Andreas Broscheid, "Ending Cooperation: A Formal Model of Organizational Change in German Pharmaceutical Interest Representation." Discussion Paper 05/9, Max-Planck Institut für Gesellschaftsforschung (MPIfG), Cologne, Germany, 2005, 6–8.

69. European Commission, *Impact on Manufacturing: Pharmaceutical Products* (Luxembourg: European Commission, 1997), 70.

70. Danzon, *Pharmaceutical Price Regulation*, 53.

71. Jane A. Sargent, "The Politics of the Pharmaceutical Price Regulation Scheme," in *Private Interest Government: Beyond Market and State*, ed. Wolfgang Streeck and Philippe C. Schmitter (London: Sage Publications, 1985), 112–117.

72. Justin Greenwood and Karsten Ronit, "Pharmaceutical Regulation in Denmark and the UK: Reformulating Interest Representation to the Transnational Level," *European Journal of Political Research* 19, no. 2-3 (1991): 340.

73. Sargent, "Politics of Pharmaceutical Price," 120–121.

74. Alan Earl-Slater and Colin Bradley, "The Inexorable Rise in the UK NHS Drugs Bill: Recent Policies, Future Prospects," *Public Administration* 74, no. 3 (1996): 398.

75. OECD, L'Industrie pharmaceutique: Questions liées aux échanges (Paris: OECD, 1985), 40.

76. Martina Garau and Adrian Towse, "Pricing and Reimbursement Policies in the UK: Current and Future Trends," in *European Medicines Pricing and Reimbursement: Now and the Future*, ed. Martina Garau and Jorge Mestre-Ferrandiz (Oxford: Radcliffe Publishing, 2007), 41.

77. Earl-Slater and Bradley, "Inexorable Rise in UK NHS Drugs Bill," 399.

78. Sargent, "Politics of Pharmaceutical Price," 122.

79. Patricia M. Danzon and Li-Wei Chao, "Does Regulation Drive Out Competition in Pharmaceutical Markets?" *Journal of Law and Economics* 43, no. 2 (2000): 320.

80. Earl-Slater and Bradley, "Inexorable Rise in UK NHS Drugs Bill, 396.

81. Lacy Glenn Thomas, "Implicit Industrial Policy: The Triumph of Britain and the Failure of France in Global Pharmaceuticals," *Industrial and Corporate Change* 3, no. 2 (2002): 460.

82. Claudio Casadio Tarabusi and Graham Vickery, "La mondalisation de l'industrie pharmaceutique," in *La Mondalisation de l'industrie: Vue d'ensemble et rapports sectoriels* (Paris: OECD, 1996), 129; Grabowski, "Regulation and International Diffusion of Pharmaceuticals," 9.

83. Earl-Slater and Bradley, "Inexorable Rise in UK NHS Drugs Bill," 400–405.

84. Greenwood and Ronit, "Pharmaceutical Regulation in Denmark and the UK," 344–345.

85. Finkelstein and Bittinger, "Price Controls," 5.

86. See, most recently, U.K. Office of Fair Trading, *The Pharmaceutical Price Regulation Scheme* (London: Office of Fair Trading, 2007), http://www.oft.gov.uk/shared _oft/reports/comp_policy/oft885.pdf.

87. Thomas, "Implicit Industrial Policy," 461.

8. COALITIONS AND COLLECTIVE ACTION

1. Mancur Olson, *The Logic of Collective Action: Public Goods and the Theory of Groups* (Cambridge, MA: Harvard University Press, 1965); Russell Hardin, *Collective Action* (Baltimore: Johns Hopkins University Press, 1982); Elinor Ostrom, "A Behavioral Approach to the Rational Choice Theory of Collective Action: Presidential Address, American Political Science Association, 1997," *American Political Science Review* 92, no. 1 (1998).

2. Claus Offe, "The Attribution of Public Status to Interest Groups: Observations on the West German Case," in *Organizing Interests*, ed. Suzanne Berger (Cambridge: Cambridge University Press, 1983), 152–153.

3. James Q. Wilson, "The Politics of Regulation," in *The Politics of Regulation*, ed. James Q. Wilson (New York: Basic Books, 1980), 370–372.

4. See David Vogel, *Trading Up: Consumer and Environmental Regulation in a Global Economy* (Cambridge, MA: Harvard University Press, 1995); Dale D. Murphy, *The Structure of Regulatory Competition: Corporations and Public Policies in a Global Economy* (Oxford: Oxford University Press, 2004).

5. Harvey M. Sapolsky, "The Politics of Product Controversies," in *Consuming Fears: The Politics of Product Risk*, ed. Harvey Sapolsky (New York: Basic Books, 1987), 183.

6. This so-called Virginia School included University of Chicago–trained public policy scholars who were granted tenure at the University of Virginia, but also at the University of Maryland and George Mason University.

7. Victoria Murillo, "Political Competition, Partisanship, and Policymaking" (unpublished book manuscript, 2008).

8. Martha Durthick and Paul J. Quirk, *The Politics of Deregulation* (Washington, DC: Brookings Press, 1985).

9. Mancur Olson, *The Rise and Decline of Nations: Economic Growth, Stagflation, and Social Rigidities* (New Haven, CT: Yale University Press, 1984).

10. Michael Piore, *Beyond Individualism: How Social Demands of the New Identity Groups Challenge American Political and Economic Life* (Cambridge, MA: Harvard University Press, 1995).

Acknowledgments

This work has drawn help and inspiration from a wide range of scholars and practitioners. I would like to thank Peter Hall, Suzanne Berger, Nicholas Ziegler, Bob Hancke, Keith Darden, Pepper Culpepper, and Orfeo Fioretos. At Harvard Business School (HBS) my colleagues in the Business, Government and International Economy (BGIE) area have provided invaluable support and suggestions. My thanks to Julio Rotemberg, Forest Reinhardt, Dick Vietor, David Moss, Rawi Abdelal, Noel Maurer, and Lou Wells. I would also like to thank Joe Bower and Tarun Khana. My appreciation as well goes to the external reviewers of the manuscript, including generous suggestions and support by Jonah Levy. My thanks to HBS for supporting this project, and to Vincent Dessain and Elena Corsi at the HBS European Research Institute in Paris. I would also like to thank Diane Choi and Caitlin Anderson for their research and editing support. Finally, my thanks to my family for supporting me and putting up with me through this project.

Index